COMMUNITY CONTROL:

THE BLACK DEMAND

FOR PARTICIPATION IN

LARGE AMERICAN CITIES

An Urban Institute publication

COMMUNITY CONTROL:

THE BLACK DEMAND

FOR PARTICIPATION IN

LARGE AMERICAN CITIES

ALAN A. ALTSHULER

PEGASUS

A DIVISION OF THE BOBBS-MERRILL COMPANY, INC.

Indianapolis • New York

This is the first volume in the "Pegasus Series
on Decentralization and the Urban Crisis," of
which Alan Altshuler is General Editor.

Pegasus
A DIVISION OF THE BOBBS-MERRILL COMPANY, INC.
Printed in the United States of America
Third Printing

CONTENTS

PREFACE

THIS IS the introductory volume in a projected series focused on the widespread demand for increased citizen participation in the governance of America's large cities. The concept of "participation" that will guide these studies is broad enough to encompass the right to be consulted at one end of the spectrum, near-absolute community control of vital public functions at the other. In addition to entreaties for a role in the exercise of public authority, demands by minority groups for a greater share of private economic power will also be considered insofar as they seem to call for public policy decisions—for example, in connection with government contracts and private projects undertaken with government-insured loans.

The present volume examines those aspects of the participation issue that cut across functional policy lines. Future volumes will consider the issue's manifestation in such functional arenas as police, education, housing, economic development, and so on. The authors of the various volumes will strive to link their studies by addressing similar issues, by making comparative observations, and, most important, by searching out opportunities for research that will yield more rigorous comparisons.

In general, it should be noted, these volumes will be the by-products of efforts by their authors to define hypotheses and research priorities preparatory to more rigorous and narrowly focused scholarship. Each volume will endeavor: (a) to analyze the main issues, viewpoints, and interests in its area; (b) to assess (from a variety of relevant perspectives, and with explicit attention to uncertainties) the more prominent and otherwise more interesting policy recommendations that have been advanced; (c) to review the substance and clarify the limits of our present relevant knowledge; and (d) to identify strategies for ameliorating the most serious gaps in our knowledge—or at least those among them that are susceptible of amelioration.

Though tentative, these surveys are being published in their present form because the issues, both political and scholarly, with which they deal are extremely pressing. Vital commitments are being made every day. Thus, the authors have deemed it appropriate to make whatever contribution to clear and informed thinking they could in timely fashion. Doubtless they will have frequent cause for embarrassment as events rush on these next few years, but that is typically the price of seeking to infuse scholarship with high policy relevance. The authors consider it worth paying.

The central questions that the series, and particularly the present volume, will address are:

(1) From whom is the demand for greater participation coming? How likely is it to persist and/or mushroom?

(2) What, precisely, do those who demand greater participation seem to mean by the term? (This is not to suggest that there is a single authoritative definition, only that the general demand encompasses a variety of specific aspirations which merit separate and detailed analysis.)

(3) How does the demand for greater participation in the governance of large cities fit into the overall framework of American politics and culture?

(4) On the critical issue of neighborhood (community) control: to what extent need this be incompatible with the objective of racial integration? What are the types of interests that would be most affected by transfers of authority to neighborhood institutions, and just how would they be affected (assuming various possible arrangements)?

(5) To what extent need enhancement of the neighborhood role in local government conflict with such
traditional "good government" values as: substi-
tuting "merit" and the ethos of neutrality for "politics" in the public service; minimizing financial
corruption; taking advantage of scale economy opportunities; controlling the baleful "neighborhood effects"
of actions dictated by narrow perspectives and
responsibilities; and guiding metropolitan development through planning?

(6) As and when neighborhood authorities are established, what are the main procedural and substantive
options with respect to: neighborhood definition?
modes of representation and accountability? fiscal
relationships? civil service regulations and job security guarantees? contracting procedures and responsibilities?

(7) Where public authority remains at the city, state,
or federal level, what are the ways in which groups
that currently feel underrepresented can be given a
greater sense that their views are being taken into
account? What are the potential costs (in terms of
delay, frustration, inefficiency, corruption) of each
likely mechanism or approach?

(8) What, if anything, might federal and state authorities do to encourage greater local government sensitivity to the viewpoints of low income and racial
minority groups? to enhance the opportunities of
racial minority groups to participate in the private
sector jobs and profits generated by government
activity? Again, what might the cost of each plausible course of action prove to be?

One final point. Though the orientation of each volume
will be analytic rather than normative, the authors do not
equate dispassion with bloodlessness. They will inevitably
conclude (and frequently differ as they do) that some claims

and proposals deserve more attention than others, that some lines of argument are a great deal more plausible than others. Insofar as possible, they will make their judgments explicit. It is hoped that this approach will contribute to the reader's interest even as it facilitates his evaluation of the analyses presented.

ACKNOWLEDGMENTS

THIS VOLUME evolved over a period of eighteen months. During the spring of 1968 I became chairman of an academic advisory committee on decentralization convened by Paul Parks, the Boston Model Cities Administrator. I had previously penned several "thinkpiece" essays on criteria that might guide a redesign of American urban governmental structure,* but my main scholarly interests lay elsewhere at this time. The committee's function, however, was merely to give Mr. Parks a private forum in which to explore emerging ideas. It did not involve much time, and I took on its chairmanship as one might any minor extracurricular activity.

The subject quickly grew on me, though, and I seized the first opportunity that arose to concentrate on it for a brief period. This proved to be a summer study on urban policy problems, financed by the U.S. Department of Housing and Urban Development, at the University of California (Berkeley) during August 1968. The summer study participants included academic social scientists, representatives (some academic, some consultants) of the infant field urban social planning, recent and current assistants to big city mayors, and black community activists. Interest in the black demand for greater neighborhood participation in big city government, then just surfacing as a major issue throughout

---

*Cf., in particular, "New Institutions to Serve the Individual," in William Ewald, ed., *Environment and Policy: The Next Fifty Years* (Indiana University Press, 1968), pp. 423–444.

the nation, ran high. The group proved an invaluable one in which to gather hypotheses, proposals, justifications of conflicting positions, and illustrative evidence about it. Serving as chairman of the summer study's committee on "participation" issues. I devoted the month to doing just that.

Toward the end of the summer study William Gorham, President of The Urban Institute, passed through. Hearing of my now intense interest in the participation issue, he invited me to write a paper for The Urban Institute on it. That prod was all it took by this time to drive me to total immersion in the subject. Upon completion of the paper originally requested, I expressed a desire to press on, and Gorham generously extended the terms of his invitation. Thus, The Urban Institute supported my work on this book from start to finish. Needless to say, it claimed no power of review and bears no responsibility for the views expressed herein.

One always incurs numerous personal debts in the preparation of a book, but I have incurred more than most on this occasion. The subject is new, the literature embryonic. Thus, an unusual amount of my learning has been by conversation and interchange of letters.

My greatest collective debt is to the public officials and black activists, mainly in Boston (though also, during August 1968, Oakland, California), who have agreed on one or another occasion to discuss the black participation movement with me or admit me to their meetings. Without their assistance, this book, and particularly chapters 1 and 4, simply could not have been written.

The work of the Boston Model Cities advisory committee played a major role in arousing my interest in the black participation movement and my initial sense of the relevant questions to ask about it. Those who took part with some regularity were Paul Parks, Anthony Kettaneh, Frank Michelman, Ithiel de Sola Pool, Daniel Richardson, Eugene Dial, John Myers, and Dorothy Sherman.

At the Berkeley summer study I spent the equivalent of several days receiving the issues examined in chapters 1 and 4 with Paul Cobb, a remarkably articulate, perceptive, and charming young Oakland activist. Mr. Cobb's contribution to my education on these matters has doubtless been greater than that of any other individual. I also accumulated notable intellectual debts at the summer study to Sherry Arnstein, William Booth, Timothy Costello, Leonard Duhl, Bernard Frieden, Marshall Kaplan, Elizabeth Howe, Donald McCullum, Melvin Mogulof, Jeffrey Pressman, Martin Rein, and Richard Strichartz.

During the year of work on this book that followed the summer study, I benefitted immeasurably from frequent conversations with my M.I.T. colleague Leonard Fein and with the following graduate students: Norman Fainstein, Susan Fainstein, Dion Diamond, Joel Rosenblatt, Jon Ellertson, and Margaret Power.

For written comments on all or portions of the manuscript, I am extremely grateful to Michael Lipsky, Christopher Jencks, Betsy Levin, Joseph Lewis, Francis Rourke, Sherry Arnstein, Leonard Duhl, Susan Fainstein, Charles Beard, Peter Marcuse, Gary Marx, Patrick Murphy, Duane Lockard, Herbert Gans, and David Cohen.

Joseph Lewis, Director of Universities Cooperation at The Urban Institute, has been an unfailing source of encouragement, administrative support, and constructive criticism.

With love and gratitude, I dedicate this volume to my wife, Julie. Her contribution to it can scarcely be overstated. On the one hand, she has been my most constant, clear-headed, and constructive critic. On the other, she has (with the enchanting assistance of Jennifer and David Altshuler) provided a setting of domestic warmth, tranquility, and delight that has both fueled and freed my mental energy for scholarly concentration.

A.A.

Cambridge, Massachusetts
December 1969

CHAPTER ONE

THE ISSUES

RECENT demands by groups that have traditionally had little power—most visibly, affluent students and low income blacks—for enhanced roles in the shaping of policies that vitally affect their lives have been widely hailed and condemned as unprecedented. In the sense of going beyond the past, they are indeed so. In the sense of constituting a sharp break with tradition, however, they are anything but. The aspiration toward more meaningful democracy, of which these demands are the latest extension, has in successive guises been a key item on the political agenda throughout American history.* There is evidence, moreover, that its headline-making explosions in the current period are but extreme symptoms of a very widespread sense of disquiet at the size, complexity, and impersonality of modern institutions. For example, it was reported during the 1968 Presidential campaign that: "Mr. Humphrey's private polls have shown that what voters of all persuasions want most is a sense of participation in the political process, a feeling that they can be heard and have their doubts addressed."[1]

At the level of general rhetoric, greater participation is now favored by those who lead or aspire to lead virtually

---

*This theme is elaborated in Chapter 2.

all our institutions. So long as it is endorsed without excessive zeal, participation ranks as a controversial issue with motherhood. At the level of action, however, chaos prevails. Greater participation conflicts at every turn with other ideals and with well-entrenched interests. No consensus has even begun to emerge about the priority it deserves or the concrete forms it ought to take.

The subject of this volume is one subset of demands for greater participation: those being advanced by the black communities of America's major cities. Its purposes are: (a) to elucidate the most pressing issues of theory and ideology that are posed by these demands; (b) to sketch their relationship to international currents, and their roots in American history; (c) to examine the most plausible suggestions that have been made for responding to them; and (d) to suggest priorities for further research.

In this chapter, I should like to set the stage: first, by making explicit what I understand the central issues to be; and second, by specifying the meanings that I attach to some key but ambiguous terms.

When black spokesmen demand greater participation in the political and economic lives of their cities, their specific agenda of reform typically includes the following: (1) devolution of as much authority as possible to neighborhood communities; (2) direct representation of such communities on the city council, the board of education, the police commission, and other significant policy bodies; (3) black representation at all levels of the public service in far more than token numbers; (4) similar representation on the labor forces of government contractors; and (5) the vigorous application of public resources to facilitate the development of black-controlled businesses.

This, of course, is only the formal agenda of objectives toward which progress can be measured fairly easily. There is also an informal agenda, which involves reorienting the spirit of government, that is at least equally important. What black leaders across the political spectrum say they want are federal, state, and local administrations which give top priority to the pursuit of racial equality, and which are genuinely committed to making policy *with* rather than *for* the people. But they insist that they want even such administrations to concentrate on helping them to obtain power and wealth of their own (and, most, though far from all, add, as communities, not simply as individuals).

To use their own language, they want to stop being colonies. They want their dependence on the benevolence of ruling outsiders (most of whom, in any case, are not very benevolent) to cease. And they will not be mollified by provisions for a few of their number—by adopting its speech and behavior patterns, and by agreeing to be instruments of its institutions—to enter that class.

It is ironic, but highly typical of modern revolutions—which tend to be products of impatience given birth by progress—that the colonial analogy should become fashionable just when its validity has become highly questionable. A few decades past, when the inferiority of Negroes was rigidly enforced by law and custom, when most (those who lived in the South) were denied even the vote, the power of the analogy was indisputable. Today, when formal discrimination has been outlawed and numerous institutions are giving blacks preferential treatment, it is at best hyperbolic, at worst seriously misleading about the nature of the problem. (Numerous whites, going further, have labelled it nonsense. I do not. Blacks remain a small and impoverished minority, subject in both the public and private sectors to institutions in which their representation at the top is negligible. The white majority, on the whole, is far from solicitous of black interests and aspirations. Thus, there is substantial reason to speak of white majority tyranny. Given recent world history, the use of the term "colonialism" by blacks to describe this phenomenon is understandable, and felicitous politically even if not analytically.[2])

The participation crisis, however, is one of *perceived* legitimacy and nationhood. The most important thing about the colonial analogy is that it is widely believed to be valid, by blacks committed to ultimate integration as well as by those bent on separatism. Moreover, even those few black activists and intellectuals who consider the language over-drawn tend to accept the conclusion. They use the language of reference groups and group politics to explain why black wealth and power are vital to the diffusion of self-respect in black communities, why mobilization is prerequisite to equality, and why equality is prerequisite to integration.

The most controversial item on the black participatory agenda is community control; and we shall devote more attention to it than any other. Most whites, liberal and con-servative both, today agree that a great deal of adminis-trative decentralization is called for in the nation's big cities, and that a decisive test of good administration is responsive-ness to reasonable client desires. What they generally have in mind, however, is the delegation of authority within bureaucracies to field officers (e.g., school principals) who will be instructed to seek "good community relations"—but who, if perchance they "go native," can be slapped down at will by their superiors at central headquarters. There are substantial variations in the degrees of client responsiveness considered desirable, but few indeed seem prepared to make client responsiveness in the big city ghettos a function of neighborhood authority as opposed to city government grace.

Some of the opposition to community control, of course, is based crudely on self-interest. Civil servants fear for their jobs and promotions, contractors for their profits, etc. But the generality of white hostility to community control is far wider than can be explained by immediate self-interest. Most whites simply disbelieve that Negroes have a legitimate com-plaint about the operation of city government. Their inclina-tion is to think that Negroes have only themselves to blame for their impoverished condition.

To illustrate: a survey conducted in fifteen large cities for the Kerner Commission in 1968 asked the following ques-tion: "On the average, Negroes in [your urban area] have worse jobs, education, and housing than white people. Do you think this is due mainly to Negroes having been discriminated against, or mainly due to something about Negroes themselves?" The white respondents answered as follows:[3]

Mainly due to discrimination 19%
Mainly due to Negroes. themselves   56
A mixture of both   19
Don't know   6

A national Harris survey conducted in 1969 produced similar findings, and highlighted the differential perceptions of white and Negro Americans.[4] The respondents were asked, first, whether they thought that, in general, black people were discriminated against in this country. Only a bare plurality of whites believed that they were (46–43 per cent). Negroes, by contrast, were virtually unanimous in thinking that they were (84–4 per cent).

The respondents were then asked whether they thought blacks faced discrimination in eleven specific areas of American life. The proportions responding positively were as follows:

Think blacks are discriminated against in getting:	Whites (per cent)	Negroes (per cent)	Difference (percentage points)
Treatment by police	19	76	57
Quality education in public schools . . .	23	72	49
Skilled labor jobs	35	83	48
White collar office jobs	38	82	44
Entry into labor unions	22	64	42
Fair wages	22	64	42
Manual labor jobs	18	58	40
Fair prices in grocery stores	12	51	39
Decent housing	46	83	37
Hotel and motel accommodations	34	67	33

Even more strikingly, a national Gallup poll conducted for *Newsweek* in 1969 found more white Americans believing that Negroes receive favored treatment than that they suffer from discrimination. The key questions and responses were as follows:[5]

Do Negroes today have a better chance or worse chance than people like yourself:

	Better (%)	Worse (%)	Same (%)
To get well-paying jobs?	44	21	31
To get a good education for their children?	41	16	41
To get good housing at a reasonable cost?	35	30	27
To get financial help from the government when they're out of work?	65	4	22

Even among those whites who believe that the disease of discrimination is real, moreover, there is a disinclination to favor the medicine of community control. The intellectual and social science critics of community control tend to fall into this category. The most important arguments that they make are the following: (1) that community control would be a step toward racial separatism; (2) that it would intensify rather than alleviate social friction; (3) that it would be anti-libertarian, in the sense of suppressing diversity within neighborhood communities; (4) that it would be inimical to governmental honesty, equity, and professionalism; (5) that it would reduce the capacity of local government for vigorous action, and for action based on citywide rather than more parochial considerations; (6) that it would prove a dead end for blacks themselves, leading them to expend a great deal of effort in return for negligible or even negative returns; and (7) that community control is today a minority demand even within the black community. To my knowledge, no single critic has developed all these arguments, but they are all advanced frequently. Let us review them, along with some key evidence and counterarguments, in turn.

WOULD COMMUNITY CONTROL BE A STEP TOWARD RACIAL SEPARATISM?

Most of those who argue that it would assume that community boundaries would be drawn to maximize racial homogeneity. (I shall contend below, on pp. 131–32, that this is improbable.) Others simply note that, given existing residential segregation, neighborhood communities would be far more racially homogeneous than the larger cities of which they were part. And they add that, once the boundaries were defined, there would be a very strong tendency for whites to flee those with Negro majorities. In the predominantly white communities, moreover, neighborhood officials might be far less solicitous of Negro interests than today's citywide officials. This would be particularly likely in working class neighborhoods with substantial Negro minorities, or threatened by ghetto expansion. These might become little Mississippis, touching off black migrations comparable to that from the original.

Other arguments advanced under the "separatist" rubric include the following. First, government bureaucracies, very much including those of the nation's large cities, are today the best integrated institutions of American society. The struggle to make them so has been long and hard—and despite their relative position, still has a long way to go. To break them up (dis-integrate them) now would be a colossal retrograde step.[6]

Second, the historic record suggests that progress toward integration is most likely when decision makers drawn from the educational elite are entrusted with power and well insulated from citizen influence. Thus, the Supreme Court has a far better record on race than Congress, and it has proven easier to integrate Catholic than Protestant churches. Similarly, Robert Crain, in a study of disputes over school integration in eight nonsouthern cities, concluded that the disposition to combat segregation tended to be a direct function of the extent to which educational decision making was insulated from citizen control.*

Third, it is pointed out that the history of efforts to combat segregation in America has been one of raising the level at which decisions were made. White segregationists are still demanding a reversal of the trend toward federal infringement upon state's rights. In this context it is sometimes pointed out that not too much faith should be placed in the formal power of state authorities to prevent communities from pursuing racist policies. The record of federal enforcement of the 13th, 14th, and 15th Amendments in the southern states is less than reassuring. And even as enforcement of the requirement of formal nondiscrimination has become more vigorous in recent years, the spirit of southern state government has remained profoundly (and quite effectively) racist.**

To all these arguments a few blacks respond, of course, that separation is indeed their goal, that the long quest for integration was both hopeless and misguided—hopeless because the white majority will never permit integration, misguided because the black subculture is superior to mainstream American culture anyway. Why should blacks, these militants ask, rigidly suppress their own personalities in order to resemble and be "accepted" by whites?

What is more important, however, is that at present most black spokesmen whose long-run objective is integration are

---

*Crain and his colleagues found that such factors as region, size of the Negro population, and socioeconomic status of the white population had little predictive value. The variables that appeared to matter were school board characteristics. In particular, appointed boards were much more receptive to integration than elected, and appointed boards composed of blue ribbon civic leaders were more receptive than those composed of professional politicians. Among *elected* officials, mayors (who could seek white support on other issues if they accommodated black demands for school integration) were more receptive than school board members.[7] Almost identical findings have been made, incidentally, with respect to the politics of fluoridation.[8]

**By racist, I mean anti-integrationist as well as tending to deny non-whites equal social and economic opportunity, equal justice, and an equal share of government benefits.

also supporters of community control (see below, pp. 60–61). They tend to answer the criticisms outlined above as follows.

First, and most important: to proclaim full integration as one's immediate and only goal is idle rhetoric. Only a tiny minority of white Americans are prepared to have their own neighborhoods and schools integrated, except in token proportions and by black families that have adopted white life styles. There is probably a national majority opposed to integration even on these terms. Thus, when open occupancy proposals have been put to American state and local electorates, they have almost invariably been voted down.*[9] When the Survey Research Center (SRC) of the University of Michigan asked a fifteen-city sample of white respondents in 1968 whether they would favor the imposition of limits on further in-migration if a single Negro family moved into their 100-family neighborhood, a majority of those who had opinions (48–40 per cent) replied that they would.** When a sample of whites living in Buffalo, New York, was asked during the winter of 1966–67 whether they favored busing to bring about school integration, only 23 per cent responded positively (vs. 59 per cent opposed).***[12]

---

*A U.C.L.A. research team which conducted surveys in Los Angeles following the Watts riot, moreover, found that open occupancy was the racial issue that most inflamed whites.[10]

**A majority of those with opinions (51–40 per cent) opposed open occupancy legislation, but a slight plurality said that they personally would not mind at all if a Negro family moved in next door (49–44 per cent). A large majority did favor equal employment legislation (67–23 per cent).[11]

***Surprisingly, upper income whites were more hostile to busing than lower income whites. By contrast, it was upper income blacks who most favored busing.

If anything, the Buffalo sample was more favorable to integration than SRC's fifteen-city sample. For example, whereas the SRC respondents opposed open occupancy legislation by a ratio of 5–4, the Buffalo sample *favored* it by a ratio of 5–2.

Comparing survey with referendum results on open housing, one is led to the conclusion that whites talk a more integrationist line than they vote. The reason is quite likely that their fears are easily stirred during referendum campaigns. On the other hand, it may simply be that whites are more prone generally to resist integration in practice than when answering pollsters.

By contrast, an overwhelming majority of blacks has supported integration in the past and continues to do so. An SRC survey in Detroit several months after the Detroit riot of 1967 found Negroes favoring the goal of integration by a ratio of 87–1.[13] In the Buffalo survey cited above, Negroes favored school busing to achieve integration by 67–17 per cent. In this survey, whereas whites said they favored the general concept of integration by 2–1 (46–23 per cent), Negroes favored it by nearly 15–1 (87–6 per cent).[14] In the fifteen-city survey of 1968, only 8 per cent of Negro respondents said that they would prefer to live in a neighborhood with no whites. Only 6 per cent said that they would prefer their children to attend majority-Negro schools. A nationwide poll conducted in mid-1969 by the Gallup organization for *Newsweek* found Negroes preferring to live in integrated neighborhoods by a ratio of 4½–1 (74–16 per cent), and preferring integrated schools for their children by almost 9–1 (78–9 per cent).[15]

Those who favor both community control and integration maintain that, if history has ever taught a lesson, it has taught that those few white liberals who genuinely desire full integration cannot deliver it—at least not in the foreseeable future. The urban ghettos are growing, not dispersing. In a study of thirteen cities that had special censuses between 1964 and 1967, Reynolds Farley and Karl Taueber found that in all but two, segregation by census tracts had increased since 1960.*[16] National census analyses show that

---

*In a previous article, Taueber had noted that: "In 1910 some ethnic groups were as segregated from native whites as Negroes were. Since 1910, however, the residential segregation of every group of European descent has been declining, whereas segregation of whites from Negroes has been increasing."

Analyzing 1960 census data from specific cities, he had also reached the following conclusions: (a) that Negroes are far more segregated than Puerto Ricans (New York) and Mexican-Americans (Los Angeles); (b) that since 1940 the segregation of Orientals from whites has markedly decreased, while that of Orientals from Negroes has markedly increased (San Francisco); (c) that less than one-eighth of segregation can be explained on the basis on Negro-white income differentials (Chicago and 15 other cities);

whites have been fleeing the central cities at an accelerating rate during the 1960's.* Meanwhile, Negroes, who managed to account for 3.4 per cent of suburban growth during the 1950's, accounted for only 1.1 per cent from 1960 to 1966. Census Bureau surveys indicate that Negroes have accounted for a much larger share of suburban growth more recently—an astonishing 14 per cent from 1966 to 1968—but the Bureau warns that high sampling variability makes this finding very suspect.[19]

Black leaders, the "moderate" proponents of community control point out, have rarely opposed integration in practice, even though some have taken to rejecting it as a goal in their rhetoric. None propose denying individual blacks the right to move to predominantly white neighborhoods today. It is still *whites* who provide the political constituency for segregation. All the blacks have done is to change tactics. They have revived the distinction between integration and equality as objectives, and determined to concentrate for the time being upon the latter.

Essentially this decision has been pragmatic. They have judged that if integration ever came about it would do so only *after* black achievement equalled white. (The traditional view, of course, accepted by the Supreme Court in the *Brown* decision, had been that integration was a prerequisite of equal achievement.) They have judged that the real key to unlocking the black potential is self-respect, and that given white resistance to integration, the most feasible way for

---

(d) that the degree of segregation tends to increase as housing vacancy rates go down, and vice versa; (e) that, consequently, segregation increased during the forties and decreased during the fifties (all cities for which the census published adequate data from 1940 through 1960); but (f) that the overall degree of segregation was slightly greater in 1960 than 1940.[17]

*On a national basis, white central city population *in*creased at an annual rate of 220,000 during the 1950's, *de*creased at an annual rate of 141,000 from 1960 to 1966, and *de*creased at an annual rate of 486,000 from 1966 to 1968.[18] These figures understate the pace of change in the cities where Negroes are concentrated, because in many of the newer cities of the South and West the Negro population share is small and the white population has continued to grow rapidly.

blacks to acquire it is to exercise responsibility in their own communities.

Similarly, they have concluded that black business is most likely to develop on the basis of ghetto markets and favorable government actions. They have judged that sympathetic government is most likely to be a product of political mobilization, and that residential segregation (even if an evil in most other respects) is a great mobilization asset.* But most of all, they have judged that white America is much more likely (though still not very) to concede a large measure of ghetto self-determination than to accept large numbers of blacks into its neighborhoods.

All black leaders and would-be leaders, moreover, are today in search of mass followings. (Perhaps more than anything else, this is what differentiates them from most civil rights leaders of the past—Marcus Garvey is a conspicuous exception—who did not consider mass followings obtainable.) None believe that the black masses can be mobilized around the remote goal of integration. Popular followings are secured and maintained by focusing on more immediate desires: jobs, physical security, better schools, better housing, more sympathetic treatment from public servants, and so on. They are also secured by establishing cultural rapport: that is, by manipulating the right symbols in the right style. The right style at the present time is militant revivalist. The right symbols are those which express pride in black, and which attempt to purge traditional black self-hatred by ridiculing the traditional aspiration for acceptance into white America.

The evidence available suggests that the calls for black pride and black power have struck responsive chords among the Negro masses, but without substantially altering the basic thrust toward equality and integration. Thus, the SRC fifteen-city survey conducted in 1968 found that, while blacks massively favored integration (see above, p. 22), 96 per cent felt that blacks should take more pride in Negro history, 70 per cent felt that Negroes should patronize Negro-

*Social science findings tend to bear this out.[20]

owned stores whenever possible, and fully 42 per cent felt
that Negro schoolchildren should study an African language.*[21] The 1967 Detroit survey, in which the ratio of
black support for integration was 87–1, also found widespread
support for the term "black power." Only 9 per cent of the
black respondents in this survey (by comparison with 39
per cent of the white) thought that "black power" implied
blacks ruling over whites. This 9 per cent, moreover, was
composed almost entirely of blacks who disapproved the term.
The supporters nearly all spoke of equity rather than superiority, and emphasized that they were *for* black people,
not against whites.[23] Gallup's 1969 *Newsweek* poll, which
found continued mass support for integration, also found a
majority of those with opinions favoring the term "black
power" (42–31 per cent). Northern respondents under thirty
endorsed the term by more than 4–1 (68–16 per cent). The
same poll showed massive support for the idea that "Negroes
have a special soul that most whites have not experienced"
(54 per cent yes, 22 per cent no).**[24]

What all this suggests is that Negroes and whites have
radically different views as to whether black power and black
pride need violate the traditionally acceptable limits of American ethnic pluralism. The rhetoric and the demands will
probably change as and if white America becomes truly receptive to integration. In the long interim, it ill behooves
white liberals to reject black-proposed ghetto improvement
schemes out of hand. So, at least, the "moderate" supporters
of community control maintain.

---

*On this point, the authors note: "We had no other question that so
clearly taps positive identification with a black heritage without at the same
time implying rejection of whites. But the support of this single proposition, which a few years ago was scarcely discussed by most Negroes and
still seems exotic and impractical to most white ears, is so impressive
that it suggests a considerable potential for the growth of black cultural
identity in America."[22]

**Of related interest is a recent Harris poll of Negro respondents in
Harlem. Fully 75 per cent maintained that they watched the program "Soul"
on a local educational television station.[25]

The critics respond, however, that the intentions of the black masses are not the issue. What *is* at issue is the prospective consequences of community control. Would it, in fact, lead down the paths forecast above? Those I have labelled the "moderate" advocates of community control tend to answer this question—or, rather, these questions—as follows.

First, as to the charge that whites would flee those neighborhoods with Negro majorities: the fact is that whites have been doing so for decades. And it is just as true that they have been trying to keep blacks out of their neighborhoods. Failing in the cities, the whites have adjourned to the suburbs, where they exercise just the sort of community control that blacks are now demanding. The fact is that more than half the whites who now live in metropolitan America live in suburbs rather than central cities. (The estimated 1968 suburban share for whites was 59 per cent; that for blacks 20 per cent. The differential tended to be greatest in the largest metropolitan areas, and in the Northeast and North Central regions.[26]) Taking all Americans together, moreover, only 22 per cent lived in local jurisdictions that had populations larger than 250,000 in 1960, fewer than half of these in cities larger than a million.

Thus, small-scale government is the American norm, even within metropolitan areas. For central city whites who value it, the option of moving to the suburbs is always open. Only blacks have been confined regardless of taste to the central cities, and told that government at a scale which permitted them majority status would be "separatist." Even if this is literally true, to apply it solely to blacks is inequitable. It is, in fact, typical of the white determination to keep blacks power-poor.*

Second, in answer to the charge that breaking up the city

---

*I prefer this term to "powerless," which implies an absolute lack of influence.

Parenthetically, this view of the white attitude toward inequality is quite widespread. In the Kerner Commission's fifteen-city survey, almost half of the black respondents who thought that whites cared at all thought that their interest was malevolent (27 per cent, vs. 29 per cent who thought that most whites would like to see Negroes get a better break). Those under

bureaucracies would be a major step away from integration: blacks are inclined to emphasize (a) the current underrepresentation at all but the menial levels of existing city bureaucracies,* (b) the current high levels of tension between city bureaucracies and ghetto populations, (c) the lack of white concern about segregated suburban bureaucracies, and (d) the contrary evidence suggesting that Negro communities would employ integrated staffs.** Given the shortage of black professionals, it would be surprising if many black communities could—even if they wished—get along with all black personnel. Their recruits, presumably, would have to meet state licensing standards. Segregation would more likely be a problem in white neighborhoods, but if Negroes are willing to take this risk it ill becomes whites to refuse it. The reason many Negroes are willing to take it is that they prefer sympathetic and responsive government at home to a few jobs "abroad."

Third, with reference to the historic record (of elites being more favorable toward integration than the citizenry at large): this is no argument for denying blacks the degree of local self-rule enjoyed by suburban whites. If whites are anxious to further integration, let them do so at the metropolitan scale, for suburban and central city communities alike. In any event, blacks are no longer satisfied with pa-

---

forty were much less likely to think whites wished Negroes well than those over forty, and the difference was particularly striking among the educated. For example, 46 per cent of Negroes over forty with at least some college education thought that most whites wished Negroes well; the comparable percentage for those under forty was 18.[27]

In the 1969 *Newsweek* survey, 51 per cent of northern respondents under thirty said they thought that most white people wanted to keep Negroes down. Another 30 per cent thought that most whites were at best indifferent to inequality.[28]

*The Kerner Commission, for example, in a survey of 28 large city police departments, found that the median percentage of Negro policemen was one-fourth (6 per cent) the median Negro share of total population (24 per cent). For the ranks of lieutenant and above, Negro underrepresentation was four to five times greater.[29]

**For example, in New York's controversial Ocean Hill-Brownsville experimental school district, the teaching staff was 80 per cent white as of June 1969.[30]

ternalism; they value self-governance even more than integration.* But it should also be recalled that the historic record is one of white mass resistance to integration, not black. The surveys suggest that among Negroes the white pattern is reversed: that is, the masses are more favorable to integration than the elites.**

Fourth, in response to the charge that the federal record of constitutional enforcement in the South provides little ground for optimism that state authorities would be able to prevent the teaching and practice of race hatred in local communities: community control supporters maintain simply that the analogy is a false one. The Southerners had a position of power in Congress that Negroes cannot hope to achieve in the state legislatures. The national majority had little interest in stamping out southern racism. By contrast, the state majorities will be waiting to pounce at the first excuse. For generations it was accepted that the federal government had little power to intervene in the affairs of southern states. The right of state governments to intervene at will in local affairs, on the other hand, is undisputed.

WOULD COMMUNITY CONTROL INTENSIFY SOCIAL FRICTION?

Some of those who charge that it would have interracial

---

*The evidence suggests that in fact this is a minority position. It commands widespread support among the young and the politically active, however. See below, pp. 56-61.

**The validity of this assertion depends heavily on how the elites are defined. Elderly Negro men of wealth would doubtless be very favorable to integration. An "elite" group consisting of young professionals, intellectuals, and community organizers would presumably include a much higher proportion of separatists (however defined) than the Negro population at large. By way of illustration, the Survey Research Center asked respondents in its fifteen-city survey whether they thought schools with mostly Negro children should have mostly Negro teachers. Overall, 10 per cent of black respondents thought that they should. Among college graduates over the age of forty, only 3 per cent thought so. Among college graduates under forty, 20 per cent thought so.[31]

and inter-neighborhood friction in mind, others intra-racial and intra-neighborhood.

Those in the first category maintain that the central cities, unlike the suburbs, are cauldrons of passion and diversity. The success of existing city governments in keeping the lid on leaves much to be desired, but there is every reason to believe that a more fragmented system would do worse. City-wide elective leaders have to hold broad coalitions together. On the whole, they strive to act in ways that, even if they fail to heal, will at least avoid aggravating the sores of intergroup friction. Neighborhood authorities, if they were not totally ineffectual, would frequently be racist.[32] Even if they were not, their actions would seem so to many of the interests they threatened—e.g., civil servants, contractors, construction workers. Recent experiments with community control (most saliently, of public education in Ocean Hill-Brownsville) and community action hardly provide ground for optimism about the calming effect of movements toward community control.

Reviewing proposals for community control of the police, James Q. Wilson has added several additional twists.[33] The suburban analogy, he contends, is over-simple. Just because the central city *is* central, it cannot be fully suburbanized. People from all over the metropolitan area use it each day. They expect the highest level of order to be maintained in it, just as they know that it contains the most highly priced land. Law enforcement cannot be responsive solely to resident norms in the central city; it must also serve businessmen, shoppers, theatergoers, students, public officials, and so on. It is also of critical importance, Wilson argues, that the central cities contain the deepest social cleavages in our urban areas. The potential for violent conflict between black ghettos and the working class white neighborhoods that lie in their paths of expansion should not be underrated. Somehow, Wilson writes, the proponents of neighborhood control seem to assume that only Negroes would gain control of the police. But in practice whites would do so as well, and their use of this power to drive and keep Negroes out would be highly probable. Wilson concludes:

> When a community is deeply divided and emotionally aroused, the proper government policy is not to arm the disputants and let them settle matters among themselves; it is, rather, to raise the level at which decisions will be made to a point sufficiently high so that neither side can prevail by *force majeure* but low enough so that responsible authorities must still listen to both sides.

In response to these charges, the supporters of community control argue as follows.

First, it is true that the cities are cauldrons of diversity, but there is every reason to believe that community control would be more conducive to peace than the present system. The discontent of blacks has repeatedly exploded into widespread civil disorder in recent years. Some way must be found to establish a form of government that is widely perceived as legitimate in the ghettos. At very least, community control should reduce tension between the citizenry and public officialdom within the ghettos.

Second, it might also tend to reduce friction between neighborhoods. The present system forces diverse groups to compete continuously for resources within a single system. A system which permitted them less frequent contact might very well lower the level of tension. This should particularly be so for neighborhoods that lack a common border. Diverse suburban populations do not confront each other in local elections or policy processes. The result, apparently, is to reduce citizen awareness of interest conflicts. It is noteworthy that conflicts over school desegregation have invariably occurred *within* school districts. This may be taken as an argument either for or against disaggregation, but it certainly supports the view that conflict is intensified when diverse groups are forced to live together.

Third, the danger that white neighborhoods would strive to keep blacks out is indeed real. They have done so for years, admittedly with greatest success in the suburbs. But no one ever said that community control would be costless. If white racism is the problem, then the white majority should deal with it by state or city (the cities being unlikely to go out of business entirely) action. In order to prevent black racism, legislation establishing community control will undoubtedly contain provisions for intervention by higher authorities under specified circumstances. Abuse of the police power to exclude blacks will clearly fall within the scope of these provisions, and black pressure groups can be expected to demand intervention. They will doubtless fail at times. Even so, white racism is no argument for maintaining domination by citywide white majorities of local government in all the neighborhoods that blacks currently occupy.

Fourth, the frictions at Ocean Hill-Brownsville were probably unusual rather than typical of what might be expected if the concept of community control were applied widely. Moreover, the pains were pains of birth and transition. Revolutions are rarely placid in their first moments, but they often produce more stable situations than those which prevailed just prior to their occurrence. At some point, those with a vested interest in denying blacks a "fair" share of local power, profits, and jobs will have to be confronted. Blacks will make sure of that. No one can really say what leadership strategy would be most conducive to minimizing turbulence. What one can say is that justice will be more likely to prevail in the end if leaders of government and public opinion work to facilitate the transition rather than prevent it. (A number of means that have been proposed to ease the pains of transition are reviewed in subsequent chapters.)

Fifth, Wilson's error is to equate the Central Business District (CBD) with the central city. No one is proposing to give the very few residents of the former jurisdiction over it. The fact is, however, that the vast majority of central city acreage is residential—and in the nature of the case, it is on these acres that people live. Industrial and commercial land uses outside the CBD would not seem to present obstacles to community control any greater than their counterparts in the suburbs. In fact, they might present less, because in setting up a new system of government it should be possible to establish a more rational system for distributing their taxes than exists in the suburbs.

It should be noted, moreover, that central cities vary enormously in their share of metropolitan population. San Francisco and Boston contain roughly one-fifth of their metropolitan area populations. New York, Chicago, and Los Angeles contain half or more, in addition to being many times larger in absolute terms.* Yet little Boston, whose current population is probably less than 600,000, is generally accounted by its journalists and governmental leaders a city of neighborhoods. The current mayor, Kevin White, has led the nation in establishing neighborhood city halls and neighborhood advisory committees. The original Model Cities plan submitted by White's administration to the city council —which rewrote it, largely at the behest of civil service and construction unions—included vital elements of community control with respect to schools, police, health, contracting, and economic development. The Boston Renewal Authority has announced a plan to give neighborhood councils a conditional veto over renewal plans for their areas. The Boston Housing Authority has contracted with tenants' groups to manage several of its buildings. All in all, there does not seem to be any inherent reason why more than a small portion of Boston has to be governed according to standards considered desirable for the CBD. Even for residential enclaves within the CBD, moreover, the need for central police control need not inhibit moves toward community control of the schools and other public services.

Let us turn now to the charge that community control would tend to exacerbate intra-neighborhood frictions. This

---

*For New York and Chicago, I am defining the metropolitan area as the Standard Metropolitan Statistical Area (SMSA) rather than the Standard Consolidated Area.

theme has been developed by Daniel Moynihan in his analysis of the Community Action experience.[34] Moynihan writes that in Syracuse and a number of other cities terrific factional battles broke out in the first year or so of the Community Action Program (CAP). The order of development, he maintains, had been as follows. First, middle class white reformers (particularly those in the Ford Foundation, the President's Committee on Juvenile Delinquency, and the Office of Economic Opportunity) set out to organize the poor. The first thing that happened was that the organizers themselves, acquiring some sense of the difficulty of bringing about major change, were radicalized. Next, there was a stirring among the poor, accompanied by heightened racial antagonism if they happened to be black. Next, there was retaliation by the larger white community, whereupon the Community Action Agency, which had promised so much, proved to be powerless. In part, the problem was that insufficient money was available, so those encouraged to participate had nothing to do but quarrel and produce inflammatory rhetoric. Where any substantial amount of money *was* made available, however, it tended to generate brutal power struggles among those determined to control it. These were generally accompanied by threats of violence or actual violence.

Moynihan adds that the frictions were particularly intense in multi-racial target areas. In these the only solution often seemed to be further disaggregation—structuring the community political process so that governing board seats and virtually all other resources were allocated on a strict population basis to each ethnic and racial group.

The pro-community control response to this line of argument is that colonial rulers have always deemed their subjects unfit for self-governance. White America has deprived the black population of political experience. It is not surprising that the transition to self-rule should involve some turbulence, though in general its degree has been far less than suggested by Moynihan—who argues from a few colorful examples.* Nor is it cause for astonishment that in a situation of extreme scarcity even limited resources should sometimes give rise to cutthroat—in the literal sense—competition. To reduce the intensity of factional strife, the needs are (a) resources on a scale that can significantly alleviate ghetto scarcity, (b) more effective oversight from higher levels of government to prevent violence and corruption, and (c) time for the new political systems to settle down.

As for the allocation of representational positions in accord with racial and ethnic group shares of the population, so what? Seats in the U. S. Congress are allotted by state, and logrolling more generally is a hoary American political tradition. So long as a particular electoral method gives each vote equal weight and conduces to peace, why carp? If a great many people are offended by the explicit recognition of ethnicity and race, however, there are alternative ways to achieve substantially the same results. When the groups live in separate enclaves, district elections can do the trick. When they do not, the answer could be proportional representation. Whichever method is chosen, it is hard to believe that the foundations of the republic will be undermined.

WOULD COMMUNITY CONTROL
BE ANTI-LIBERTARIAN?

The argument that it would—following Madison, Tocqueville, and Hofstadter—is that small community size and populistic democracy are both antagonistic to the toleration of political and intellectual competition.** Combined, they

---

*The kind of systematic evidence that would be needed to settle this question is at present unavailable. Research designed to acquire it merits top priority, in my view, on any community control research agenda.

**Madison emphasized the danger of rule by faction in small communities. Tocqueville stressed the danger of majority tyranny in a nation as committed to egalitarian democracy as the United States. Hofstadter introduced the now conventional theme that American populism has historically been marred by a passion for stamping out diversity and dissent—and accusing those who stand in its way (e.g., defenders of the Bill of Rights) of affiliation with sinister conspiracies.[35]

are almost impossible to overcome. The nation's political and intellectual elites have sought to constrain these tendencies by emphasizing the concept of limited government—which is to say, limits upon the power of majorities. The key mechanisms of limited government have been (a) the power of the judiciary, especially the federal judiciary, to invalidate actions by other governmental bodies deemed inimical to free intellectual competition; and, increasingly in the present century, (b) professionalism, as a way of infusing the (typically ambiguous) democratic will with rationality, consistency, and respect for the overall constitutional tradition.

The Joe McCarthy experience, together with an enhanced awareness of white majority tyranny in the South, greatly reinforced the intellectuals' distrust of unfiltered democracy in the fifties. Social analysts of the time were fond of pointing out that the American failure to prepare in advance for World Wars I and II, and to help preserve the peace after the former, had been manifestations of democracy in action. Among their pet themes with regard to local politics were the following: that the Salem witchhunt, and lynchings throughout our history, had been expressions of local democracy; that in our time experimental evidence had shown the pressures toward consensus to be far greater in small than in large groups; that, perhaps for this reason, local communities seemed unable to support organized competition among political parties or factions; that attempts to purge the schools and libraries (not to mention the magazine counters, bookstores, and theaters) of controversial ideas and symbols were frequent in local communities (and much more so in small than in large jurisdictions); and so on.

Judith May has recently traced the impact of this period on the democratic theories of two leading social scientists:

> Both [Seymour Martin] Lipset and [Robert] Dahl are committed to "democracy," but in response to impelling political events—McCarthyism and the Cold War—revised their conception of which aspects of democracy should be maximized. When they were primarily con-

cerned with . . . distinguishing between dictatorship and democracy, they sought to maximize participation (and majoritarianism). When their concern shifted to tolerance for civil liberties and protection of democratic forms against extremist onslaughts, they sought to maximize responsible leadership. Evidence of political stratification which had previously been viewed with alarm became positively valued out of fear of participants inadequately socialized in the "rules of the game." Previously noted differences between the interests of leaders and followers were overlooked in new formulations of "indirect democracy" that pointed out it was in the leader's interests to serve his followers' interests.[36]

Similarly, Leonard Fein has recently noted that the predominant intellectual view on the organization of public education *circa* 1960 was that local democratic control tends toward "the same kind of intellectual protectionism that characterizes schools in totalitarian countries."[37] Those who today oppose community control on libertarian grounds are in essence maintaining that the lessons of the fifties remain good. Many would contend indeed that, in the current atmosphere of racial passion and polarization, their relevance is greater than ever.

The counterarguments are general and by now familiar. Community control is alive and healthy outside the nation's large cities.* The intellectuals' distaste for small-scale local

---

*Thus, with respect to education, Fein writes: "Just as intellectuals were concerned with structural reforms [c. 1960] which would temper the parochializing power of local communities, so were those communities increasingly alarmed at the prospect of a decrease in their autonomy. These were the post-Sputnik years, and talk of national standards and federal involvement was widespread. Against such pressures, communities asserted their own historic jurisdiction, and were, in the main, successful—largely by virtue of their movement toward the called-for reforms within the prevailing structures."[38]

It should be noted that these were reforms that had to do with technical effectiveness (i.e., the teaching of skills) rather than with encouraging intellectual or racial diversity in the schools.

government has not notably slowed the trend toward urban Balkanization by suburbanization. One can be sure that higher level (white-dominated) governments will hold ghetto communities to at least comparable standards of respect for diversity as white. The autonomous citywide bureaucracies have traditionally suppressed expressions of the *majority* culture in black communities—for example, by discriminating against civil service candidates with "Negro" speech patterns, by adopting textbooks which ignored or disparaged Negro history, by firing teachers who introduced their students to militant black perspectives. The overriding fact is that black Americans are demanding equality. Liberty will have to be protected by other means than denying it—just as it has been protected until now by other means than abolishing local government. The intellectuals, finally, should recognize that their arguments against local democracy receive a hearing in the corridors of power only when they provide a convenient rationale for keeping blacks down.

WOULD COMMUNITY CONTROL BE INIMICAL TO GOVERNMENTAL HONESTY, EQUITY, AND PROFESSIONALISM?

The argument that it would has been made most effectively by James Q. Wilson. In his book, *Varieties of Police Behavior*,[39] Wilson maintains that, historically, the local precinct house—oriented more toward the support of ward politicians than of bureaucratic superiors—was the main locus of police bribery, third degree interrogations, and prison shakedowns. The ward-oriented police were indeed tolerant of neighborhood variations from citywide norms (particularly if the neighborhoods were Irish), and they were kind to the friends of ward politicians. But by the same token they were inclined to disregard the rights of friendless minorities (e.g., suspects in cases involving heinous crimes, sexual deviates, political radicals, and Negroes), to protect illicit enterprises, and to conceal official corruption.

The modern professional department, by contrast, tends to be honest and to treat all citizens alike. It does concentrate its surveillance on suspicious-looking individuals (the young, the poor, the black, and especially individuals who combine these characteristics), but it has statistical justification for doing so. Most criminals do fall into these categories. It will be zealous in enforcing the law, and thus make a great many arrests. It will emphasize that it lacks discretion to overlook "minor" offenses or to vary its application of the law to suit neighborhood norms. This zeal will engender a great deal of hostility in the groups most subject to arrest. But the member of such a group, once arrested, will benefit as he is charged, booked, and jailed in an orderly manner without infringement of his legal rights.

The reality, Wilson admits, falls somewhat short of the ideal just stated. The police are poorly educated, poorly paid, and all too human. They bring the attitudes of their own subcultures (primarily white, working class, ethnic) with them to the job. Thus, racism, brutality, and corruption persist. But they are far less frequent today than in the past; and they are least frequent in the most highly professionalized departments.

Ghetto residents want more than honesty and equity from the police, of course. They want these in a context of effective crime control. This objective as well, the critics of community control maintain, requires increased centralization. Patrick Murphy, for example, has recently written as follows:

> The crime control system in the United States is not working well. It is seriously breaking down in some cities. It is a locally controlled "non-system," minimally influenced by the states and negligibly influenced by the federal government. Fragmentation is at its worst in policing. . . .
>
> The poor quality of policing in the nation results not only from our uniquely fragmented local arrangement (40,000 separate, uncoordinated departments) but from the underdeveloped state of the police career. The closed

personnel systems and lack of educational standards have resulted in low levels of education among chiefs as well as policemen. . . .

Fragmentation of city police departments could weaken crime control. . . . More black policemen are needed. More black police superior officers are needed. Much better relationships between ghetto residents and police are needed. Much more participation by citizens in crime control is needed. Representative citizen advisory committees at department and precinct levels are needed. . . .

[But] the best interests of the ghetto communities, which have the greatest stake in better crime control . . . , would not be served by separation. They could expect less police protection, even if blacker. . . .[40]

Honesty, equity, and effectiveness, then, the critics argue, all tend to be functions of professionalism. And professionalism tends to depend, *inter alia,* upon insulation from politics and upon large scale. The community control model seems antithetical to both.

A further word of explanation is in order here about the relationship of scale to professionalism. In part, the link is that scale permits the support of specialized recruitment and training programs, of highly paid and high-powered top managers, and of interesting career opportunities for ambitious young men. In part it is that larger systems permit the frequent scrambling of personnel, so that tight cliques (able to protect the inefficient and corrupt) have little chance to develop. And in part it is simply that larger systems— perhaps because they are more complex, perhaps because they are more remote from the ordinary citizen in any event, perhaps because they attract elite participants—have always led the way toward public management reform. Adjustments have to be made for historic and constituency characteristics—in particular, older and poorer communities tend to be less amenable to professionalism—but they provide no comfort for the advocates of community control. Within any given city, one can expect a reduction in scale to mean a reduction in professionalism—least severe in high income neighborhoods, more severe in low. The low income neighborhoods, moreover, are the ones in which rackets are most prone to flourish, providing unusual inducements for the police to become corrupt. It is in precisely these neighborhoods that close central supervision and frequent transfers are most needed.[41]

By way of rebuttal, community control advocates contend that the central issue in the ghettos at present is legitimacy, not efficiency. This is particularly true of Wilson's subject, the police. In the 1969 *Newsweek* poll, fully 46 per cent of the national sample thought that local police were harmful to Negro rights. Among northern respondents under thirty, 70 per cent thought that on balance the police were a force for harm in their communities.[42] If a choice had to be made, it would be justifiable in this situation to trade off some efficiency, and even some honesty, for an alleviation of social tension.

As it happens, however, few Negroes believe that enhanced community control would involve reduced efficiency or honesty. With respect to the former, it bears unceasing repetition that effective law enforcement is impossible without community support. It is senseless to justify a system on the basis of its elaborate testing system or its capacity for rapid response to alarms when its substantive product is poor. The police have themselves become a source of tension, a provocation to disorder, in the ghettos. As Burton Levy has noted:

> Virtually every incident of threatened or actual civil disorder in the urban ghetto began with an encounter between a police officer and a Negro citizen. Whatever the factual reality is—as contrasted to the belief systems —clearly the cops serve as the "flash point" for black anger, mob formation, and civil disorder.[43]

In no other field of public activity, moreover, does the

colonial analogy strike such a responsive chord. Joseph Lohman took this as the theme of one of his final articles.

> The young, the poor, and the minority groups [he wrote] have frequently viewed the law as not of their making nor to their interest; the law is that of a foreign power and the police is an army of occupation.

This sense of oppression burned most fiercely, he added, among those "thrice defined in their exclusion and deprivation." The current hostility of ghetto communities to the police was having a "disabling effect upon the law enforcement function." Nor was this hostility gratuitous. The police, he had found, did indeed tend to support the racial status quo with greater zeal than seemed necessary. In general, they blamed all demonstrations on "troublemakers" and pursued a racial "double standard" of law enforcement. The main components of this double standard were a number of assumptions, "taken for granted, like the air they breathe, by many police personnel." Central among these assumptions were the following:

1. The inevitability of vice or law violation when there are contacts between persons of differing racial extraction which are not a customary and accepted pattern of that community.
2. The necessity to enforce with police power the social customs and traditions of the community, apart from law (de facto segregation).
3. The necessity to invoke special action against minority groups which is not invoked against members of the majority group. Demonstrations, stop and frisk practices, and confinement of individuals to special districts are instances of the double standard.
4. The necessity to regard all instances of civil disobedience as without any differentiating characteristics . . .[44]

Wilson would say that such abuses have declined, and will disappear in time, with increased professionalism. But

Negroes are impatient, and can point to eminent white observers who disagree, if not with Wilson's trend report, at least with his forecast. Burton Levy, for example, writes that until recently he was a champion of the "professionalism" approach. During 1966 and 1967, however, he had an opportunity for intensive observation of police work in all parts of the nation as a consultant to the U. S. Department of Justice in establishing its police-community relations program. On the basis of this experience, together with his analysis of newly published studies, he has recently (late 1967) "completely reversed" his position. His current judgment is that:

> The problem is not one of a few "bad eggs" in a police department of 1,000 or 10,000 men, but rather of a police system that recruits a significant number of bigots, reinforces the bigotry through the department's value system and socialization with older officers, and then takes the worst of the officers and puts them on duty in the ghetto, where the opportunity to act out the prejudice is always available.[45]

Levy saw no evidence that recruitment, training, or community relations were anywhere having a significant impact on police practice.

In another recent study, Arthur Niederhoffer has noted that "a defeat is looming" for the advocates of professionalism. Only in periods of economic depression have the police ever been able to recruit middle class, college-educated men. It is these who have provided the thrust toward professionalism. In the current period of prosperity, the recruitment base is essentially confined to working class young men who are anxious for security but who have lacked the means or drive to graduate from college. Such men readily become part of the police subculture, but formal training and indoctrination intended to change that subculture have negligible impact on them.[46]

Even where professionalism is most advanced, its veneer

has regularly proven too thin to cope with racial tensions. For example, Wilson cites Oakland as one of the most "professional" forces in the nation, but shortly after his book appeared, it was Oakland police who wantonly shot up the local Black Panther headquarters.[47] In the most thorough study that has been made of the Oakland force, Jerome Skolnick concluded that strong anti-Negro prejudice was a norm among its members, and that a white policeman who failed to share it would be resented by his fellows.[48] During the tenure of Chief William H. Parker, the Los Angeles police force was regularly accounted the most "professional" in the country, but it was infused with racism from top to bottom. Reviewing its performance during the Watts riot, Gary Marx concluded that its "refusal to negotiate or use strategies other than a white show of force may have had disastrous consequences."[49]

Turning from the issue of efficiency to that of honesty, Negroes are inclined to say that here, too, professionalism has been overrated. From their vantage points in the ghettos, they claim to observe a great deal of protection of illicit enterprises. When it is argued that the police may lack authority to shut down these enterprises, or that the courts insist on standards of proof that the police cannot meet, they respond that this merely shows where the real problem of corruption in modern America lies: at the top. They take it for granted that the laws themselves are instruments of power, and have been shaped to serve the interests of rich versus poor, seller versus buyer, lender versus borrower, employer versus employee, white versus black. This is why even the "moderates" consider it vital for blacks to become a thoroughly mobilized pressure group in American politics, and why the more extreme look toward establishment of a separate black nation. (If the 1969 *Newsweek* poll can be believed, nearly one-quarter of American Negroes who have an opinion believe that Negroes should have a separate nation within the United States—21 per cent yes, 69 per cent no.[50])

Returning to ground level, they argue that, even if corruption is not the explanation, the police do tend to herd "undesirable" activities into special districts, and that these, almost invariably, happen to be occupied by Negroes. Suburban police, by contrast, just drive them out; and Negro communities want authority to do the same. The issue, once again, is equality.

Would actual corruption be greater in community-controlled than in citywide police forces? The supporters of community control are inclined to respond in the negative. Tight central control and frequent transfers may be one way to limit corruption, but another is to conduct frequent outside audits and undercover investigations. It seems most probable that a system of community control would be accompanied by vigorous surveillance along these lines. White journalists and legislators would be waiting to blow every scandal out of proportion, and to use it as a pretext for takeover. Being fully aware of the precariousness of their autonomy, Negro neighborhoods would be especially zealous in their own efforts to avert scandal.

The preceding discussion has focused on the police; but of course they present the hardest case. In other local bureaucracies, the threats of brutality, inequity, and corruption are less severe; organization along tight military lines and the systematic use of transfers to prevent clique formation are less common. This is an appropriate place to add, moreover, (a) *that community control should be conceived as a continuum rather than an absolute,* (b) *that its degree will inevitably vary from one field of activity to the next,* and (c) *that its degree may also vary from one dimension of any given policy arena to the next.* Thus, one might reasonably judge that community influence over the police should be less than that over the schools, or that supervision of the police from above with respect to fiscal probity should be greater than that with respect to determining tolerable levels of street disorder.

WOULD COMMUNITY CONTROL REDUCE THE CAPACITY OF LOCAL GOVERNMENT FOR VIGOROUS ACTION, AND FOR ACTION BASED ON CITYWIDE RATHER THAN MORE PAROCHIAL CONSIDERATIONS?

Some who maintain that it would are primarily fearful of excessive citizen participation, others of excessive fragmentation of authority among organized political units.

Those in the first category emphasize the difficulty of getting large numbers of citizens to agree, particularly on programs that might inconvenience some of them. In any group of men, it is charged, the capacity to act falls off sharply as the number of people who have to agree increases. But groups of laymen—and especially groups of poorly educated laymen with little or no administrative experience—have particular handicaps as decision makers. They have little time to devote to consideration of the issues; their concerns are selfish and immediate; they lack technical competence; they are both timid and suspicious—which is to say, they are easily frightened of anything unfamiliar; they are unwilling to delegate any responsibility to staff; and they are unable to make hard choices. Their deliberations tend to be endless. If policies are ever adopted, they tend to be extremely short run and conservative—giving each interest a little bit more of what it already knows and values. As the typical citizen values effective government much more than he values participation, however, the result of trying to involve and please everyone may be to please no one.

Sidney Verba, for example, writes that the greatest dilemma of participation is its apparent conflict with the efficient attainment of other social goals:

> Effective governmental programs may require slow and careful planning, technical control, and a willingness to defer gratification. Programs based on widespread participation are likely to represent greater compromise

and less careful planning and technical control, and to be aimed at relatively rapid gratification. The best calculated plans of urban developers are shattered in clashes with the residents whom the development displaces; the calculations of educators for curriculum-reform are often thrown off by complaints from parents' groups. . . . It will not do to ignore the "irrationalities" introduced into planning that come from widespread participation: the intrusion of uninformed opinions, the need to satisfy a widespread clientele which dilutes the major purpose of programs, and so forth.[51]

Those critics who emphasize the need for large geographic scale tend also to favor high concentrations of power within local jurisdictions. Many argue that excessive fragmentation is already the Achilles heel of our local government system. The typical urban region, they note, consists of scores or hundreds of overlapping general and specific purpose governments; and the typical big city general purpose government is fragmented into hosts of semi-autonomous functional fiefdoms. The system's characteristic response to new problems, moreover, has been to proliferate autonomous single purpose authorities.[52] There has been a trend toward strengthening chief executives in recent decades, but this has been more than offset by the movement of population to independent suburbs, the multiplication of functional authorities, and the decline of political parties.[53]

Yet the great problems of our urban areas—ranging from poverty and segregation to air pollution, the protection of open space, and transportation—call for regional solutions, and for solutions predicated upon the full range of metropolitan values rather than narrow functional assignments. As Robert Wood has noted, the primary consequence of fragmentation is to leave the private sector dominant in metropolitan affairs.* Its secondary effect is to weaken local by comparison with state and national governments.

---

*Having reviewed the various policies pursued by local governments in the New York region, Wood concludes as follows: "Not one . . . has important implications for the private sector of the Region taken as an

Community control would further fragment and incapacitate local government. To the extent that it does so, most city residents, black as well as white, will feel more frustrated than they do now. Their tendency, already marked, to look toward state and national authorities for solutions to local problems will become more accentuated. The upshot will be a diminished local role rather than the enhancement of participation in American politics viewed whole. Even at this stage, moreover, the residents of large and tightly organized jurisdictions will benefit, because these will perform most effectively as lobbyists and grant applicants.[55]

Neighborhood control advocates tend to counter the above arguments as follows.

First, there is no question but that decision making is slower, and that many large projects cannot secure approval at all, in a system that allows for widespread participation. In part, this is a cost that supporters of democracy and strong local government have always had to consider. But in the present circumstance it is also a benefit. The black sense of grievance in the cities has been produced significantly by large projects that would have better been left undone. Fewer highway and slum clearance projects are exactly what the cities need. They have inconvenienced the poor to benefit the affluent. The whole purpose of the participation movement is to redirect public policy so that at least such outrages are impossible. This is not to say that no highways

---

entity. An industry barred from one locality can in all probability find a hospitable reception in another with equivalent economic advantages. . . . With so many different constituencies, many options are open for firms and households alike, and though the process of industrial and population diffusion may occasionally be skewed, the forces are not, in general, thwarted, turned aside, or guided.

"[The policies] engender a pattern of behavior more closely approximating rivalries in world economic affairs than a domestic system of government intent on aiding the processes of economic development. Because particular combinations of strategies may be effective for any one jurisdiction, there is a strong tendency for each to 'go it alone.' . . . The development of hundreds of separate policies, in various combinations, among hundreds of jurisdictions engenders a spirit of contentiousness and competition. . . . They management of the political economy goes forward in ways localized, limited, and largely negative in character."[54]

should ever be built or slums cleared. But it is to say that the proponents of such projects should have to persuade the neighborhoods most affected before calling out the bull-dozers. This will take time; it will cost money; and it may often prove unfeasible. So be it. (Some take a softer line, and are willing to consider the use of extraordinary procedures to override recalcitrant communities. Where there is unanimity is on the desirability of greater community power to hinder large projects than currently prevails.)

Second, it is true that citizen participation tends to reduce the weight placed upon long-run and technical considera-tions, not to mention the values of consistency and compre-hensiveness, in decision making. In return, however, par-ticipation prevents technicians from spinning out their designs in blatant disregard of their consequences for ordi-nary citizens. Participation increases feedback; it encourages learning and adjustment as experience is gained with new policies; it compels the recognition of diversity. As Sidney Verba has written:

> Widespread participation may lead into something re-sembling chaos, but it is chaotic because there are many different values operating at the same time, and there are many different people involved with many different goals. Under such circumstances, clear-cut policies are difficult to achieve. But such are the circumstances of democracy.[56]

What is vital to keep in mind, moreover, is that the planners have never been able to impose their conception of ration-ality on the major participants in American politics.[57] Log-rolling, inconsistency, shortsightedness, neglect of complexity: these have always characterized the process and its policy outputs. Only the powerless have been left to the tender mercies of technicians—within limits, of course, set by the objectives and the reluctance to pay taxes of the powerful. Now at least some of the powerless, those who are black, are determined to get into the game on equal terms.

Third, disaggregation need not strengthen the status quo. Although stronger governments are in a better position to force change, they are also in a better position to prevent it. As the status quo has many dimensions, they may do both at the same time. In Chicago, for example, where influence is more tightly centralized than in any other large American city, the government is remarkably effective at securing federal grants. When these are for combatting poverty, the poor benefit. When they can be utilized to serve the rich and powerful, the poor often get buffeted around.

The machine is benevolent, but in the manner of a padrone. It gives the poor what *it* judges they should want. What it will not do, or permit others to do, is to challenge the fundamental pattern of segregation and inequality. Its leaders have been enormously successful in the existing environment; they tend to consider it good, and to fear change. The machine is a coalition of groups that despise and fear one another. Its counterparts nearly everywhere else have gone into oblivion. How long can their own balancing act go on? They are not sure, but anyone who wants to rearrange the underpinnings is a threat.

The power they have concentrated enables them to be remarkably effective in protecting the fundamental status quo. James Q. Wilson has described, for example, how the Dawson machine kept the local NAACP on "safe" paths during the 1950's. On the one occasion when it felt threatened, it simply took out 400 memberships for its precinct workers, enough to control the annual election. It did not elect one of its own people president, but merely ensured that the successful candidate was someone it considered acceptable.[58] The machine's capacity to block reform was illustrated much more grandly in 1965, when the U. S. Office of Education froze $32 million in federal aid that had been earmarked for the Chicago public schools. The funds were to be withheld pending further investigation of charges that the Chicago Board of Education had gerrymandered district boundaries to maximize *de facto* segregation. Mayor

Daley phoned President Johnson, the funds were "thawed" with dispatch, and the federal investigation was abruptly discontinued.*

Fourth, let us suppose that breaking up the large cities led to an increase in federal relative to local power. Blacks would benefit doubly. Income redistribution is almost exclusively a federal function in the American system, and the federal government is the major force for integration in American politics. Thus, the enhanced federal role would probably benefit Negroes, as would the increase in their share of surviving local power.

Fifth, the tradeoff between concentration and disaggregation within the local arena need not be as harsh as the critics suggest. The policy realms over which black (and some white) communities are demanding control are quite different from those that urban intellectuals believe require metropolitan solutions. Nor do the partisans of community control hold any brief for functional fragmentation, which prevents mayors from ruling their own houses.

What is most striking, then, is that the arguments in apparent conflict do not meet. They point in opposite directions, but they are in different policy dimensions. If the advocates of each wished to forge an alliance, they might do so without compromising the key objectives of either. Their joint program might consist of the following: (a) elimination of all special districts, leaving a simple two- or three-tier system of general purpose governments within each urban region; (b) the top tier, regional in scale, to exercise responsibility for such functions as pollution control, general land use and transportation planning, the equalization of public services (via grants-in-aid), and securing integration opportunities for those who wished to exploit them; (c) the bottom tier to exercise the kinds of responsibility that sub-

---

*The Nixon Administration announced that it was reviving this investigation in mid-1969. At the same time, it accused the Chicago School Board of maintaining an illegal system of faculty segregation.[59]

urbs now exercise;* (d) each tier, or at least the top two, to be organized along strong mayor lines, with all agency heads serving at the pleasure of the mayor; and (e) civil service regulations to be made far more flexible, so as to enable chief executives to combat the three bureaucratic diseases of stagnation, unresponsiveness, and racial imbalance.

This is not to deny that there are genuine sources of potential conflict between the two camps. Where blacks hoped to achieve a central city majority within the foreseeable future, they would be likely to oppose any transfer of its functions to the metropolitan level.** (As the prospect be-

---

*Where a middle tier—the central city—persisted, neighborhoods within it would continue to exercise less authority than suburbs. Thus, the neatest and most equitable arrangement would be two tiers if it were feasible. A two-tier system, of course, might be one in which the suburbs themselves had substantially less power—e.g., to exclude low income housing, to maintain lily-white schools—than at present.

**Even where this prospect has not existed, Negroes have invariably provided heavy majorities against metropolitan government in referenda to date. But metropolitan government was not part of a package that included community control in any of these referenda.[60]

It should be noted that among Negro activists of all stripes at present, there is virtual unanimity that whites favor metropolitan government only when it serves to dilute Negro power. If one states the thesis a bit less strongly—that in most large urban areas white *majorities* for metropolitan government will be available (if ever) only when the issue is black control of the central city—it is difficult indeed to dispute.

To date, it should be noted, metropolitan government has come in America only to single-county urban areas, where it could be achieved by transfers of authority from one existing unit of government to another. Normally, state legislatures have required referenda to bring the change about. Majorities have been rare, and none has ever been achieved in a county whose population at the time exceeded one million.

There remain the possibilities (a) that federal aid might change the balance of inducements, (b) that state legislatures, confronted by severe urban unrest, might impose "package" solutions, and (c) that new program packages might produce new voting configurations.

In practice, federal aid has produced the recent proliferation of metropolitan councils of governments (see below, pp. 183–84), and the strategy of those metropolitan government movements that remain active has shifted to securing direct legislative enactment. This approach bore fruit in the Indianapolis area in 1969 (one county, population 900,000), and has

came imminent, Negroes would probably lose interest in community control itself. By the same token, white central city residents would be likely to acquire some.*) Even aside from this source of dispute, the coalition partners would have numerous disagreements on priorities and details. Their personal differences of style and outlook would make continued cooperation difficult. And their alliance would be strained severely whenever an opportunity arose to move toward one of the twin goal sets—i.e., concentration and community control—unaccompanied by any assurance that it would soon be balanced with equivalent moves toward the other.

The maintenance of our hypothetical coalition, then, would require a strong determination on both sides to avoid a break. Life within the family would be far from tranquil. To note this, however, is not to suggest that remarkable ingenuity would be required to conceive acceptable compromises. Far from it. Those most dissatisfied with the suburban and functional fragmentation of existing local institutions tend also to be appalled by the ravages that the urban renewal and highway programs were permitted to perpetrate in the late fifties and early sixties. They are not at all inclined to say that city and regional authorities should be empowered to run roughshod over minority interests. As for the blacks, they will need white liberal allies if community

---

produced important steps toward metropolitan government in the Minneapolis-St. Paul area over the past several years (seven counties, combined population 1.8 million).

*Research bearing on this double-edged hypothesis would shed very useful light on the degree to which the demand for community control is a simple manifestation of the racial distribution of power.

It bears mention, incidentally, that a white neighborhood of 36,000 in Gary (which became, in 1968, one of the nation's first two major cities to elect a Negro mayor) has already taken several steps toward secession from the city. It secured state legislation in 1969 that would permit it to "disaffiliate" from the city on petition by 51 per cent of its property owners or the owners of 51 per cent of its property (by assessed value). No referendum would be required, and no counter-petitions have legal standing. The disaffiliation petitions are actively circulating at this writing. If the requisite number of signatures are acquired, a court battle over the constitutionality of the state law is expected.

control is ever to become a reality; and it is hard to conceive of a program at once more compatible with community control and more likely to attract them. Politics has made far stranger bedfellows in the past.

WOULD COMMUNITY CONTROL PROVE
A DEAD END FOR BLACKS THEMSELVES?

Those who believe that it would tend to argue as follows. Participation is one thing, power to improve ghetto conditions quite another. The danger is great that low income communities will have their attention and energy absorbed by processes that have little potential for improving their lives. Ironically, the primary benefit of community control might accrue to whites. It could provide them with a respite from black pressure, by diverting Negroes into a fruitless competition for control of the impoverished ghettos. In this vein Martin Rein has written that:

> The fundamental problem is evidently not the manner in which institutions function, but their inability to function at all. The employment services do not have the jobs to offer, the schools cannot pay enough good teachers, the housing authorities cannot build decent cheap homes in attractive neighborhoods. The services themselves are as impoverished as those who use them. . . . *As a cause of poverty, the weakness of the redistribution mechanisms in American society seems much more crucial that the shortcomings of institutional procedures.*[61]

Writing of the federal Community Action Program, Rein argues that without large resources it has been unable to bring about more than marginal improvements in service delivery. Daniel P. Moynihan presents an even bleaker picture. He writes that in general the CAP election turnouts were pitiful; the representatives, once chosen, were ineffective; and the process tended to bog down in endless quarreling over trivial details.[62] S. M. Miller maintains that:

Most experience with participation in the Sixties has been at the planning stage. Where there has been participation at the operational stage as in CAP programs, ineffective delivery of services has been common. . . . There is a tradeoff to some extent between participation and delivery; an important issue, then, is how much loss in delivery is "acceptable" for a gain in participation? [63]

David Cohen and Christopher Jencks, perhaps the two scholars who have most carefully reviewed the evidence bearing on proposed ghetto education strategies, both conclude that there is no solid basis for predicting that community control would improve student achievement.* [64]

---

*There is room for a great deal of dispute about the relevance of the data on which their conclusion rests. The most elaborate and direct attempt to test the relationship between parental participation and student educational achievement was made in the Coleman study. Unfortunately, the measure of parental participation on which it relied was PTA attendance. Noting this, Betsy Levin has observed: "Whatever meaningful participation by ghetto parents may mean, it clearly does *not* mean membership in the PTA. What we need are new strategies of parental involvement, and new definitions and measures of parent participation. Until these are developed, tried, and evaluated, however, parent participation as a mechanism for affecting pupil achievement cannot be dismissed." [65]

In his forthcoming book in the present series, Cohen will partially rebut this argument by reporting analyses of the relation between school district size and pupil achievement. He has found no correlation between the two variables, when student and school characteristics are held constant.

Needless to say, jurisdictional size is not a direct measure of citizen participation. It is the primary measure of community control on which we are focusing in this book, however.

When size of jurisdiction is held constant, the degree of participation appears to be primarily a function of the social class, educational achievement, and ethnic culture of the citizenry. Until recently, all these factors would have led one to expect low rates of participation in ghetto jurisdictions by comparison with affluent suburban units of similar size.

The civil rights revolution has had a profound impact on the political culture of black communities, however. Formerly the least organized of American "ethnic" groups, blacks are today among the better organized. When average incomes and years of education are taken into account, the political vitality of their communities is particularly striking. Should the trend continue strong, and receive a fillip from the coming of legal community control, it could well invalidate the forecasts of backward-looking social scientists. Some community control advocates would add that even if the chance is slim it must be taken—because only this sort of cultural transformation, spreading from politics into many other fields, can enable blacks to make rapid progress toward equality.

In rebuttal, community control advocates maintain, first, that they are fully aware of the difference between the right to participate and the power to achieve one's objectives. The more militant among them have led the way toward popularizing this distinction in recent years by opting out of participation on terms defined by established institutions. They recognize as well that community control cannot substitute for resources. But they believe that community control can facilitate ghetto mobilization to bring pressure to bear on the institutions of the larger society.

Community election campaigns would provide frequent occasions for organizing and building group consciousness. Elected community leaders would have official status and indisputable claims to "representativeness" as they lobbied in the corridors of state and national power. Community-controlled institutions would concentrate on building citizen self-respect rather than destroying it. The sight of Negroes in key positions would give a tremendous fillip to black pride. The experience of getting some results from participation (whether complaining about garbage pickup or helping to shape school policy) would bolster citizens' sense of efficacy. Combined and given time, these features of community control should enhance the organizability of the black community, and hence its potency as a pressure group in the larger governmental system. Community control may bring whites a respite from certain black demands, but not from the demand for resources. That demand, if anything, will be made more sharply and urgently when blacks have their own local governments to speak for them.

Turning to the question of effectiveness, it is possible to cite the same authors cited by the prosecution in defense of community control, and in fact most of these authors are themselves on balance sympathetic to community control. Even Moynihan, the exception to this latter characterization, reports that by mid-1967 many mayors had concluded that if Community Action Agencies did not exist, they would have to be invented. They provided a source of liaison with the smouldering ghettos; they and the mayors had learned to live with each other; and they were playing essential roles in the administration of the new programs (Head Start, Neighborhood Youth Corps, Legal Services, etc.) brought into being by the federal "war" on poverty.[66]

Among the more sympathetic analysts, Rein maintains that the Community Action Agencies did effectuate "marginal" improvements. Miller notes that in the present atmosphere participation is probably necessary if many services are to continue to function at all. One does, after all, have to deal with the angry ghettos as they are, not as white liberals might wish them to be. Cohen and Jencks see no reason to fear that community control would reduce educational achievement, and they note that it might produce substantial benefits outside the realm of measured skill achievement—for example, in terms of community satisfaction and student self-respect.*

Many community control advocates would consider the above projections at the extreme pessimistic end of the spectrum. They believe that community control is a vital step on the path to developing black pride, political skill, and organization. Over time, these should transform the black community, enabling its young to learn, its adults to keep their public servants responsive, and its leaders to secure greater resources from the larger society. These results will not be apparent overnight. But this just highlights the need to take the long view in estimating the potential impact of community control on service efficiency.

IS COMMUNITY CONTROL A MINORITY DEMAND WITHIN THE BLACK COMMUNITY?

In support of the charge that it is, one can cite numerous

---

*With regard to the alleged dangers of deterioration in quality and increased racial separatism, Jencks finds some ground for reassurance in the record of Catholic parochial education. A large-scale recent survey has shown that, when adjustments are made for student socioeconomic backgrounds, parochial school Catholics end up more observant in religion (community solidarity), no less tolerant, with slightly more education, and with slightly better jobs than public school Catholics.[67] Since parochial school parents are self-selected, it should be added, the difference could well be due to unmeasured family background characteristics.

survey findings; but most of them are ambiguous and, even where clear, their significance is difficult to assess. Community control is a new issue, and repeat surveys asking the same questions over time are unavailable. A single survey provides no guidance as to trends. It rarely provides much basis for distinguishing the views of political activists and opinion leaders from the general public. It fails to record the intensity with which views are held, or the willingness to expend energy and take risks on their behalf. If taken at a time when most people have thought little about an issue, it is an unreliable indicator of how they would choose at the end of a hard-fought referendum campaign. Having stated the issue with one configuration of words, it may be highly misleading when applied to another statement that most outside observers would consider quite similar.

In support of the charge, one can cite such findings as these: Gallup's national survey for *Newsweek* (1969) found only 13 per cent of Negroes agreeing that "Negroes will make more progress by running their own schools and businesses and living in their own neighborhoods than by integrating" (78 per cent disagreed).[68] A Center for Urban Education poll conducted in Bedford-Stuyvesant during the summer of 1967 reported only 34 per cent of Negro respondents maintaining that parents should have a say in the hiring of teachers and principals (vs. 52 per cent who believed that parents should have no say).[69] The fifteen-city Kerner Commission survey (1968) found only small minorities agreeing with the following statements: stores in Negro neighborhoods should be owned and run by Negroes (18 per cent), schools with mostly Negro pupils should have Negro principals (14 per cent), such schools should have mostly Negro teachers (10 per cent), and there should be a separate black nation here (6 per cent).[70]

These findings are more ambiguous than they appear at first glance, however. Gallup's question loaded the dice by combining rejection of integration with support of community control. The importance that this anti-integration feature must have had is suggested by the fact that a higher proportion of respondents favored establishment of a separate black nation (21 per cent) than appeared to favor community control. Some respondents may have viewed the black nation as an option that should be available to Negroes who wanted it, but which would not foreclose the option of integration for others. Parenthetically, although the two polls are not quite comparable, it is noteworthy that the *Newsweek* poll showed three and one-half times as many respondents favoring establishment of a black nation as had the Kerner Commission poll 16 months earlier (21 per cent vs. 6 per cent).*

The Bedford-Stuyvesant poll is already dated, but it did show two-fifths of Negro respondents who had an opinion believing that parents should have a say in the hiring of teachers and principals. When the question was turned around, and they were asked whether parents should have a say in replacing unsatisfactory teachers and principals, the proportions were almost reversed. Nearly three-fifths of those with an opinion thought so (50 per cent yes, 37 per cent no with respect to teachers; 49 per cent yes, 37 per cent no with respect to principals). Moreover, the issue of direct parent involvement in personnel decisions is quite different from that of the larger political structure within which these decisions are made. When the residents of Newton and Brookline defend the separation of their school systems from that of Boston, they are not endorsing *ad hoc* intervention by parents in school decision making. What they are endorsing is the exercise of local democracy in relatively small (under 100,000 in the examples cited) jurisdictions.

The Kerner Commission questions seem more relevant to the issue of separatism than that of community control. Even those who have exercised control in Ocean Hill-

---

*The sample variations may well have produced an understatement of the change. The Kerner Commission sample was drawn from fifteen large northern cities. The *Newsweek* sample was national. One would have expected black nationalism to register with substantially greater strength in the former.

Brownsville, after all, have disclaimed any desire to pack the district with black teachers and principals.*

The most striking bit of evidence for the defense, however, comes from a Harris poll conducted in New York City during late November and early December 1968. This was less than one month after the end of the long New York City teachers' strike over community control, and at a time when New York City school decentralization was the hottest issue before the New York State legislature. The Harris organization asked the following question of 1,087 elementary and secondary school parents distributed throughout the city: "Generally, do you feel the community has too much influence in the running of the schools in this neighborhood, too little influence, or just about the right amount of influence . . . ?" Of those who had an opinion, nearly half felt that the community had too little influence (37 per cent, vs. 39 per cent who opted for the other two positions combined). Among Negroes, the ratio was more than 4–1 (66–15 per cent). The comparable percentages for other groups were: Puerto Rican, 31–38; Jewish, 43–41; white Catholic, 22–51. In general, support for an enhanced community role was greatest among parents who were college graduates and those who were under thirty.[72]

The parents were also asked whom they had supported in the recent strike, the community's representatives or the teachers' union.** One-third of the respondents felt unable

---

*David Cohen notes that what they have desired is personnel who would stick by the community in disputes with the city Board of Education and the United Federation of Teachers.[71] Such a "loyalty" test may be obnoxious. On the other hand, both the Board and the union expected teachers to act in accord with *their* directives in disputes with the experimental district. What was at issue, in other words, was the relative legitimacy of contending authorities. Given sufficient power, each was prepared to make loyalty the first, the indispensable, qualification for employment.

**The precise wording of the question was as follows: "There was a controversy in New York City recently in the Ocean Hill-Brownsville School District with the Local Governing Board and the Unit Administrator on one side and the teachers and their union on the other. From what you know or have heard about this situation, did you tend to support the Governing Board and the Administrator, or the teachers and the union in the strike?"

to take sides, but the remainder supported the union by 2½–1 (47–19 per cent). There were enormous differences among key social groups, however. In particular, Negroes sided with the *community* by a ratio of 8–1 (46–8 per cent), whereas whites sided with the *union* by nearly 6–1 (62–11 per cent). White Catholics favored the union by 13–1 (65–5 per cent), Jews by 4–1 (63–16 per cent), and Puerto Ricans by 1½–1 (29–19 per cent).[73]

In sum, the evidence from New York suggests that support for an enhanced community role in education is widespread, but very unevenly distributed among the city's major social groups. Even more important, it suggests that when the battle is joined the races will polarize even further.

New York is by no means the nation, however, and we have seen that the survey data from elsewhere are ambiguous.* What does seem clear, though, is that *politically active* Negroes throughout the nation favor community control. A few prominent individuals dissent, but the organizational leaders present a united front. To illustrate: the Urban League and the National Association for the Advancement of Colored People (NAACP) are generally accounted the most "moderate" of the major civil rights organizations. Yet both adopted strong community control resolutions at their 1969 national conventions. Both rejected the view that community control is a "separatist" program. The main NAACP resolution, for example, read as follows:

> We strongly support the concept of community control of public schools, particularly in the big-city school systems of the North and West, as a means of achieving fundamental changes in the schools and insuring accountability. . . .

---

*In drawing up an urban participation research program, I would give absolute top priority to the carrying out of surveys comparing black and white, leadership and mass, suburban and central city attitudes toward participation, proper local government scale, and neighborhood government within large cities.

> *We do not believe that community control and desegregation are inherently incompatible* or in conflict unless they are made to be by the advocates, white or black, of racial separatism.[74]

Speaking with less formality, Whitney Young, Executive Director of the National Urban League, has recently stated that: "Community control is the most crucial issue right now. Institutions have failed because control isn't in the hands of the people who live in the communities."[75]

What also seems clear is that the passionate supporters of community control are not offset by comparably motivated opponents. The more traditional among the black masses may deplore stridency and mass agitation, but for the most part they are people whom history has run over rather than people who are trying to grab the steering wheel. The political activists set the agenda of demands (except when the angry but nonpolitical young act spontaneously), and when the racial confrontations take place even the traditionalists find themselves rooting for the "brothers." At least, most do. The breadth of latent support on which initiators of confrontations can count is indicated by the response to a question in the fifteen-city Kerner Commission survey. Respondents were asked: "Even if you didn't join in [a riot], would you feel in sympathy with Negroes who did choose to join, or would you feel unsympathetic toward them?" Excluding the respondents who had indicated (in response to a previous question) that they would join in themselves— 8 per cent—more than two-thirds of those with an opinion indicated that they would be sympathetic (54 per cent vs. 24 per cent). *[76]

---

*It should be noted that only 3 per cent indicated that they had already participated in a riot. A related study concluded, however, that in cities that had experienced major disorders, participation had been much higher: roughly, one-sixth of all riot area residents aged 10–59 in Newark, one-ninth in Detroit. In the prime sex-age group, males aged 15–35, participation rates were roughly three times these overall figures.[77]

DEFINITIONS OF KEY TERMS

When political issues are new, and when political concepts become popular symbols, the key terms are prone to lack generally agreed meanings. Both these forces for ambiguity are vigorously operative in the area under discussion, and some explicit definitions are essential if the ensuing pages are to clarify rather than confuse. I have already hazarded a number, as seemed necessary, above. What I propose here is to bring these together, to elaborate the distinctions on which they rest, and to add a number of others.

In its general sense—that which embraces but is not confined to the political—*participation* means having a share of, or taking part in, something. One may participate in the ownership of a business, in the use of a car, in painting a barn, in the exercise of political authority. Participation is a matter of degree; one can have a very small share or a very large one.

Power means the capacity to induce others to act in accord with one's will. It is divisible into two categories, authority and influence.

Authority is the legal right to command others to act in accord with one's will. For all but total dictators, its exercise is hedged about by specifications of the values to be served and the sorts of commands that may be issued. These specifications take the following forms: statutes, judicial precedents, and administrative regulations. *Discretion* is the amount of leeway permitted an official (or body of officials) by these specifications.

Influence is all power that rests on other foundations than authority.[78]

Political power means the capacity to bring about governmental actions that accord with one's will.

Political participation means sharing in the exercise of political power. This definition excludes a good deal that rulers around the world seek to palm off as political participation—for example, voting in an election where to do so is compulsory and there is no choice of candidates.

Political participation becomes an issue when significant groups of citizens claim that they have inequitable shares of power to affect important governmental decisions. Importance, of course, is in the eye of the observer—a product of his priorities and perceptions of causality.

Political participation may be viewed as a competitive game, one whose rules are defined by law and custom. When groups of citizens feel shut out of the decision process, or judge that the rules systematically bias the game against them, they are likely to cheat—that is, to employ means that law and custom define as illegitimate. If they are disorganized and lack a protest ideology, they will act as individual "criminals." If they are organized and have a rationale for protest, they will more often act openly, with an air of righteousness, contending that the rules are inequitable. In some cases, their point will carry; the rules will be revised. This is the normal process, it should be emphasized, by which the rules evolve. But, like the process of evolution in nature, it has more in common with warfare than with reasoned debate. In democratic societies, however, the latter may play an important role.

The current crisis of political participation in American society is in part about the substantive distribution of power (who has it, with respect to what), but it is also about the legitimacy of specific participatory modes—ranging from sit-ins through strikes by key public employees to riots. The crisis is particularly acute, as Sidney Verba has noted, because all aspects of the game are at issue on numerous fronts at the same time: new people want to participate; they are raising many new as well as old issues; and they are insisting on the legitimacy of many hitherto-prohibited modes.[79] Those raising the issue range from welfare mothers to members of the U. S. Senate. The policy arenas in which it is being raised range from the operation of nursery schools to the commitment of American honor and military manpower abroad.

Early in this chapter (p. 14), I sought to make explicit my understanding of the specific claims to larger shares that make up *the issue of black participation in large American cities.* These claims seem to focus on three values: political authority, group representation in public bureaucracies, and the private income (wages and profits) generated by governmental activity. Thus, although the primary focus of this study is on the first, its subject matter includes the other two. This may not be the most elegant way to employ the term "participation," but for the set of controversies here under review it is the way that best corresponds with everyday usage.

To *decentralize* means to distribute authority more widely —that is, to a greater number of individuals. Decentralization can take many forms. One of the most vital is to substitute decisions by individuals in the marketplace for decisions by governmental officials. We shall be concerned in this volume, however, with a specific type of decentralization: that within government, from officials at the center of a jurisdiction to those in geographically defined subjurisdictions (i.e., states within the nation, localities within states, and so on).

Within this type, it is of crucial importance to distinguish *administrative* decentralization from *political* decentralization. The former involves delegation from superior to subordinate officials within a bureaucracy. The organizing principle of the bureaucracy remains hierarchical. The top officials remain free to revoke the delegation at any time. The subordinate officials remain dependent in numerous ways upon the pleasure of their superiors. Political decentralization, by contrast, involves the transfer of authority to officials whose dependence is upon the subjurisdictional electorate, or, more narrowly, a subjurisdictional clientele. The assumption must be that such officials will not be manipulable by the former possessors of the transferred authority.

Community control means the exercise of authority by the democratically organized government of a neighborhood-sized jurisdiction. There is no consensus on how neighborhoods should be defined (see below, pp. 124–34). Nor is there any consensus about the precise amount of authority that such a government would have to possess in any given policy arena for the label "community control" to be justified. What the term does clearly denote is a category of proposed reforms: transfers of authority from the governments of large cities to the governments of much smaller subunits within them. Such transfers would constitute political decentralization. At the same time, it should be emphasized that they would remain subject to modification by higher levels of government—just as are the charters of cities and suburbs today.

CHAPTER TWO

THE FRAMEWORK

Fᴿᴏᴍ one perspective, the urban participation movement is a very specific manifestation of the American race problem at this moment in time. (The thrust for participatory reform is not coming exclusively from blacks, but in the cities—as opposed to the universities, for example—they supply its overwhelming share of passion, and thus of political significance.) From another, however, it is a local manifestation of a worldwide current, and it has myriad roots in American history. The particular and general perspectives are both legitimate; neither alone is sufficient. The predominant focus of this volume is on the former, but we should risk severe distortion if we ignored the latter entirely. Hence the discussion which follows—sketchy and highly tentative, but intended at least to indicate the wider contexts.

Scholarly efforts to place this American reform movement in international context have not yet begun to appear. One need only follow the headlines, however, to observe that racial prejudice, ethnic nationalism, and dissatisfaction with the size, unresponsiveness, and impersonality of modern public bureaucracies are worldwide phenomena. The first is probably declining, but it remains of overwhelming importance in almost every country with a substantial minority population. (The partial exceptions are all Latin American.) The second has been one of the very few most potent forces for world change over the past 150 years. What is new is simply its resurgence over the past decade within the developed nations of western Europe and North America. The third, too, has a long history, but its capacity to unite intellectuals of the left and right, and to command mass support, is of very recent origin.[1]

The one serious—though journalistic and very brief—effort to place the American movement for local participation in world context that has so far appeared is by Nathan Glazer.[2] Glazer, a profound student of American ethnicity and an inveterate world traveler, begins by noting that:

> The same issues are rising everywhere. . . . One cannot help feeling that we are in the grip of a movement against bureaucracy and centralization—particularly where ethnic and racial divisions are involved—that in some way has to be taken into account. Thus, the association of this movement in the United States with the black and the poor . . . may conceal from many of us its real power and seriousness.

He then maintains that the growth of ethnic passions seems unrelated to "objective" degrees of cultural heterogeneity, inequality, or oppression. Thus, although the Flemings of Belgium are rapidly improving their relative economic position and are already dominant politically, their resentment of alleged Walloon domination seems to be waxing rather than waning. The drive for separatism has acquired such strength that the University of Louvain is to be separated into two parts, with the French-speaking division being relocated at great expense outside the geographic zone of Flemish dominance.

An even more astonishing example is the separatist movement among the French-speaking citizens of the German-speaking canton of Bern, Switzerland. The Swiss government system provides greater opportunity for citizen participation than probably any other in the world. The country is small and militantly democratic. Its central government is almost powerless. Even the small cantons delegate most of their powers to local units within them. And these latter "are dominated by the direct voting of citizens on every conceivable issue." Nonetheless, a separatist movement is flourishing among the French speakers of Bern. The passion it inspires among its members has been sufficient to produce several recent bombings.

Glazer's other illustrations of his thesis are Welsh, Scottish, and French Canadian nationalism. He concludes that:

> In all these cases—and in many more I could refer to— we find not only the demand for cultural opportunity, economic equality, political consideration in proportion to one's numbers in a unitary state but what to me is the irrational demand that the "foreigners," the "others," with whom one has been associated in an integrated state for centuries, be removed . . . a demand, now coming from the ostensibly dominated rather than the domineering groups, for the clearing out of the dominators, so that the formerly inferior group can conduct its own life, without involvement with others. And, of course, we see the same demand developing in black communities in this country. Undoubtedly this [like its counterparts elsewhere] is at present the demand of a minority. But the majority is confused, passionless— and for the most part, silent.

For all that I admire Glazer and find his examples provocative, this analysis strikes me as severely unbalanced. For one thing, it implies that the movement for neighborhood power in American cities is aggressively separatist. This is a gross oversimplification. To illustrate: in the New York City Harris poll cited above (p. 59), it will be recalled that Negro respondents favored a larger neighborhood role in education by more than 4–1. At the same time, they favored racial integration of their own children's schools by a margin of 11–1 (86–8 per cent).

Second, it implies that the grievances of American Negroes are trivial, that Negroes have not in fact been the victims of severe hostility and exclusion by the majority.

Third, it ignores the long history of efforts by lower class groups to acquire greater control over their immediate environments (e.g., factory working conditions) and to improve their socioeconomic circumstances. In this connection, Charles Tilly's review of collective violence (the extreme protest model) in the history of western Europe over the past several centuries seems highly relevant. Tilly maintains that violent protests have generally had political roots. Far from being just youthful rampages or irrational by-products of social change, they have typically expressed lower class demands "for established places in the structure of power." The evidence for this proposition is that collective violence has not been randomly distributed among lower class groups. It has, rather, been produced almost invariably by groups whose peaceful efforts to alter the structure of power had been gathering force for some time.[3]

Although he denies that it is random or capricious, Tilly does not deny that collective violence is associated with rapid change. On the contrary, he contends that it clusters in periods when change has generated many new claimants of power and has dramatically shifted the distribution of political resources among social groups. "Violence flows from politics," he concludes, "and more precisely from political change."[4]

He adds that collective violence is an interactive phenomenon, most frequently between the political authorities and protestors against the status quo. The authorities have substantial discretion in responding to illegal protests that are not intrinsically violent. If they are sufficiently brutal, like the governments of Hitler and Franco, they can suppress almost all expressions of protest. In systems where their response is more problematic, their choice in concrete situations is frequently the critical determinant of whether large-scale violence occurs. Summing up, Tilly writes that:

> A large proportion of the European disturbances we
> have been surveying turned violent at exactly the moment
> when the authorities intervened to stop an illegal but
> non-violent action. . . . Furthermore, the great bulk of
> the killing and wounding in those same disturbances
> was done by troops or police rather than by insurgents
> or demonstrators. The demonstrators, on the other hand,
> did the bulk of the damage to property.[5]

Fourth, Glazer neglects the cases that might be cited of
ethnic separatism gathering force—which is to say, intensity
and mass support—in response to genuine exclusion or oppression by the majority. The cases of Biafran and Zionist
nationalism, to wit, seem at least as relevant as those of
Welsh and French Canadian nationalism. So, though colonial
rule was more patronizing than harsh, do the rebellions that
have reshaped the maps of Asia and Africa over the past
quarter century, and that have had such a profound impact
on the American Negro consciousness.

Fifth, Glazer disregards frequent examples that might be
cited of *dominant* groups in modern nations stressing the
theme of ethnic purification. The Nazi experience is not
very many decades behind us. Scanning the world scene
as this is written, the longstanding South African and Rho-
desian cases, and the recent explosion of official anti-Semitism
in Poland, are particularly salient. Literally hosts of less
extreme examples might be cited, though since the fall of
Hitler ethnic persecution has tended to be cloaked in somewhat euphemistic rhetoric.

What Glazer has provided, then, is a controversial hypothesis (that ethnic passion is unrelated to the actual degree
of ethnic difference, repression, or inferiority) and a few
proposed topics for the comparative portion of the needed
participatory research agenda. Though only suggestive,
these offerings are by no means to be spurned. Developing
and addressing this section of the agenda is absolutely essential if we are to distinguish meaningfully between the unique
and the near-universal in the American movement for urban
participation.

Let us now turn to the roots of this movement in our national history. They are numerous and profound. The most significant among them appear to be: (1) the high value that Americans from the start have placed on citizen participation in politics; (2) the long exclusion of blacks from full membership in American society; (3) the persistence of ethnicity as a vital distinction in American society; (4) the strong taste of Americans for decentralized government; and (5) the American unwillingness to forego political representation in dealing with public bureaucracies.

I propose to review these in turn.

THE IDEAL OF WIDESPREAD POLITICAL PARTICIPATION

This has probably been the most persistent theme in American history. Generation after generation, movements have arisen with the aim of improving the common man's ability to control his governors. Such movements have also arisen elsewhere, but in no other country has the democratic principle been given such priority or met so little opposition—at least, with respect to the organization of governments and the participation of whites.

Even before the Revolution, American state and local governments were the most democratic in the world. The Crown's appointed governors imposed taxes to help meet the cost of defense—only in the last two decades, after the French had been expelled from North America, did many come to view it as the cost of occupation—but otherwise they played a secondary role to the elected legislatures. Property qualifications for voting and officeholding were the rule, but most whites were able to meet them.[6]

The paramount trend of American eighteenth-century politics was the growing reluctance of the colonists to be taxed except by their own elected representatives. To virtually all the British ruling class and even many Americans, this seemed wildly radical. But the upshot, of course, was the first modern anti-colonial revolution. (Is it unreasonable to ask whether the grievances of the colonists against the Crown were comparable to those of black Americans more recently against white?)

In the first half of the nineteenth century, as a substantial landless class developed (with the emergence of cities) for the first time, attention turned to the abolition of property requirements. Of this movement William Riker has written: "As recently as the middle of the 19th century, both the name and practice of democracy were anathema to respectable people. For bourgeois minds the word identified both Jacobin terror and Jacksonian vulgarity." Yet by 1840 universal male suffrage (still, of course, confined to whites) was the American rule, nearly half a century before it became so in France or England, nearly a century ahead of Germany, Italy, and the Scandinavian countries.[7]

The thrust toward democratization was also one toward politicization in the age of Jackson. The common man was king. Deference (outside the South) was dead, the spirit of equality was ascendant. Democracy was young, the aspirations of its partisans unlimited. The agenda of reform was to fill as many offices, including judicial, as possible by election, the remainder by patronage. Experience, formal training, dispassion, continuity: to cite these as values to be stressed in staffing the government was to appear antidemocratic. The common man (like today's militant black) wanted his own kind in office; such criteria would tend to exclude them. Fortunately, the functions of government were few, the age of professionalization was yet to come. The total politicization of government had a price, but it was undoubtedly easier to pay then than later.

In retrospect, we can see that the absorption of the masses into politics involved substantial upheaval everywhere. Relatively few nations have made the transition to mass politics without experiencing dictatorship, let alone spoilsmanship.

Even in Great Britain, where it might appear to the casual eye that stable mass democracy was achieved with remarkable grace and dispatch, the transition was scarcely uneventful. In many respects, of course, it dates back to the bloody civil wars of the mid-seventeenth century, in which the monarchy was overthrown and Charles I beheaded. Three decades after Cromwell's death and the restoration of the monarchy, another reigning monarch was overthrown. In the following century, wrote Elie Halevy:

> England, the sole European country where the reigning dynasty had been set up as the result of a successful rebellion, [was] the home of insurrection. . . . A Government without a police force was powerless either to prevent these outrages or repress them promptly. The right to riot or, as it was termed by the lawyers, "the right of resistance," was an integral part of the national tradition.[8]

Following the French Revolution, the English masses were even more restive and the ruling classes more frightened. Tilly notes that the establishment of professional police forces during the second quarter of the nineteenth century was explicitly perceived in crowd-control as well as crime-control terms. He quotes Benjamin Disraeli, looking back from 1862:

> There arose Luddite mobs, meal mobs, farm riots, riots everywhere; Captain Swing and his rickburners, Peterloo "massacres," Bristol conflagrations, and all the ugly sights and rumours which made young lads, thirty or forty years ago, believe (and not so wrongly) that "the masses were their natural enemies, and they might have to fight, any year, or any day, for the safety of their property and the honour of their sisters."[9]

The first decades of the twentieth century, following achievement of universal manhood suffrage, were if anything more unsettled. In the streets, mass demonstrations, frequently accompanied by violence, were occurring regularly on behalf of union demands, women's suffrage, temperance, and (till 1914) disarmament. On the political front, the Liberals were going down before the onslaught of a new party tied organizationally to the labor unions and dedicated to socialism. In 1926 the country experienced a general strike. Historians doubt that revolution was ever an immediate possibility. Contemporaries may be pardoned if they occasionally had their doubts (as many did).

Returning to the American scene: Jacksonian reform fragmented legal authority in the name of popular rule. In the spoils system, however, it also provided tangible resources and an outlook on the proper use of authority that could be utilized to achieve high concentrations of extra-legal influence. And, of course, utilized they were. With mass immigration, industrialization, and urbanization in the latter third of the nineteenth century, the resources available to local "machines" were greatly expanded even as their character deteriorated—away from democratic zeal, toward careerism and corruption.

Still, there were many who viewed the machines as legitimate incarnations of democracy: they were composed of common men; they survived by speaking the various languages of the polyglot mass electorate and providing large numbers of voters with specific favors. Others perceived them as monstrous perversions of democracy. Though they distributed favors widely, they concentrated power tightly. Though their little favors went to little men, the big favors went to land speculators, public utility franchise holders, government contractors, illicit businessmen, and of course the leading members of the machines themselves.

Members of the rising middle class disliked them because they were corrupt and vulgar. Social reformers disliked them because, ultimately, they were bulwarks of conservatism. The bosses were entrepreneurs, not revolutionaries. They provided specific opportunities for individual representatives of deprived groups, but they never questioned the basic distribution of resources in society. Their methods of raising revenue tended toward regressivity. On the whole, the lower classes paid for their own favors. What they got was a *style* of government with which they could feel at home. What the more affluent classes got, though relatively few of them appreciated it, was a form of government which kept the newly enfranchised masses content without threatening the socioeconomic status quo.

When reform came, its banner was again democracy. Partisanship and patronage, the Progressives believed, enabled bosses to manipulate the democratic will rather than serve it. The answers were nonpartisanship and civil service. Spoilsmanship and corruption wasted the public's resources; career bureaucracies founded on merit would implement the public's directives with economy and efficiency. Ward elections encouraged both voters and their representatives to think parochially; enlightened democracy, expressing itself in at-large elections, would address the larger issues (generally conceived, one hastens to add, in geographic rather than socioeconomic terms).

It is fashionable at present, following Lincoln Steffens, to romanticize the machine and disparage the priggish Progressives. This revisionism has some solid justification. The Progressive reforms did tend to enthrone the middle class at the expense of the lower, and to paper over rather than genuinely mediate differences.[10] As Robert Salisbury has noted, their standard was a "consensual, integrated" community:

> A proper city [they believed] should manifest no deep-seated social or economic cleavages. Groups and classes with opposing interests are considered dangerous to the continued tranquility of the polity. When they exist, as they increasingly did in the industrial city of turn-of-the-century America, it becomes necessary to adopt programs, such as universal education, and institutions, such as nonpartisan local government or at-large elections, that overcome the threatening heterogeneity.[11]

What this quote makes clear, by the way, is that the Progressives did have a program for dealing with diversity.* It was assimilation via institutions that would educate the young and focus the attention of voters on issues which united rather than divided them. Was this Progressive program naïve? Perhaps, but it was far from absurd in the context of what was known *circa* 1900. What is more relevant is to ask whether it bears scrutiny today—because the program remains ascendant,** and it increasingly divides black from white Americans. The latter, in general, seem firmly inclined to stand pat with it.

Before leaving the Progressives, it should be noted (a) that they were an unusually diverse lot, and—what is of particular relevance to the present discussion—(b) that they were advanced Jacksonians in their attitude toward the ballot box.

(a) Though Progressive rhetoric at the local level was often a cover for enhancing business and middle class influence, Progressivism in its heartland had more the flavor of a rural small town crusade against concentrations of *both* business and political power. National Progressive leaders such as Norris and La Follette were prominent campaigners in favor of the progressive income tax, antitrust legislation, pure food

---

*And also, it should be added, with poverty. Salisbury writes: "The common school, later the high school, and now the community college have been urged and supported as mechanisms for equalizing the life chances of everyone in the community. To introduce programs for one group that were not available to another . . . would cultivate group and class differences at the twig-bending stage which would lead to deeper socio-economic cleavages in the adult community. Most people, it seemed, never considered the possibility that the have-not groups might receive *more* and *better* education than the middle class. It looked like the poor could only get shortchanged in a system of differentiated education and a caste system would result."[12]

**In 1967, e.g., more than three times as many cities with populations over 10,000 elected their councilmen at large (68 per cent) as did so by districts (19 per cent). The remainder elected some one way and some the other. In cities of over one-half million, the ratio of "pure" at-large to "pure" district systems was 2-1 (46-23 per cent). In cities of one-quarter to one-half million, the ratio was 10-1 (70-7 per cent).[13]

and drug laws, and so on. This helps explain why, to most social reformers, Progressivism seemed considerably less suspect than boss rule.

(b) On the state and local level, Progressive reformers championed the initiative, recall, referendum, and nominating primary as ways of enhancing the citizen's role in government. They favored short rather than long ballots, but this was because something had been learned about the limits of citizen attentiveness since the days of Jackson. (Though not enough, the critics of Progressive reform have charged. Even as the Progressives required less of citizens by shortening the ballot, they required more by dispensing with party labels.) Nationally, the Progressives helped secure the direct election of senators and female suffrage—via constitutional amendment in 1913 and 1920 respectively.

In the 1930's, the focus of the participation issue shifted from state and local government to the great bureaucracies of the modern corporation and national state. In the public sector, as regulatory activities proliferated, increasing use was made of committees representing, in one fashion or another, the interested parties. As Grant McConnell has noted, the American ideal was regulation by voluntary agreement rather than by law:

> Since there were too many people to address individually, they must get together in their own associations and agree—voluntarily. Then government could put its stamp upon their own informal, cooperative, and free decisions. Government would thus have achieved the purpose of a free people, and without coercion.[14]

Herbert Hoover was the great articulator of this doctrine in the 1920's, before the explosion of governmental activity. The New Deal made it a central feature of American government. It has increasingly been applied to the distribution of benefits as well as regulation.

It directly conflicts, of course, with the Progressive ideal of having all government decisions made by representatives of the whole public. It has been much criticized for opening the way to rule by special interests, with little regard for the general good or even for the good of the less well organized among the parties most profoundly affected. (This, in fact, is a central theme of McConnell's.) At the same time, it recognizes the need for disaggregation to make large-scale government amenable to citizen influence. Theodore J. Lowi has recently labelled this doctrine "interest-group liberalism" and argued that it has been the predominant force for change in American governmental arrangements since 1933:

> The new halo words alone imply the extent to which the new type of claim now dominates: "interest representation," "cooperation," "partnership," "self-regulation," "delegation of power," "local option," "grass roots," "creative federalism," "community action," "maximum feasible participation," and that odd contribution from the New Left—which seems unable to escape established thought patterns—"participatory democracy."[15]

What this litany makes clear is the extent to which the growth of national power has been accompanied by efforts to enhance participation within the national system. Traditional geographic federalism has been transformed and supplemented by new modes of political decentralization. It also makes clear that current black demands for greater self-government within the large system, even while receiving greater infusions of funds from it, are squarely in the mainstream of recent governmental reform.

In the private sector, the great issue of the thirties was the right of workers, powerless as individuals, to participate collectively in the determination of their wages, fringe benefits, and working conditions. The labor issue, of course, had been brewing for many decades. And labor organization had been resisted at least as bitterly as black demands are resisted today. Lewis Lorwin commented in 1933 that:

Employers in no other [Western] country, with the possible exception of those in the metal and machine trades of France, have so persistently, so vigorously, at such costs, and with such a conviction of serving a cause opposed and fought trade unions as the American employing class. In no other Western country have employers been so much aided in their opposition to unions by the civil authorities, the armed forces of government, and their courts.[16]

More recently, Philip Taft and Philip Ross have written that: "The United States has had the bloodiest and most violent labor history of any industrial nation in the world."[17] They judge that this violence was mainly a product of the nation's ideology and law, which had long exalted the rights of property and made public power available to suppress the effective modes of labor protest—i.e., those which kept plants from operating. As the ideology and law changed, violence declined, until today it is extremely rare.*

In a similar vein, David Greenstone has recently speculated about the sources of American resistance to labor organization. The bitter hostility to unions, he writes,

may have reflected the relatively late emergence of American capitalism and the repressiveness typically associated with the first years of heavy capital accumulation. But the righteous antiunionism of the almost entirely Protestant entrepreneurial class may have also

---

*The authors sum up as follows: "The melancholy record shows that no section of the United States was free from industrial violence, that its origin and nature were not due to the influence of the immigrant or the frontier, nor did it reflect the darker side of the American character. . . . The virtual absence at present of violence in the coal and copper mines, breeding grounds for the more dramatic and tragic episodes, are eloquent testimony that labor violence from the 1870's to the 1930's was essentially shaped by prevailing attitudes on the relations between employer and employee. Once these were changed, a change accomplished partly by legal compulsion, violence was sharply reduced."[18]

reflected the unchallenged Protestant individualism that had earlier produced the peculiar harshness of American slavery. . . . [In addition], because American capitalists after the Civil War did not have to compete with an older elite of birth or rank, workers could not ally with either antibusiness Tory radicals or antiaristocratic liberal businessmen . . .[18a]

Public authorities so regularly and brutally broke strikes, he adds, that "even the strongly antisocialist leaders of the AFL accepted Marx's judgment that in America the state was indeed the creature of the bourgeoisie."[19]

The Great Depression brought a dramatic change in national policy, and spurred the burst of organizing—an increase in union membership from 2½ million in 1932 to 9 million in 1939—that created the labor movement we know today. Without belaboring the analogy, it merits note that similar shifts in national policy during the fifties and sixties—from the *Brown* decision of 1954 through passage of the anti-poverty and civil rights acts of 1964–65*—have played a vital role in generating the current surge of black militance and organization.**

The reaction of the nation's great industries to the explosion of organizing that followed passage of the National Industrial Recovery Act, incidentally, bears comparison with deep southern resistance to the *Brown* decision. In Greenstone's words:

Two years later, the intense and often violent opposition of large corporations elevated the infant CIO's struggle to establish industrial unions into a central symbol of revolt against the existing economic order. Management not only infiltrated union locals with spies, but resorted

---

*Those of greatest significance were the Economic Opportunity Act of 1964, the Civil Rights Act of 1964, and the Voting Rights Act of 1965.

**The mechanisms of impact, it merits note, have often been more symbolic than tangible. They have spotlighted and given official sanction to new ideas—e.g., racial equality, maximum feasible participation—even when the government's own will to implement them has proven weak.

to systematic violence, including the murder and injury of workers in the Little Steel Strike. In 1937, in one of the most carefully documented cases of employer violence, Walter Reuther and other Autoworker leaders were brutally beaten by former criminals and prize fighters employed by the Ford Motor Company.[20]

As in the sit-ins and most civil disorders of the past decade, moreover, the protestors of the thirties frequently violated the rights of property; the killing and maiming were perpetrated mainly by defenders of the status quo.*

It is tempting, for all the risk, to speculate about still other resemblances between the labor and civil rights issues. For example:

When the government decided to establish rules for collective bargaining, the definition of bargaining units posed questions scarcely less challenging than those of neighborhood definition today (see below, pp. 124–34). What the Wagner Act did was to set up a regulatory commission, the National Labor Relations Board (NLRB), and empower it to deal with the question. It provided as well for the NLRB to supervise elections in which the majority of each bargaining unit might choose a union to act as exclusive bargaining agent for all its members. This solution was far from neat, but it gradually acquired substance over the years, and the issue ceased to perturb the body politic.

When labor became a mass movement in the 1930's, it was radicalized. Prior to the New Deal, labor unions organized only the most skilled (and to their employers, indispensable) members of the blue-collar labor force. Semi-skilled and

---

*With respect to the more recent experience, the Kerner Commission reported that of 83 persons killed in the 75 disorders it investigated, public officials, mainly policemen and firemen, made up 10 per cent. The "overwhelming majority" of those killed and injured were Negroes.[21]

Gary Marx concludes his review of the evidence more pointedly: "Up to the end of the summer of 1967 . . . police, not rioters, were responsible for most of the more than 100 deaths that have occurred. Similarly, in a related context, the more than 100 civil rights murders of recent years have been matched by almost no murders of racist whites."[22]

unskilled whites were excluded then, just as nonwhites have been by many unions (and particularly those craft unions that predate the New Deal) more recently. By the 1920's and 1930's, the craft union members had become *petit bourgeois,* preoccupied with preserving their relative positions, bitterly suspicious of appeals to working class solidarity, hostile to calls for the transformation of society. The Great Depression shook these attitudes, but not for long. John L. Lewis was able to commence industrial organizing under the AFL banner during the early New Deal, but the new industrial unions were expelled from the AFL in 1936. As the industrial workers were organized, their unconventional tactics (e.g., the sit-down strike), their disrespect for prevailing definitions of the rights of management, their militant passion, and their extreme egalitarian rhetoric terrified great numbers of less aggrieved Americans.*

Politically, labor's support—again like that of the civil

---

*It merits note in this connection that a general relationship between increased participation and support for "radical" ideas has been observed by students of voting. The causal flow can run in either direction. The emergence of new political movements may energize previously apathetic voters. Similarly, the enfranchisement of new voters may provide substantial political markets for ideas whose support had hitherto appeared negligible.

Thus, although precise figures are unavailable, it is generally agreed that Jefferson's triumph in 1800 was achieved largely by drawing large numbers of new voters to the polls. We can specify more precisely that Jackson's victory in 1828 coincided with a near-quadrupling of the vote over the previous election.[23] The opposite side of the coin is that the suppression of class issues between the elections of 1896 and 1932 coincided with a sharp decline in voting turnout—from a consistent 75 per cent plus during the fifty years ending 1896 to an average of 52 per cent for the three elections of the 1920's. This figure rose to 59 per cent for the Roosevelt elections, and has increased only slightly since.[24] Over the past two decades, of course, the most striking increase in voter participation has been among Negroes.

In a more specific analysis, Thomas Pettigrew and Kurt Back have found that George Wallace's strong showing in the Presidential primaries of Wisconsin, Indiana, and Maryland in 1964 was attributable mainly to increased turnout rather than to shifts—i.e., "white backlash"—among those who had voted in previous primaries. They found the same phenomenon operative in the showing of Louise Day Hicks in the 1963 Boston School Committee election.[25]

rights movement today—came most strikingly from the young and the intellectuals.

History alone will tell whether the demands of black Americans can be absorbed and the civil rights issue can be tamed in ways that resemble the nation's experience with labor. It has long been the mark of an optimist to believe that they can.*

Let us conclude this capsule history of the drive for participation in American history with dispatch, as the recent chapters are the most familiar. The central postwar focus, of course, has been on civil rights. Until the late sixties, the salient issues were voting rights and the right to participate in the use of public accommodations. In the sixties, the Supreme Court returned the issue of *white* suffrage to the center stage of American politics with its reapportionment rulings.[27] As the first half of the sixties came to a close, white politicians were learning to live with equal apportionment and black leaders were abruptly confronted with the challenge of what to do now that Congress had enacted all their recommendations developed over several decades.

The civil rights movement—here defined as the entire movement to improve the condition of blacks in the United States, not merely that portion of it preoccupied with legal rights—enjoyed a brief and unprecedented moment of unity as the battle for strong national civil rights legislation reached its climax in 1963–64. Since then, a hundred flowers have bloomed, and the impatient fury of the young has greatly intensified. The movement's program of formal rights, enacted whole by Congress in 1964 and 1965, had little impact on the segregated, impoverished lives of most American Negroes. Increasingly, black leaders—those who

---

*The analogy was particularly fashionable in the heady first days of the poverty program. Its chief advocate was Jack Conway, fresh from thirty years as a labor organizer (in the early days of the United Auto Workers) and official. Early in 1964 he became co-chairman of the task force assigned to develop guidelines for the Community Action Program. A year later he became Deputy Director of the Office of Economic Opportunity (OEO).[26]

wished to create followings, those who wished to hold them, those who wished to enlarge them—began to articulate demands that they claimed *would* touch these lives. And they sought to develop styles that would appeal—not to potential white contributors and allies, nor to older, more traditional, more cautious blacks—but to the angry young blacks on the northern ghetto streets. Such phrases as "black power," "black pride," "black consciousness," and (perhaps most significant, given the history of black self-hatred) "Black is beautiful" came into fashion. Programmatically, the emphasis shifted from the integration of individuals to the equality of blacks *as a group* with whites: equality of power and income as well as formal rights before the law. Tactically, the emphasis shifted from setting a moral example and troubling the white conscience to stridently demanding, threatening, and mobilizing, thus hoping to stir the white sense of prudence.

These, at least, seem to be the common threads in the uncommonly diverse, still emerging pattern. As has been noted previously (p. 57), the militants are still a minority. One striking, stylistic, indicator is the preference for race labels. If Gallup's 1969 poll for *Newsweek* can be believed, the partisans of "Negro" and "colored" still outnumber those of "black" and "Afro-American" by two to one.* But then, it has always been minorities that have made revolutions. More mundanely, it has always been minorities that have made majorities. And the trend toward mass involvement and militance among blacks has been rather steep from the start of the Montgomery bus boycott (1955) to date. Moreover, it has proven contagious. Indeed, the issue of the terms of

---

*The percentages were as follows:[28]

	Like Most	Like Least
Negro	38	11
Colored	20	31
Black	19	25
Afro-American	10	11
Don't Care	6	6
Not Sure	7	16

political participation has become a thread that binds nearly every issue in American politics, from Head Start to Vietnam.

THE EXCLUSION OF BLACKS FROM FULL MEMBERSHIP IN AMERICAN SOCIETY

This has been scarcely less notable than the long drive for enhanced participation in American history. Prior to the Civil War, such exclusion was *de jure*. The vast majority of American Negroes who were slaves did not have the legal status of human beings, let alone of citizens. To aid one who had a will to freedom was to participate in an act of theft. The Declaration of Independence and the Constitution no more applied to slaves than to horses or mules. As Frederick Douglass told a white Independence Day audience in 1852:

> To [the slave], your celebration is a sham . . .; your denunciation of tyrants, brass fronted impudence; your shouts of liberty and equality, hollow mockery; your prayers and hymns, your sermons and thanksgivings . . . a thin veil to cover up crimes which would disgrace a nation of savages . . .
>
> You invite to your shores fugitives from oppression abroad, honor them with banquets, greet them with ovations, cheer them, toast them, salute them, protect them, and pour out your money to them like water; but the fugitives from your own land you advertise, hunt, arrest, shoot, and kill. . . . You shed tears over fallen Hungary, and make the sad story of her wrongs the theme of your poets, statesmen, and orators, till your gallant sons are ready to fly to arms to vindicate her cause against the oppressor; but, in regard to the ten thousand wrongs to the American slave, you would enforce the strictest silence and would hail him as an enemy of the nation who dares to make those wrongs the subject of public discourse.[29]

Even free Negroes in most states were barred from voting, owning property, or testifying in courts of law.

Following passage of the 13th, 14th, and 15th Amendments, new legal fictions were developed—for example, that compulsory segregation did not imply legal inequality—but the system of caste and segregation increasingly came to rest on practice that had no explicit sanction in law. This *de facto* pattern was able to persist because many white Americans insisted on it, the vast majority approved, and no more than a handful were outspoken in their opposition. Government agencies, far from combatting discrimination, actively practiced it—often with savage violence in the South (and in precinct houses everywhere), with somewhat greater restraint elsewhere. Until the past two decades, Negroes could no more obtain Federal Housing Administration (FHA) mortgages to purchase homes in predominantly white neighborhoods than they could vote in Mississippi.[30]

Thus, although it is plausible to argue that Negroes today are like white immigrants yesterday,[31] this has not been true historically. If Negroes today are no more disadvantaged than the Irish a century ago, it has taken them 300 years to get there. If the long denial of full citizenship has led a militant minority to deny its worth, and to champion their own analogy—that of colonialism—there would seem to be little cause for surprise.

In fact, the thesis that integration is a futile strategy is far from new.[32] As early as 1788, the Negro Union of Newport, Rhode Island, suggested that emigration was a more viable strategy. This idea attracted widespread white support during the first six decades of the nineteenth century. Among its public advocates were James Madison, James Monroe, Andrew Jackson, Daniel Webster, Henry Clay, and (as late as 1862) Abraham Lincoln. Noting that the vast majority of free Negroes were indifferent to or opposed it, Theodore Draper has labelled the emigration movement "a white man's fantasy for Negroes."[33] But it did attract thousands of blacks, particularly the better educated and particularly during periods of white reaction. It attained its peak of Negro support in the dismal decade just preceding the Civil War. This was the decade of the Fugitive Slave Act, the *Dred*

Scott decision, and the Kansas-Nebraska Act (which reopened northern territory to slavery). These were also years of massive immigration from Europe. As Bennett writes, the

> white immigrants depressed wages and eliminated Negroes as competitors in several fields. Hundreds of Negroes were stoned in anti-Negro riots; thousands more fled America in panic. . . . A mood of bitterness and hostility moved over the ghetto which trembled on the brink of suicidal revolt. . . . Black nationalism reached such a peak in these years that no Negro leader could denounce it outright.[34]

One of those who mirrored the shift was Martin Delaney. A leading anti-migrationist in the forties, he explained his 1852 move to the opposite camp in the following words:

> I am not in favor of caste, nor a separation of the brotherhood of mankind, and would as willingly live among white men as black, if I had an equal possession and enjoyment of privileges. . . . If there were any probability of this, I would be willing to remain in this country, fighting and struggling on. . . . But I must admit, that I have no hopes in this country—no confidence in the American people, with a few excellent exceptions. . . . Heathenism and Liberty, before Christianity and Slavery.[35]

Negro nationalism receded from sight during the Civil War and Reconstruction. The decades following the Bargain of '76, however, were in many ways more bitter than the fifties. The Supreme Court and Congress were again courting the white South. Immigration from Europe was again heavy. The hostility of white workers to competition from Negroes was again severe. (During the eighties, more than fifty strikes were recorded in the North against the employment of Negro workers.) The difference was that such cause had been given for hope.

During these years the first movements flourished for limited Negro self-determination within the American polity. The most interesting was that led by Edwin McCabe, a former state auditor of Kansas, to create a Negro state in the Oklahoma territory. A number of Negro municipalities were in fact chartered both North and South. Emigrationism, of course, revived. And a few began to advocate the violent defense, if necessary, of Negro rights. But the most prominent alternative to integrationism that emerged in this period was accommodationism—meaning accommodation to the white insistence on superiority and segregation. As Booker T. Washington expressed the accommodationist program, Negroes should reject the goal of integration and eschew politics. They should concentrate on improving their character and learning the manual trades that they might hope to be permitted to practice. In return for being permitted to do these things in peace, they should "manifest their gratefulness by showing a spirit of meekness and added usefulness." [36]

Like the Civil War, World War I aroused great hopes which soon were brutally dashed. It was fought under the banner of lofty Wilsonian rhetoric, and its prosperity generated the first great burst of Negro migration north. The white response was a wave of savage anti-Negro riots in 1919, the first year following the war. The norm was for local police to participate in these riots rather than to endeavor to protect their victims. The partiality of the courts was almost equally notorious. [37]

The decade following the war witnessed the rise and fall of the first Negro mass movement of any kind. Its leader was Marcus Garvey, and its theme was a return to "Mother Africa." Garvey maintained that no strategy could possibly alter the basic situation of Negroes in the United States. To be free of injustice, Negroes needed power, and the key source of power in the modern world was national sovereignty. In order to achieve nationhood, the Negroes of America would have to join with those of Africa in overthrowing African colonialism. The movement's slogan was "Africa for the Africans at Home and Abroad."

During the interim before nationhood was achieved, Garvey stated, Negroes should develop their strength here through racial pride and unity. A great organizer and showman, Garvey established branches of his United Improvement Association in cities throughout the nation. Within the Association he created an elite African Legion for the men and Black Star Nurses Corps for the women. The former wore red and blue uniforms embellished with swords and riding crops; they policed all Garveyite meetings. The nurses' uniform was white, to symbolize their purity. The Association's flag was black, red, and green—for the skin, blood, and hope of the race respectively. Countering the myth of Negro inferiority, Garvey proclaimed Negro superiority:

> When Europe was inhabited by a race of cannibals [he stated], a race of savages, naked men, heathen, and pagans, Africa was peopled with a race of cultured black men, who were masters in art, science, and literature. . . . Black men, you were once great; you shall be great again.[38]

The Garvey movement's appeal, like that of the Nation of Islam more recently, was to those near the bottom of the Negro social structure rather than the top. One of its essential arms was the African Orthodox Church, a tenet of which was that God is black. Within the movement, black was a symbol of everything good: beauty, virtue, strength, etc. Responding to attacks from the integrationist NAACP, Garvey admitted that its demands were just but contended that "the great white majority will not grant them, and thus we march on to danger."[39] The danger to which Garvey himself marched was a mail fraud conviction in 1925 and deportation—he was a Jamaican—upon completion of his sentence. With the leader's departure, the movement collapsed.

Little more, surprisingly, was heard of black nationalism until the late 1950's, when the Nation of Islam burst upon the national consciousness and the end of colonial rule in Africa created a stir among black intellectuals. Separatist movements were not lacking in the intervening decades—the Nation itself was founded in 1934—but they failed to attract either large followings or highly articulate leaders. Educated Negroes who despaired of integration in this period were more likely to go Communist than separatist.

One who tried all these paths was W. E. B. DuBois, the firebrand integrationist who had been a key founder of the NAACP and the leading public critic of both Booker T. Washington and Marcus Garvey. Breaking with the NAACP in 1934, he noted that segregation had become worse during the quarter century of its existence. It was time, he argued, to recognize that the pursuit of integration was futile. Given the inevitability of segregation, Negroes should exploit it to build economic, social, and political power. They should organize producer and consumer cooperatives, develop their skills, tighten their social structure, and get out their votes.

After World War II, DuBois's interests turned to Pan-African nationalism and peace. In connection with the latter, he increasingly worked with Communists and endorsed Communist positions, though he took pains to make clear that he himself was not a Communist. In 1951, as chairman of the Peace Information Center, he was indicted by a federal grand jury for failure to register that organization as an agent of a foreign power. Though acquitted, he was more embittered than ever before. In the years that followed he was lionized by the nations of the Communist and Third Worlds, but almost totally isolated at home. Unwilling to sign a non-Communist affidavit on principle, he couldn't even obtain an American passport to accept the invitations he received from foreign leaders. Finally, at the age of ninety-two (in 1960), he secured a passport and moved to Ghana. A year later he joined the American Communist Party. Shortly before his death in 1963, he concluded his political journey by adopting Ghanaian citizenship.

The recurrent waves of black support for nonintegrationist

strategies seem to have risen mainly during periods of white reaction following periods of Negro gain. Even the first migrationist movement fits this description. During the Revolution, free Negroes successfully opposed an effort to bar them from the Continental Army. During the war most northern states abolished slavery. In its immediate aftermath, many slaveholders freed their slaves and the first abolitionist societies were organized. A few Negroes also rose to national prominence in the larger society during this period—e.g., Joshua Bishop and Lemual Haynes, who pastored white churches; Benjamin Banneker, the surveyor and astronomer who helped lay out the District of Columbia; and Phillis Wheatley, the poet. The cooling of American revolutionary ardor, however, the invention of the cotton gin (which greatly increased the profitability of slavery), the excesses of the French Revolution, and the black revolution in Haiti all combined to nip this drift toward racial liberalization in the bud.

The evidence for the thesis with respect to the 1850's and the periods following Reconstruction and World War I has already been discussed. How about the current wave of black support for nonintegrationist strategies? It dates most conveniently from the Meredith march through Mississippi of June 1966. James Meredith, it will be recalled, had announced that he wished to demonstrate that a Negro could walk without fear through Mississippi. He was shot within hours after crossing the state line. Shortly thereafter, as he recuperated, numerous others, including many of the nation's most prominent civil rights leaders, took up his line of march. As they went, Stokely Carmichael, the new chairman of the Student Non-Violent Coordinating Committee (SNCC), took the national spotlight with his reiterated (if imprecise) demands for Black Power. Within weeks, a national controversy over the term had begun which continues to the present.[40]

No one can say with confidence why Carmichael's slogan struck such a responsive chord among young blacks, or why the more general shift among black activists toward emphasizing ghetto improvement over integration has continued to gather force in the three years (as this is written) since the Meredith march. The crucial points here, however, would seem to be: (a) that Negro hopes had been raised dramatically by the Johnson Administration's rhetoric and legislative accomplishments in 1964–65, and (b) that 1966 was a year of sharp national pullback from the grand promises made to the poor and black in the previous two years. As John Donovan has written, 1966 was the year in which "the war on poverty became the first domestic casualty of the war in Vietnam."[41] The rapid escalation of the latter war begun early in 1965 had by the end of that year severely unbalanced the federal budget and produced alarming signs of inflation. The pressure in Congress to hold down federal spending was overwhelming. The war on poverty, which had just commenced its projected steep spending takeoff, would have been an obvious target in any event. The raucous militancy of many "representatives of the poor" in the Community Action Program made it all the more so.*

The congressional and city government reaction to the Community Action Program, and the failure of the war on poverty to escalate, were particularly unfortunate because some disillusion on the civil rights front was inevitable. The Civil Rights Acts of 1964 and 1965 did open public accommodations and voting booths to Negroes throughout the South, but they had no visible impact at all in the northern ghettos. Any vigorous attempt to move the North toward *de facto* integration (rather than just to bring the South up to the North's *de jure* standards) was more likely to produce a congressional majority against civil rights than to promote the goal sought. With all its tactical resources focused on

---

*In the event, the war on poverty's appropriation for fiscal 1967 was 7½ per cent higher than for fiscal 1966. This fell far short of what had originally been anticipated, however, and actually caused a reduction in the spending rate reached by the spring of 1966. Moreover, Congress earmarked most of the money for the least controversial anti-poverty activities (most notably, Head Start), leaving only about 20 per cent to be spent at the discretion of local Community Action Agencies. The total appropriation for fiscal 1967 was $1.6 billion.

maintaining support for its Asian policy, the administration was particularly unwilling to contemplate such an effort after 1965, but it would have been improbable in any event.

This suggests a final point. The war in Vietnam aside, there was almost surely more support in white America for heavy spending to alleviate poverty than for vigorous efforts to combat *de facto* segregation. In other words, ghetto improvement is a more feasible objective (at least politically) in the current period than integration. Or, as some blacks would put it, to place equality before integration is just good politics in white-dominated America.

At the same time, it is helpful to recall that the persistence of race as a vital social distinction is only the most extreme instance of a more general phenomenon, explored in the following section.

THE PERSISTENCE OF ETHNICITY IN AMERICAN SOCIETY

As Glazer and Moynihan have indicated, it is time now for analysis to proceed beyond the melting pot analogy.[42] Though the differences among them have grown more subtle over time, the major ethnic groups in American life continue to act as magnets for their members. Most social and family life continues to take place within them.[43] And thus they retain distinctive identities, carrying norms of child rearing, politics, religion, and so on from one generation to the next.*

---

*They do not do so, it should be noted, with equal effectiveness in all circumstances. Ethnicity seems to be most salient in northern cities from Chicago on east, and least salient in the new cities of the West and Southwest. This may be because the settlers of the newer cities have been emigrants from other American locales. By their very willingness to move, they have manifested their low ethnic attachments as individuals. They have arrived with none of the language and few of the cultural distinctions that compelled high ethnic consciousness in the years of high immigration from other lands. In part for these reasons, and perhaps in part because the social structures of the newer cities have had less chance to rigidify than those of the Northeast had had even a century ago, they have encountered little hostility or exclusion.[44]

Michael Parenti has argued that it is crucial to distinguish between the "acculturation" and "assimilation" of American ethnic groups.[45] "Acculturation" refers to acquisition of the styles and customs of the larger society, particularly those of relevance to behavior outside family and close friendship groups; "assimilation" refers to the loss of group identity. Parenti maintains that American ethnic groups have quickly —by the second generation—become Americanized in their cultural practices and have lost interest in Old World culture. Nonetheless, they have retained their identities. They have evolved as units within the larger societal whole, becoming more alike but remaining still sufficiently different so that their members feel most comfortable in ethnically homogeneous social groups. The ethnic dimension—a combination of the closely linked variables of religion, national origin, and race—cuts across those of income and occupation; and it is no less significant as a social distinction than they. In general, moreover, ethnic groups tend to have quite stable class positions:

> A comparison of first and second generational occupational statuses as reported in the 1950 national census shows no evidence of any substantial convergence of intergroup status levels. . . . If today's ethnics enjoy a better living standard than did their parents, it is because there has been an across-the-board rise throughout America. Fewer pick-and-shovel jobs and more white collar positions for minority members are less the result of ethnic mobility than of an over-all structural transition in our national economy . . .[46]

Glazer and Moynihan develop the same theme in *Beyond the Melting Pot,* but take greater care to note that the Jewish and Oriental groups are great exceptions—mainly because of their exceptional aptitudes (rooted in their traditions, carried by their child-rearing practices) for formal education.[47] Despite their occupational mobility, of course, the Jewish, Chinese, and Japanese groups have retained exceptional vitality as social units.

One of the most striking findings of recent social science is that ethnic political awareness has tended to be greater in the second and later generations than the first. Wolfinger explains this in terms of the need to develop a middle class with resources and political skills. Members of this class provide the group with leadership and secure party nominations for it. These nominations will typically come first from a party that feels it needs the ethnic group's support, and they will tend to fix the ethnic group's political affiliation. At some later point a great issue is likely to shake that affiliation, but even then the group will probably shift *en masse.*[48]

Beyond a certain threshold point, there is no evidence that the proportion of middle class members within a group heightens political awareness. What is perhaps more striking, however, is the lack of evidence that time, occupational mobility, or suburbanization significantly erodes that awareness. Ethnic groups do differ, of course, in their rate of assimilation. Wolfinger notes that the large Irish and German immigrations were simultaneous, but that the former group retains a far greater sense of ethnic awareness today. The Germans have truly, and almost uniquely, progressed far toward assimilation. Near the other extreme, the French Canadians of Quebec, whose ties to the mother country ended with the French and Indian War in 1763, show few signs of assimilating.[49]

It was widely forecast a few years back that suburbanization would spell the end of ethnicity as a significant force in American life. It appears, however, that ethnic groups do cluster in the suburbs, and that those most highly segregated from other groups in the central cities are also most concentrated in the suburbs. It also appears that ethnic identity can be sustained in the absence of residential segregation. Members of an ethnic group may constitute only one-fourth the population of a suburb, but still do nearly all their socializing with one another. Parenti speculates that:

> the new "affluence," often cited as a conductor of greater assimilation, may actually provide minorities with the

financial and psychological wherewithal for building
even more elaborate parallel sub-societal structures, including those needed for political action. In prosperous
suburban locales, while the oldest and most exclusive
country clubs belong to old-stock Protestant families,
the newer clubs are of Jewish or varying Catholic-ethnic
antecedents. . . . Increasing prosperity among Catholics
has been accompanied by an increase in Catholic institutional and social organizations including a vast
parochial education system, and the proliferation in
sectarian higher education often means a heightened
consciousness.[50]

He adds that this persistence of ethnic identity is bolstered
by the continued resistance of the white Protestant majority
to assimilation. This resistance is strongest in the case of
Negroes, and in fact is an omnipresent factor in their consciousness. One would expect those most rejected by other
groups to maintain the highest degree of in-group solidarity.
And so they seem to do—beginning at the time when their
middle class reaches the threshold size referred to previously
as a requisite for mobilization.

This is not to deny that ethnicity as a social and political
factor may decline in importance over the next two or three
generations. But it is to place the current surge of black
ethnic consciousness—at just the time that the Negro middle
class has become a substantial proportion of the overall Negro
population—in the larger context of American ethnic pluralism.

POLITICAL DECENTRALIZATION

The strong preference of Americans for political decentralization has also shaped a good deal of the nation's history. This preference has rested in part on a general belief
that government should be kept as close to the people as
possible, and in part on the desire of particular subgroups
within the national system to exercise as much self-rule as
possible.

The origin of American federalism itself illustrates this argument. On the one hand, as Martin Diamond has shown, the founders were much influenced by Montesquieu's theory that liberty depended on small territorial scale. The ancients had contended that small scale, in the form of the city-state, was essential to the good life and the full development of virtue. Montesquieu revised the argument to emphasize that large scale presupposed despotic authority. Only a despot could hope to wield a large empire into a coherent political unit. Citizen self-rule could survive only in the small republic, where the interest of the whole was easier to grasp, where conspiracies were easier to guard against, and where each individual had a large enough share of responsibility to inspire political virtue.[51]

The founders were even more revisionist than Montesquieu. They were little impressed with the alleged positive virtues of small scale, but they very much feared the despotic potential of a national government. Not all of them feared it equally, of course. The members of the Constitutional Convention were among the Americans of their time who feared it least, and those who dominated the convention were in the nationalist wing of even this group. The convention was carried by Madison's argument, later presented in *The Federalist*, Number 10, that in fact the national government would be less prone to rule by faction than the states and localities, and that it could help guarantee their continued republicanism.[52]

Even so, the Constitution they produced assigned the national government only a specific list of enumerated powers. Not only did it leave most domestic functions to the states, provide for equality of state representation in the Senate, and provide for the election of Presidents by state electoral colleges, but it also left such crucial functions as legislative apportionment and the determination of voting rights to the states. Only with the end of Isolation and the vigorous emergence of the positive state in the twentieth century did the national features of the Constitution come clearly to predominate over the federal.

The federal component was so great in the first place, and remained paramount so long, because most Americans were not nationalists. They recognized the need for national representation in foreign affairs, but they wanted as little to do with foreign affairs as possible. With Montesquieu, they feared the despotic potential of large-scale government, and as radical democrats they believed that government was most sensitive to the people's desires when it was very close to them. They were acutely aware, moreover, of interest conflicts among the nation's states and regions. And as state patriots they were reluctant to have these conflicts arbitrated by any higher authority.

To sum up, the federal union could not have come into existence at all had it given less recognition to the power of separatist sentiments among the state citizenries. The political identities of the states have now persisted even longer than the ethnic identities discussed in the previous section. Though they are clearly less strong than a century ago, they give no signs of dying out. They have caused a good deal of perhaps unnecessary friction over the years. Yet by recognizing that national and state loyalties were not mutually exclusive, by compromising with those who preferred a weak confederation of states, the nationalists of 1787 were able to set the country on the long path to subjective nationhood.

Jumping to the present, what is most striking about American federalism is the national-state-local sharing of responsibility in virtually every arena of domestic policy. As Morton Grodzins has shown, even at the height of the New Deal Congress maintained a determination to have the states administer new federal programs, and to do so with a very large amount of discretion.[53] National and state officials are in no sense the hierarchical superiors of local officials, but their approval or acquiescence is frequently necessary before the latter can act. The relationship of national to state officials is similar. State or local authority with respect to a given problem does not imply "sovereignty" in the American system. It rather implies a legally defined and significant role in the political system's scheme of organization for handling the problem. This tolerance for sharing, vague delineation, and overlap in the American federal system is its most distinctive characteristic, and probably its greatest strength. I shall argue below that a similar tolerance is called for in dealing with the community control movement.

At the local level, the American preference for small scale is reflected in the continued predominance of less than mammoth jurisdictions. In 1960, only five American cities had populations larger than one million, and fewer than 10 per cent of all Americans lived in them. The sixteen cities with populations between 500,000 and 1 million accounted for just another 6 per cent.* A 1966 Gallup poll provides more direct evidence of the public taste. A national sample was asked the following question: "If you could live anywhere in the United States that you wanted to, would you prefer a city, a suburban area, small town, or farm?" Only

---

*This total of 16 per cent living in cities larger than one-half million is expected to hold about steady in the 1970 census. The most reliable estimates available as this is written suggest that such cities will average about 75 per cent white in 1970, but that they will include 36-37 per cent of all black Americans by comparison with 13-14 per cent of all white Americans.[54]

Of related interest are the following Census Bureau figures for 1968:[55]

	Per cent of all American whites	Per cent of all American Negroes
Metropolitan Areas of one million or more:	34	42
Central Cities:	13	34
Suburban Rings:	22	8
Metropolitan Areas smaller than one million:	30	27
Central Cities:	13	20
Suburban Rings:	16	7
Combined Totals:		
Central Cities:	26	54
Suburban Rings:	38	15
Outside Metropolitan Areas:	36	31

22 per cent said that they would like to live in a city. Nearly two-thirds of those who currently resided in cities larger than 50,000 said that they would prefer to live elsewhere than a city. By contrast, only about one in thirty of those who currently lived elsewhere wished that they could live in a city.* No racial breakdown was provided, but it seems reasonable to assume that a far higher proportion of white than black large city residents are there by choice.

THE AMERICAN UNWILLINGNESS TO FOREGO POLITICAL REPRESENTATION IN DEALING WITH PUBLIC BUREAUCRACIES

This reluctance has shaped American practice in ways that are of high relevance to the community control issue. Elected officials, for example, have valued the prerogative of intervening on behalf of their aggrieved constituents. Consequently, they have resisted proposals to insulate the bureaucracies fully from political influence and to establish such internal grievance mechanisms as the ombudsman.** Over time, in response to scandals, the spread of middle class norms, and

---

*The precise figures were as follows:[56]

Current Resident	Preference (per cent)				
	City	**Suburb**	**Small Town**	**Farm**	**Don't Know**
City larger than ½ million	36	37	21	5	1
City 50–500 thousand:	34	31	24	9	2
City 2.5–50 thousand:	6	24	60	9	1
Under 2.5 thousand and rural:	1	7	23	69	–
National:	22	28	31	18	1

**Within the United States, there have been important class differences of emphasis, though even middle-class WASP's have probably been less willing on balance to dispense with political representation than the citizens of numerous other countries. Of these internal American differences, Banfield and Wilson write: "The assimilation of lower-class people into the

the growing volume of business, they have gradually given ground. But this country still lags well behind most other developed nations in the "judicialization" of its public bureaucracies.

Perceiving this, Americans are far more likely than the citizens of other nations to adopt political, as opposed to legalistic, strategies in dealing with government agencies. They are also more likely to feel that they can do something about an unjust government decision. Thus, in the five-nation survey conducted by Almond and Verba in 1959–60, the percentages who thought they might be able to do something about an unjust regulation were as follows:[58]

Nation	Local Regulation	National Regulation
United States	77	75
United Kingdom	78	62
Germany	62	38
Italy	51	28
Mexico	52	38

The American advantage, then, is particularly marked at the national level. This is also true, at least by comparison with the United Kingdom, of the American propensity to rely on political strategies. Asked how they would go about trying to correct the unjust *local* regulation, the respondents who had indicated that they might be able to do something answered as follows:[59]

---

middle class has, of course, entailed their assimilation to the political ethos of the Anglo-Saxon Protestant elite, the central idea of which is that politics should be based on public rather than on private motives and, accordingly, should stress the virtues of honesty, impartiality, and efficiency.

"Wherever the middle class is dominant, this ethos prevails and fixes the character of the political system . . .

"Meanwhile, there remain enclaves that are heavily lower-class in all of the central cities and many of the older suburbs. In these, machine-style politics is as popular as ever. It does not flourish as of old, however, because of restraints and impediments imposed by the middle class, which constitutes the majority in the metropolitan area if not in the city proper, controls the legislatures, and has a virtual monopoly on federal office, both elective and appointive."[57]

Strategy	U.S.	U.K.	Germany	Italy	Mexico
Organize friends and neighbors; work through party or pressure group:	59	36	21	9	28
Acting alone, contact political leaders or press:	20	45	15	12	15
Acting alone, vote against offending officials at next election:	14	4	1	1	--
Acting alone, contact administrative officials; consult lawyer; appeal through courts:	3	4	34	14	20
Other:	2	3	1	16	6
Total percentage who might act:	77	78	62	51	53

Asked how they would go about trying to correct the unjust *national* regulation, the respondents who had indicated that they might be able to do something answered as follows:[60]

Strategy	U.S.	U.K.	Germany	Italy	Mexico
Organize friends and neighbors; work through party or pressure group:	32	22	19	10	20
Acting alone, contact political leaders or press:	57	44	12	7	8
Acting alone, vote against offending officials at next election	7	3	4	1	--
Acting alone, contact administrative officials; consult lawyer; appeal through courts	--	1	5	5	10

Strategy	U.S.	U.K.	Germany	Italy	Mexico
Other:	--	2	2	6	7
Total percentage who might act:	75	62	38	28	38

Americans also rank high in their expectation of equal treatment from administrative officials,* but they do not rank particularly high in their expectation that an expression of their views will be taken seriously by public bureaucrats in the absence of pressure. Almond and Verba posed their respondents two hypothetical questions: (1) "Suppose there were some question that you had to take to a government office—for example, a tax question or a housing regulation. If you explained your point of view to the officials, what effect do you think it would have? Would they give your point of view serious consideration, would they pay only a little attention, or would they ignore what you had to say?" (2) Suppose "you had some trouble with the police—a traffic violation maybe, or were accused of a minor offense . . . [same choices as before]?" The responses were as follows:[61]

	U.S.		U.K.		Germany		Italy		Mexico	
Expectation	Bur.	Pol.**	Bur.	Pol.	Bur.	Pol.	Bur.	Pol.	Bur.	Pol.
Serious consideration for point of view:	48	56	59	74	53	59	35	35	14	12
A little attention:	31	22	22	13	18	11	15	13	48	46
To be ignored:	6	11	5	5	5	4	11	12	27	29
Depends:	11	9	10	6	15	13	21	20	6	7
Other and Don't Know:	4	2	2	1	9	13	18	20	3	5
Total per cent:	100	100	98	99	100	100	100	100	98	99

---

*It should be noted that equal treatment is compatible with unreasonable policies. It may be that Americans fear bureaucratic stupidity and rigidity more than discrimination. If so, they presumably consider political representation essential not to secure equality, but rather to infuse public activity with flexible common sense.

**Government Bureau; Police.

What is particularly striking about the American pattern is the discrepancy between what Almond and Verba call "perceived citizen competence" and "perceived subject competence." Their key measure of the former is the percentage of citizens in each country who think they might be able to do something about *both* an unjust local law and an unjust national law. Their measure of the latter is the percentage who expect serious consideration of their viewpoint both in a government office and from the police. The figures are as follows:[62]

Nation	Citizen Competence	Subject Competence
United States	66	37
United Kingdom	56	50
Germany	33	43
Italy	27	27
Mexico	33	8

One might expect that this discrepancy in the United States would produce a substantial sense of disquiet on the part of any group which felt compelled to rely more than most on the good faith and good sense of administrative officials. If the group felt culturally apart from the rest of American society, if it viewed itself as having distinctive interests, and/or if it believed that many administrative officials bore it malice, one would expect this disquiet to be magnified. The sort of group, then, which one would expect to find most aggrieved is a minority subculture which had long experienced prejudice, and which found itself forced to share representation with members of the cultural majority who outnumbered it. The members of such a group would almost invariably find themselves in the minority. Coming to view the electoral deck as stacked against them, they would press for revision of the governmental scheme. If they were sufficiently aggrieved, they might press for separate nationhood. If this drastic remedy appeared unfeasible or worse than the disease, they would be likely to press (1) for a drawing of election district and local government boundaries which permitted most of them to live in political subunits where the group constituted a majority, and (2) for as much delegation of authority to the level at which they enjoyed self-rule as possible.*

In this context, whether or not the demand for community control seems justified, it is easily comprehensible.

---

*If the group were not clustered geographically, of course, different strategies would be called for—e.g., insistence upon the use of proportional representation in elections at all levels of government.

CHAPTER THREE

THE INTERESTS

IN Chapter I we reviewed the key arguments against community control. Let us now turn to the concrete interests, real and alleged, of key actors who have frequently opposed community control.

First, there is the supposed interest of citywide elective officials in holding onto as much power as they can. It would seem, however, that community control might cut either way in this respect—depending on the local political climate, on the community control scheme adopted, on each politician's objectives, and on the nature of his political base. Let us consider a few hypothetical examples.

A is a councilman in a city that currently has district elections and a strong mayor system. He is the preeminent local political actor in his district, but he is unlikely ever to win a citywide election. His basic instinct is to oppose any change in the existing governmental structure, but he recognizes the need for some response to the intense black pressure for community control. It strikes him that the city might adopt a community control scheme which made use of existing ward boundaries and which provided for (or permitted) the same man to act as neighborhood "mayor" and city councilman. Though the American norm is to forbid dual officeholding, it might be justified in this case as an answer to the argument that community control would increase the fragmentation of power. If authority were devolved upon the neighborhoods, and A became the chief executive as well as city-wide representative of his neighborhood, his power would be greater than at present. He had always aspired to be a chief executive, with power to act rather than merely to vote. He had once thought in grander terms, but here was the best opportunity that was likely to come his way. To favor community control so long as it did not fragment power too severely would also be a rather statesmanlike position, one which creatively blended responsiveness to the new demands with a concern for effective public management. If dual officeholding proved unacceptable, he could with perfect consistency vote against community control in the end.

B, on the other hand, is a councilman in a city that currently has at-large elections. The ethnic group to which he belongs is dominant citywide but not in his own neighborhood. He lives in the better part of town, moreover, and several of his fellow incumbent councilmen live nearby. He has little reason to believe that he could dominate his neighborhood politically, or interest in doing so. He believes that the existing city government structure is fine, and he knows that his own political resources are well adapted to it. The simple addition of neighborhood governments and devolution of authority to them would, in his view, dilute the city's problem-solving capacity and generate a great deal of unnecessary conflict. Any linkage of neighborhood government to a citywide district system would imperil his own city council seat as well. On top of all this, his support in past elections has included a great many civil servants, along with their families and friends, and few Negroes. Thus, even rhetorically, his best bet is to speak out against community control.

C's position is more complicated. His city has a combination of district and at-large elections to the city council. He is a liberal who currently occupies an at-large seat, won with a combination of most of the city's Negro votes and a minority of its white votes. He has been prominently mentioned for mayor, and the Negro vote—about 25 per cent currently—is rapidly increasing as a share of the citywide total. He is basically in favor of concentrating rather than fragmenting local government power, and he has been frightened by the racial vituperation that has characterized the community control controversy. On the other hand, he worries that intensified black frustration may produce a new round of civil violence. He has always favored responding to black aspirations with movement toward integration and redistribution, but at present little progress seems possible toward either. Community control does not involve integration and need not be expensive; perhaps it is the only black demand to which a (limited) positive response is possible.

Returning to his own political future, however, white backlash is in the air. "Law and order" candidates have prevailed in several cities hitherto considered liberal during the current year (1969). Perhaps the best bet would be to oppose community control in the name of integration. Given his likely opposition in the next mayoral election, Negroes would have little choice but to support him anyway. Most whites would recognize his position as code language for doing nothing with minimal offense to the black community. It would be likely to enhance his "respectability" while assuring the white community that he was "safe." The trouble is that, with events moving so fast, C doubts that fine calculations like these have much predictive value. Perhaps a year hence most whites will be preoccupied with other issues, while Negroes sit out the election in the absence of a community control candidate. This is just one of countless possibilities that leave C inclined to vote his conscience—except that he is not sure what it dictates.

And then there are the mayors themselves. John Lindsay of New York has linked community control with the broader issue of whether the functional bureaucracies should be subject to political control. With it as his lever he succeeded for a time in taking control of the New York City Board of

Education—only to have the teachers' union succeed in persuading the state legislature to take it away from him again.* At a moment when Lindsay's prospects in this endeavor still appeared fair, Herbert Kaufman forecast quite plausibly that:

> . . . Groups clamoring for local control of administrative programs, confronted with the suspicion and resentment of bureaucracies . . . will probably discover that they get their most sympathetic hearings from chief executives, especially from big-city mayors. For such groups can provide the executives with counterweights to the bureaucracies: they constitute an alternative channel of information about administrative performance, reducing executive dependence on the bureaucracies. . . . Chief executives probably could not create the groups if they set out deliberately to do so, but it would be surprising if they did not eventually perceive the advantages of collaborating with them now that a variety of complaints has brought the groups spontaneously into being.**[2]

It would be rash, I think, to dismiss this scenario out of

---

*State legislation passed in April 1969 replaced the city school board appointed by the mayor with an interim board to be appointed by the presidents of the city's five boroughs. This board in turn was to be replaced in mid-1970 by one composed of two mayoral appointees and one elected representative of each borough. This bill also provided for the establishment of 30 to 33 "community school" districts in the city, each with no fewer than 20,000 pupils; it ensured that nearly all control would remain with the central board, however.[1]

**The passage continues as follows: "It will be an uneasy, mutually wary relationship. To neighborhood and community associations, the paradox of turning to remote chief executives in a quest for local control will be disturbing. To chief executives, the risks of opening a Pandora's box and releasing uncontrollable disintegrative forces will give pause. Yet each can gain so much from an alliance with the other that it is hard to avoid the feeling the attractions will overcome the anxieties. I do not mean to imply the alliance will be formal or structured. I mean only to suggest each side will turn to the other as appropriate occasions arise, and that the occasions will arise with increasing frequency in the years ahead."

hand in consequence of Lindsay's rout in the state legislature. He led the way, and prepared the ground rather carelessly. Those who follow will proceed with the caution of astronauts. They will proceed with less enthusiasm than astronauts, because they will recognize that the community control issue *is* a Pandora's box. They will proceed at all (those who do) because they will recognize that the box is already open. They will consider that total unresponsiveness to black demands is as risky as total identification with them. As activists, they will be driven to seek workable compromises, which incidentally enhance their own local roles. They will not simple-mindedly associate community control with dilution of their own power, because they will be preoccupied with existing constraints upon that power. In particular, they may judge that they will be stronger as brokers between the neighborhoods and the city bureaucracies than as prisoners of the latter.

They will care more, in other words, about the actual power than the formal authority of their office. They are likely to have even greater immediate interest in whether particular steps in the direction of community control will reduce or heighten racial tensions, win grudging acceptance from or outrage the public bureaucracies, improve or imperil their own reelection prospects. The limited experience to date, of course, from the federal Community Action Program to the New York Ocean Hill-Brownsville experiment, suggests that even quite limited support for community control is a poor risk on all counts. But, to repeat, unresponsiveness to black demands is also risky, so the search for paths to reconciliation is bound to continue.

Nor is the national experience quite as negative as the highly visible (at this writing) Ocean Hill-Brownsville case. The Community Action Program in its youthful heyday angered many mayors because it seemed almost a pure exercise in mobilization of the poor against them. As viewed from the ghettos, the program was federally financed and locally opposed. The Community Action Agencies (CAA's) often had no official tie to the city government, nor did their funding depend upon local approval. By the same token, however, they typically exercised no governmental authority and distributed only token resources. Thus, all the program really provided was a fillip to ghetto aspirations and a mechanism through which demands might be more effectively articulated.

Since passage of the Green Amendment in December 1967,* however, cities have had the option of bringing Community Action under their official control. Though few have

---

*By late 1967 there were more than 1,000 CAA's. About four-fifths of these were private, nonprofit organizations which had no public officials on their governing boards. The Office of Economic Opportunity (OEO) had funded them directly, rather than through state or local government channels.

The Green Amendment provided that each CAA should be a state or local government, *unless* the state or local government chose to designate a nonprofit organization as its CAA. Each CAA was to have a governing board, which would establish its program, fiscal, and personnel policies. One-third of the governing board members were to be public officials *(unless* the state or local government opted for a smaller proportion), one-third were to be democratically selected representatives of the target area, and one-third were to be representatives of organized groups. These rules were effective as of July 1, 1968.

Congressional Quarterly reported that passage of the Green Amendment was probably necessary to prevent dismemberment of the OEO as a whole. The Republicans proposed many transfers of OEO programs to other agencies, all of which failed because the southern Democrats either voted against them or abstained. Their price, *inter alia,* was the Green Amendment. Some northern big city Democrats might also have favored these proposals in the absence of the amendment.

Congresswoman Green (D. Ore.) summed up the normative case for her amendment as follows: "What a tragedy it would be if community action against poverty becomes perverted to an attack on local government—as though it were the cause or even held the cure for the problem." In a somewhat more hardnosed vein, Representative Sam Gibbons (D. Fla.), who had been floor manager of the 1965 and 1966 anti-poverty bills, said he did not think "you should turn over the whole war on poverty to the poor any more than you should turn the hospitals over to the sick."[3]

It should be emphasized that the amendment by no means constituted a general repudiation of "maximum feasible participation." On the contrary, it placed Congress squarely on record as favoring a specific interpretation of that vague phrase, one quite generous by the standards of all previous

exercised this option, its availability seems to have taken most of the heat out of mayoral opposition to the program.*

The Model Cities experience to date is even more encouraging. This program has involved almost as much citizen participation as the Community Action Program, though its enabling legislation—passed in 1966, after two years experience with Community Action—stipulates that no application for aid can receive federal consideration unless it has city government approval. With this inducement to city-neighborhood cooperation (based on the principle of ultimate city authority), the program has managed to get through its first three years without making many enemies. There have been city-neighborhood deadlocks in a number of cities, of course, and there is widespread fear that the program will receive inadequate funding to satisfy even minimally the hopes that have been aroused. But the important point in the present context is that the mayors consider the program worth lobbying for, and with some passion.

A moment ago I mentioned that Community Action had provided little more than a fillip to ghetto aspirations and a mechanism through which demands might be articulated. A transfer of substantial authority to neighborhood institutions would provide these in even greater degree, of course; but it would provide much more as well. Perhaps its most

---

periods and other programs. Considering that the phrase had originally slipped through Congress without being noticed, and had been under continuous fire ever since, this might have been considered a victory—i.e., it consolidated gains that had been made during an extraordinary period of progressive reform, on terms better than had been expected only a short while before.[4]

*As of December 31, 1968, 96.7 per cent (883 out of 913) of reporting local governments intended to continue operating their poverty programs through the existing Community Action Agencies. Moynihan's comment cited previously should also be recalled here, that by late 1966 most mayors realized that the CAA's were playing a vital liaison role between the ghettos and themselves—so vital, in fact, that if they did not exist something like them would have had to be created.

important positive potential, from the standpoint of citywide elected officials, would be to divert much of the force of community dissatisfaction from them to neighborhood leaders. There would still be pressure on the citywide leaders to find resources for the decentralized functions, but they would be far less vulnerable than currently to blame for day-to-day operations.

The community leaders who came to the fore, moreover, in a genuine system of neighborhood government would probably be more moderate than today's most visible ghetto spokesmen, who achieve renown primarily through the militancy of their rhetoric. The general experience of ghetto elections to date has been that few far-out radicals run, and that those who do are defeated. The drudgery of local government has little attraction for radicals, and they have little attraction for ghetto voters.*

Responsibility for the operation of complex services would be likely to sober the successful candidates in neighborhood elections still further, and in any event to absorb much of the ghetto's political energy. These hypotheses are far from certain, needless to say, but they receive strong support from the records of today's black mayors and legislators (ranging from city councilmen to Congressmen). At very least, they seem as plausible as the hypotheses that seem to be guiding most white mayors and legislators today.

City officials who supported limited devolutions of authority to the neighborhood level would be likely to reap a harvest of good will in the black community and (in the case of mayors) of good publicity nationally. The force of white backlash on the other side of the ledger would depend upon

---

*Systematic research on these propositions is lacking, but there is fairly general consensus on their validity among informed observers.

There is a critical need for more precise and certain information on this point. I would maintain that studies of the impact of various selection systems upon the types of representatives produced by ghetto communities merit absolute top priority on the urban participation research agenda.

a multitude of factors, but of these the two that city officials could do most about would probably be the following: (a) the extent to which civil servants were persuaded that their tenure rights would be respected, and (b) the extent to which the interest of white city residents in exercising community control was aroused.

We shall deal with the former at some length below. In connection with the latter, it seems appropriate to emphasize once more that white suburbanites value community control highly; why should not their central city brethren? At present the issue is being posed racially, but this may prove susceptible to change.*

A number of close and sympathetic observers of Mayor Lindsay's efforts in New York have emphasized the improbability that community control can be "sold" so long as the market for it is predominantly black. Robert Dentler, for example, the highly respected sociologist and director of the Center for Urban Education, recalled in September 1968 that he had three years previous reported to the city School Board that school decentralization could only succeed if it were instituted citywide. His reasoning was that piecemeal decentralization would (a) permit the organizations hostile to reform to concentrate their fire on one or a few weak targets, and (b) fail to mobilize the widespread potential (but unorganized) support for it.[5]

Doubtless seeking to arouse some of this alleged potential, William Haddad, speaking as a new Lindsay appointee to

---

*What does not seem likely is that the passion of central city whites for community control will ever equal that of Negroes. Whites lack the senses of injustice and exclusion that drive the black movement, and those who most value small-scale local government have the easy option of moving to the suburbs.

More precise comparisons of black with white attitudes toward local government scale in general, and community control within the big cities more specifically, would be of enormous value, however. In addition to improving our understanding, well-designed surveys would be likely to suggest numerous hypotheses about the most fruitful ways to court white interest in community control.

the New York City Board of Education in the late summer
of 1968, responded as follows to a reporter who asked
whether he thought Board members should send their children to the public schools:

> I think the city school system is a disgrace. I think that
> they will inhibit a child. I wouldn't penalize my kid by
> sending him to school here if I could raise the money
> [to send him to private school]. . . . If we had local con-
> trol of the schools on the West Side of Manhattan, I
> would feel a lot better about putting my kids in the
> schools here because I could make that system work for
> me. . . . If I got mad enough, I'd go down there and I'd
> damn well make that school function for me.[6]

Almost a year later, reflecting on the Ocean Hill-Brownsville experience, Herman Badillo, the retiring borough president of the Bronx, urged that future experiments with community control should be undertaken first in white middle
class neighborhoods. In these, community control would
doubtless work most smoothly, and their experience would
help build citywide support for the concept.[7]

Let us turn now from the fears of elected officials to those
of career civil servants. We shall deal with these concerns at
greater length in the next chapter, but a few words are in
order here.

Community control is unlikely to be adopted anywhere
without strong job security guarantees. The most effective
community control strategy would probably be to accept
these but to urge that they be supplemented by a vesting
of pension rights and an offer of early retirement opportunities, to facilitate voluntary withdrawal by those civil servants
who feel uncomfortable about working under community
authority.

If we focus on teachers, whose fears have dominated the
news recently, it is worth keeping in mind that their spokesmen have been less than united in opposition to community

control. The president of the National Education Association took a strong stand in favor of community control in the midst of the New York strike, unqualified by any statement of support for the strike. In Washington, D.C., which began an experiment in community control (involving first one, currently two, elementary schools) in September 1967, the local teachers union—like that of New York, an affiliate of the American Federation of Teachers—has taken a supportive position. In a recent survey, the *New York Times* found top school administrators in Detroit, Philadelphia, and Cincinnati (as well as New York and D.C.) contending that substantial moves toward community control were inevitable and desirable.[8]

The promotional issue is much more difficult than that of job security. Most teachers, to stick with them as our example, have no expectation of promotion; but those who do have typically invested many years perfecting their mastery of an existing career "game." During this period, the cardinal objective of their professional associations has been to "get politics out of education." It is not surprising, then, that they believe it would be highly immoral to change the rules now—with the explicit aim, no less, of enhancing political control.

It seems unlikely that this group will be won over, but three responses to their criticism may be suggested: (1) that these are changing times, in which career-long stability in anything is the exception rather than the rule; (2) that, to move from the abstract to the concrete, we are in the midst of a national crisis which both threatens civil war and poses far more substantial issues of equity than those of concern to them; and (3) that every effort will be made to mitigate the force of the blow. The last might include, again, total vesting of pension rights, so that promotional opportunities elsewhere could be taken up without financial sacrifice. They might also include employment of a consultant by the city to help those who wished to search for jobs with more promising futures in other jurisdictions. To have to change employers in order to secure promotion is an inconvenience, but hardly an American tragedy. It should be added that in most cities community control (or other mechanisms for bringing nonwhites along quickly) would only reduce the number of promotional opportunities available to whites, not eliminate them. Thus, if an adequate portion (which would vary with the plan adopted and the nonwhite population share) of the white candidates departed, the relative position of the remainder could remain as good as before. Considering the unpleasantness that white administrators in nonwhite districts currently face, one would expect a substantial portion to be grateful for the opportunity to depart without loss of pension benefits—unless, that is, they believe that their skills are not saleable anywhere else.

In addition to the interests of elected officials and civil servants, there are those of numerous institutions that have well-oiled relationships with existing city agencies. Most prominent among these are government contractors and public service unions.

Assuming that some contracting (a term I use to encompass all government purchasing from the private sector) were decentralized, and that neighborhood officials tended to favor neighborhood enterprises, some currently successful vendors would indeed be hurt. This could hardly be avoided, as a central purpose of the reform would be to open the contracting game to new players. How might the blow to the old players be softened, so as to mitigate the force of their opposition? The most obvious compromise would be to devolve purchasing authority only in part, and that gradually. Given an expanding public sector, neighborhood agencies might fairly quickly increase their relative share of contracting volume while the absolute level of spending by citywide agencies (taken collectively) fell only slightly or not at all.

Nor would the citywide contractors likely be shut out of neighborhood business entirely. The typical citywide firm would have some neighborhood bases of strength of its own. On larger contracts, neighborhood agencies would probably be required to use competitive bidding procedures. Citywide firms might remain the only vendors of certain specialized goods and services. And, more generally, the citywide firms would be free to adapt by developing ties with neighborhood enterprises and manpower programs.

Turning to the unions: a strong case can be made that community control would strengthen rather than weaken them as institutions. If one examines the history of labor-management relations, few lessons are so clear as that the potential for union dominance is greatest where one union faces numerous employers. In this situation, it can generally pursue a "whipsaw" strategy, focusing its attack upon a single employer at contract time, assuming that if he gives in the others will have no choice but to follow. A strike against one employer can be supported indefinitely by levies on the wages of the members who are still working. The key constraints upon such unions in the private sector are competitive pressures upon the employers with whom they deal—from nonunion enterprises, from other industries, from foreign countries. None of these constraints are significant in the public sector.

What public service unions must beware of is the wrath of government. The way to avert this danger is to cultivate public support. Here again, disaggregation can be a help. A strike that paralyzes a neighborhood is less likely to enrage public opinion than one which paralyzes a large city. More generally, it follows that where a large portion of the public desires community control, such unions will do well to bend with the wind—so long as they can do so without sacrificing other vital interests.

The problem today, of course, is that community control is associated with black militance, which in turn is associated with threats to job security, to the merit principle, and to professional autonomy. This suggests that the path to reconciliation, insofar as one exists at all, lies in combining community control with citywide guarantees of these key union values. In fact, most of the community control schemes being discussed today do this and more. They typically provide that bargaining over hiring and promotional standards, pay, fringe benefits, and tenure rights will continue to be citywide. With respect to these, the unions would remain as free to threaten citywide strike action as they now are. (Public employee strikes are illegal almost everywhere, it should be noted, but the severity of the penalties and the determination of public officials to enforce the law vary from state to state.)

None of this is to suggest that the demand for community control can be assuaged without any union concessions. At very least, community control will involve some reinterpretation of the merit principle, some reduction in professional autonomy, and substantial adjustment to new relationships. But it is to suggest that the policy objectives of both parties can be met simultaneously in high degree, and that the cost of compromise in cities with large nonwhite populations is likely to be minor by comparison with the cost of protracted warfare.

Finally, there is the interest of those whites who simply oppose full integration. Speaking realistically, that means almost all whites—if one includes the vast majority of even that minority who would be happy to have a few middle class Negroes in their neighborhoods. This "interest" is too important a factor in the political process to ignore, dictates of good taste to the contrary.

As noted previously, the white preference for separatism in large part accounts for the nature of current black demands. The current white hostility to community control as well suggests a determination to keep blacks in subjugation, but the primary reasons for this hostility are probably: (a) the association of community control with black militance, (b) the publicity given to anti-white rhetoric by some black militants, and (c) thus, the association of community control with racial warfare.

The greater probability, however, is that community control would suit the interests of these whites to a T. It offers a way of demonstrating responsiveness to black demands and

of providing a safety valve for black frustrations, while rein-
forcing the present black deemphasis on integration. Only
a couple of years ago, one who championed the neighborhood school was anti-black. Now, if he is willing to subject
the neighborhood school to neighborhood control, he can
claim an identity of objectives with most black leaders. Nor,
as noted previously, should it be forgotten that community
control has a good deal of potential appeal in its own right
to the residents of big city white neighborhoods.

It would be rash indeed to forecast with confidence that
community control would be a force for peace rather than
racial warfare. But there are substantial reasons for thinking
that it might. In addition to eliminating numerous issues that
have proven insoluble (e.g., large-scale busing to achieve
school integration), it would create a substantial class of
black politicians with jobs to do other than agitating. These
politicians, moreover, would have unassailable claims to being
treated by the larger society as the legitimate spokesmen and
negotiators for their communities.

Their jobs and their selection by popular vote would tend
to place them among the moderate activists in the black
community. It has been noted, moreover, that representatives
of the poor who have regular dealings with the institutions
of the larger society are highly susceptible to being co-opted.
They tend to be more hungry for the patronage that these
institutions can dispense, and less closely monitored by their
constituents, than the representatives of more affluent
groups.[9] The more obscure the position, the more one would
expect to find this tendency operative—and most neighborhood
positions will be quite obscure. The top positions are more
likely to be occupied by affluent and sophisticated black
professionals—at least in the beginning*—but experience with
black mayors and congressmen to date would suggest that
they, too, will be easy men with whom to deal. This is not

---

*Later on, the pattern of other small and medium-sized localities, whose
politics attract few such people, may become dominant.

to imply that they will ask little, only that they are likely to be subdued and reasonable—and, once in office, to steal the thunder from more radical black activists.

More generally, Banfield and Wilson note that the militance of black politicians on racial issues tends to be in direct proportion to the paucity of tangible benefits that they have to offer their constituents.[10] Almond and Verba report that participation does indeed seem, as Americans have long believed, conducive to political satisfaction. And they add that a political system has little potential for stability if large numbers of its citizens consider it illegitimate.[11]

Michael Parenti adds the encouraging note that the Black Muslims have become an increasingly conservative force as they have secured—without integration—improved psychological and material conditions for their members. He observes that the willingness of social movements to risk violence has traditionally declined as they achieved a measure of recognition, some possessions, and a regularized organizational pattern. The Muslims, he predicts, will prove too weak to achieve their dream (of an autonomous nation), too functional to wither away, and too realistic to invite war with vastly superior forces. Thus, they will go the way of the early Church and of European socialist movements. Their prophets will become bishops, their symbolic sacrifices of blood will be consummated with wine.[12]

Community control might not lead in these directions, quite obviously. Over the years, it might enhance ghetto mobilization and radicalism at the same time. This would be most likely in the following circumstances: (1) if the larger society neglected redistribution as well as integration; (2) if community control seriously impaired service delivery; and (3) if community control significantly reduced the amount of integration that would otherwise have occurred. With regard to the former two, the finding of Almond and Verba is relevant that, for all the conduciveness of participation to public satisfaction, it cannot compensate for poor system performance (as perceived by the citizenry).[13] Whether in fact community control would reduce perceived system performance or prevent much integration that would otherwise have taken place is a question on which the best informed analysts may disagree. It is not even clear that pilot projects would provide much indication, for they would be acutely subject to Hawthorne effects.*

---

*A "Hawthorne effect" is the impact upon a subject's actions of knowing that he is being closely studied. Its origin is a study of worker productivity at the Hawthorne plant of the Western Electric Company in the 1930's.[14] More generally, the term is today applied to many situations in which the fact of being new or special has a critical impact on the way something is done.

CHAPTER FOUR

PLAUSIBLE OPTIONS

THIS volume would grow to inordinate length if I sought to review all the intriguing community control designs that have been suggested, not to mention their likely impact on every arena of local public policy. As a rationing device, therefore, I propose to concentrate on a limited number of issues that cut across functional lines, and of proposals that strike me as representative of the more plausible that are in the air.* I shall also focus on designs for multi-purpose neighborhood government rather than on piecemeal mechanisms for enhancing client influence over specific programs. Future volumes in this series will deal with many of the latter. The topics to be discussed are: (1) the definition of

---

*By "functions," I have in mind such activities—around which local agencies are typically organized—as educating the young, combatting crime and disorder, providing welfare services to the poor, etc. By "plausible" proposals, I mean those that seem to be based on an appreciation of American political realities. No community control proposals are even probably feasible, but a good many have struck me as almost certainly unfeasible. As some basis for screening has seemed necessary, it is the latter that I have chosen to neglect.

neighborhoods, (2) mechanisms of representation and accountability, (3) finance, (4) personnel, (5) contracting, and (6) the federal role.

*   *   *

THE DEFINITION OF NEIGHBORHOODS

The issue of whether to establish neighborhood subgovernments within large cities is controversial but simple. It soon leads, however, to much more complicated questions about their boundaries, powers, and procedures, questions which require detailed and precise answers. For this very reason, no two men are likely to come up with quite the same ones. Let us consider the key options with respect to boundary definition in this section. We shall be concerned with neighborhood powers and procedures throughout the remainder of this chapter.

One might kick off the definitional process in a city by surveying popular perceptions of neighborhood boundaries. The results would be quite inconclusive, however. Most people perceive different neighborhoods for different purposes, and view their own home as the focal point for each. Moreover, the neighborhoods of greatest concern are quite tiny: the few closest houses to one's own, one or several blocks, an elementary school district.[1] Nor is there any consensus among social scientists on how neighborhoods should be defined. Suzanne Keller reports finding four distinct types of definition in the literature: those based on "natural" geographic boundaries, those based on evidence as to the users of neighborhood facilities, those based on the cultural characteristics of residents, and those based on resident perceptions.[2]

In both everyday and social science usage, moreover, the terms "community" and "neighborhood" are quite distinct. The former, as Robert Nisbet has written, refers to ties that "are characterized by a high degree of personal intimacy, emotional depth, moral commitment, social cohesion, and continuity in time."* The most common bases for such ties in contemporary America are family, religion, ethnicity, race (the ethnicity of Afro-Americans), occupation, and income class. The essence of "neighborhood," by contrast, is spatial contiguity.

This has led some critics of the movement for community control to pose the question: Are neighborhoods relevant? To be more precise, they have suggested that contemporary neighborhoods lack *both* the scale to deal with the problems that people care about and the sense of community that might make the exercise of political responsibility within them a source of profound satisfaction to their members.

The demand for participation, in this view, cannot be satisfied by providing for the expression of just any small community interests. The needs are to cultivate community life along the social dimensions that most matter to people, and to imbue the whole political system with an ethic stressing active consultation and responsiveness. The sorts of organizations they have in mind are churches, labor unions, ethnic and racial associations, professional associations, and so on. Whether participation should involve formal delegations of public authority to such groups is another matter. Most adherents of this position think not.

In response, it can be argued as follows:

First, structural reform is often prerequisite to spiritual, and disaggregation is a program of those who feel they lack power to shape the spirit of the whole. There is a great deal of precedent for believing that a group's sense of unity can be cultivated by treating it as a group—i.e., by assigning it tasks that require collective decision making and intense

---

*He goes on: "Community is founded on man conceived in his wholeness rather than in one or another of the roles, taken separately, that he may hold in a social order. . . . It achieves its fulfillment in a submergence of individual will that is not possible in unions of mere convenience or rational assent. . . . Its archetype, both historically and symbolically, is the family, and in almost every type of genuine community the nomenclature of family is prominent."[3]

interaction among its members, by distributing benefits through group channels and in accord with group policies, by refusing to negotiate except with official group spokesmen, and so on. Preexisting antagonisms among subgroups can wreck this strategy, but it has worked tolerably well in most American localities. The reasons it has failed in the big cities are: (a) white separatism and discrimination, (b) the consequent black sense of being an oppressed, permanent minority, and (c) the excessive size of these cities as primary local jurisdictions.

Second, the sense of participation varies with the immediacy of linkage between activity and decision. Thus, it is not surprising that the demand which touches a profoundly responsive chord in the ghettos is for community power to *decide* in some areas of intense concern, not just to appear at a few more hearings. If one considers this demand reasonable, he is led to ask whether Negroes must always experience minority status in their localities. Given the American tradition of small-scale local government, and the residential concentration of Negroes, the answer would seem to be that they needn't. One may argue about whether the jurisdictional boundaries should be drawn to maximize racial homogeneity, or whether it would suffice to design a structure that did not strike Negroes as a systematic gerrymander against them. (If Negroes are sensitive on this score, it should be recalled that gerrymandering is another hoary American tradition.) But the basic case, in terms of racial equity and accommodation, for extending the suburban pattern to the central cities would seem unassailable.

Third, people do care intensely about what happens in their neighborhoods—which they define for various purposes as the blocks they regularly walk, the district boundaries of their children's schools, their church parishes, the area with which they think their property values are bound up, and so on. In addition, of course, some cities have strong neighborhood traditions. H. L. Ross found, for example, that in an old Boston neighborhood two-thirds of the residents knew its conventional name, and four-fifths could name at least three of its four conventional boundaries.[4]

Propinquity creates strong common interests and concerns, even aside from other bases of community that neighbors may have in common. In practice, moreover, there are powerful tendencies toward residential clustering by race, religion, class, and ethnicity; and study after study has shown that people want to live among neighbors whose life styles and child-rearing patterns are similar to their own.[5] The opposite side of the coin is even more sharply etched. Few American passions are so strong as that to escape residential propinquity with those whose life styles and child-rearing patterns are perceived as radically different.

Groups vary widely, of course, in the substance of their neighborhood desires and the strength of their neighborhood commitments. What is most striking, however, is that poor people and black people (and thus particularly poor black people) have the greatest stake in their particular "turfs." Affluent whites can abandon any particular locale with ease if it becomes uncongenial. This has been, in fact, their most important mode of urban political expression over the past generation. And, despite their mobility, they defend with passion the political independence of their new "neighborhoods." The poor, on the other hand, tend to move within much smaller radii. They find changes of neighborhood both difficult and discomforting. They are also less likely to have cars; and even when they do, the friends and relatives with whom they visit are much more likely to live close by.[6]

Melvin and Carolyn Webber have noted that the population can be laid along a continuum in terms of its perceptions and uses of space. At one extreme, the intellectual elite communicates along networks of specialization over enormous distances. Its channels are the telephone, academic conventions, professional publications, and so on. Although face-to-face contact may be infrequent, the quality of interaction is quite intense. Membership in the professional community is a vital part of each member's identity. Moreover, "it is these spatially dispersed peers who will understand his work and, in evaluation, convey the rewards that matter most to him."[7]

But at the other end of the continuum, the Webbers write, may be found the "working-class locals." The consistent findings of social science studies indicate that these people, "whether residents of central city slums or suburban housing tracts, have retained the 'intense localism' and the limited 'close-knit networks' of social relations that are also found in many peasant societies." The critical distinction between the cosmopolite and the local is not whether he lives in an urban or rural place, but rather his income, education, occupation, and outlook. The forest ranger is likely to be well along toward the cosmopolite end of the spectrum; the central city day laborer will tend to be near the local end. Generally speaking, it can be said that among working class locals, "in striking contrast to middle-class groups, social organization (encompassing both family and friends) is territorially coterminous with the neighborhood place." The authors continue as follows:

> The members of these societies rarely leave their spatial environs. Of course, the job holder may have to leave the neighborhood daily, but he follows a fixed transit course to his destination, and returns with little intercourse en route. The family may make a trip to visit an upwardly mobile member of the family who has moved some distance away; but such journeys are rare, even if the distance is only a few miles. . . .
> . . . This sort of parochialism is seen in its extreme form in the localities of the male, teen-age gangs who fight to defend the turf of their street corner or candy shop against the threat of invasion by gangs from the immediately adjacent but foreign blocks. . . . In the highly personalized life of the working-class neighborhood, where one's experiences are largely limited to social contacts with others who are but minutes away, the physical space and the physical buildings become reified as aspects of the social group. One's conception of himself and of his place in society is thus subtly merged

with his conceptions of the spatially limited territory of limited social interaction.[8]

The studies to which the Webbers refer deal mainly with whites. At all income levels in American society, however, the social lives of blacks are more spatially concentrated than those of whites. It is even true, despite the popular stereotype, that they move less—at least, between locales. Dire economic necessity has forced a great migration from countryside to city, and from South to North, upon American Negroes in the present century. The most careful survey to date has found, though, that once Negroes find a city in which there is any work at all, they tend to stay put. They are much less prone to move about the country in response merely to *improved* job opportunities than whites.*

There is little reason for surprise, then, either that ghetto residents think neighborhoods *are* relevant, or that a good many intellectual critics consider them obsolete. What is surprising is that so little notice has been taken of the paradox that, among American urban residents, those whose perspectives are most limited spatially are concentrated in the largest jurisdictions—or, to put it another way, that those to whom neighborhood means the most enjoy opportunities for neighborhood self-government the least.

---

*To repeat, the measure being applied here is interlocal moves. Negroes do make more intra-local moves than whites, a phenomenon which can be explained statistically by their lower incomes and rates of home ownership. Some of the poorest urban families, who have few white counterparts in modern America, exercise a disproportionate influence on the overall rate by the astonishing frequency—up to several times yearly—of their intra-local moves.

At the time of the 1960 census, 16.8 per cent of American whites were living in a different county from five years earlier, by comparison with only 8.5 per cent of nonwhites.

Among family heads who had experienced occasional or frequent unemployment, the white rate of movement had been nearly twice the Negro rate (23-12 per cent). Among family heads who had been steadily employed during the five-year period, the white rate of movement was seven times the Negro (21-3 per cent).[9]

To establish that neighborhoods matter, of course, is quite something else from determining their boundaries. In performing the second task, it would be necessary to reconcile the overlapping perceptions of residents and, even more important, to balance these perceptions against numerous considerations of scale, simplicity, diversity, and capacity to evolve. To illustrate:

Scale Neighborhoods of 500 or even 5,000 people would be unlikely delegatees of significant public authority—if only because the argument that city dwellers deserve comparable treatment to suburbanites would lose most of its force at this scale. It would also be argued that most city services have economies of scale that call for populations much larger than this. The returns from increasing scale seem to diminish sharply, however, above about 50,000 population.[10] This is not to deny that certain public functions require larger absolute or relative scale, particularly the latter. The most obvious examples are air and water pollution control. Their technologies do not require populations above 50,000; but to be effective, the agencies charged with these functions do need jurisdiction over all pollution sources. Thus, in a larger metropolitan area they need larger scale. We are talking here, however, of neighborhood subunits within very large city or metropolitan governments. It would be superfluous for them to be capable of exploiting all potential benefits of scale.

Simplicity Fifty or 100 neighborhoods in a city would be likely to overload the channels of communication and negotiation to City Hall. Depending on their absolute size and on the strength of natural barriers marking them off from one another, such proliferation might also present unmanageable problems of cooperation and conflict management among neighborhoods.

Given these considerations of scale and simplicity, my own preference would be for units in the 50–75 thousand range in cities of up to 2 million. Only three American cities had populations significantly larger than 2 million in 1960. Two of these, Chicago and Los Angeles, might have been nicely accommodated by units in the 100,000 range, as their populations were 3.6 and 2.5 million respectively. New York, with its 8 million people, is a unique case, and it seems a tossup whether larger districts or a greater number of districts would be preferable. If local government structures were revised to create metropolitan cities, placing today's suburbs and central city "neighborhoods" on a par, the problem of very large size would become more widespread. Even so, only nine Standard Metropolitan Statistical Areas (SMSA's) had populations significantly larger than 2 million in 1960. Of these, five had populations larger than 3 million, and three had populations larger than 6 million. Each reader will doubtless have his own view of how these criteria should be balanced. I have expressed mine only to illustrate the sorts of tradeoffs that would have to be made, and the frequency with which they would likely become very painful.

Diversity and Capacity to Evolve   These are ultimately far more important considerations than either scale or simplicity. Should neighborhood boundaries be drawn to maximize ethnic, class, and especially racial homogeneity, or should the criteria be geographic compactness and equal population size? Should the assumption be permanence (as with current suburban boundaries) or periodic reapportionment (as with legislative district boundaries)? These are tightly linked choices.

Given the potential explosiveness of the homogeneity question, I would judge that the only viable strategy for the proponents of community control would be to label it irrelevant. How might this be done? Quite simply, by maintaining that the key issue is scale, and that once it has been determined in any city, neighborhoods should be shaped geographically and evolved in the same manner as legislative districts. (In reality, of course, it is not quite so simple. The scale of districts will affect, often critically, their probable diversity.) Like any system of district representation, this one would express existing residential patterns at any time. It would retain its democratic vitality, however, so long as the desire for suburban-scale government within large cities persisted. Another advantage of this position (elaborated below, pp. 134–36) is that it would greatly facilitate the linkage of neighborhood to city council and state legislative district boundaries.

Who should take part, and what procedures should be used, in the initial process of neighborhood definition? Here as elsewhere, it would be rash indeed to venture a detailed prescription. The main elements of the sort of process that could possibly win general acceptance, however, are fairly clear. Let us concentrate on the local portion of the process, though state action would generally be required as well.

The process would be iterative, one in which successive approximations were developed and debated; it would have tight deadlines (to refute the charge of stalling); and it would be open.

In stage one, a broadly representative commission or a city council committee would conduct hearings on the general criteria that should guide neighborhood definition. Anyone who had detailed proposals would also be free to submit them. The hearings would be held at convenient times for working people, and at locations throughout the city.

In stage two, a commission would be formed if it had not been previously. It would probably be appointed by the mayor, but the mode of selection would be less important than its flavor of representativeness. All key groups, hopefully, would have been consulted, and their wishes accorded enough weight to keep them from being outraged. (This will often be unfeasible, but it should certainly be a prime objective.) The function of this commission would be to develop a detailed proposal for submission to the mayor and city council. It would be instructed to announce tentative decisions on broad criteria fairly quickly, and then to hold brief further hearings at which citizens might react to them. It would then present its final recommendations on criteria to the mayor and city council. After these authorities had a chance to react (the mere passage of a few weeks without negative reaction might suffice), the commission would proceed to draft a detailed plan. If it were politically adept, it would maintain close informal liaison with the mayor, with other elected officials, and with key grass roots leaders (including particularly representatives of the major Negro factions and public employee unions) throughout the drafting process, so that potential objections might be discovered and negotiated before public stances became necessary.

In stage three, the commission plan having been published and widely discussed, the mayor would present it or (more likely) his own variant to the city council for decision. It would conduct further hearings, probably make further revisions, and then, if àll went well, enact an ordinance. The ordinance would establish neighborhood boundaries, specify a good deal of the structure of neighborhood government, indicate when and how periodic reapportionment would take place, and provide a method for the activation of neighborhood authorities. With regard to the last, three broad options are apparent: neighborhood authorities might come into being on a specified date by citywide order; a citywide referendum on the issue of activation might be held, with the majority in each neighborhood determining its own course; or a referendum might be held in each neighborhood as and when a specified percentage of eligible voters petitioned for one. If the second method were used initially, something like the third would be needed to enable neighborhoods to change their minds thereafter.

One final point before leaving the subject of neighborhood definition. Form and substance continuously interact and shape each other. Viewed historically, they are inseparable. There are solid reasons, nonetheless, for trying to keep them *conceptually* distinct in the process of planning for decentralization. The substance of decentralization—that is, the specific powers delegated to neighborhood units—will change constantly, and perhaps quite radically within a few years. The form is likely to prove rather constant—especially if one considers the regularized reapportionment procedure as part of the form. The aim, then, should be to bring into being a form that can easily accommodate a wide range of substantive options. This is not to suggest that a form can be presented to the public without some proposals for immediate delegation of power. It is only to stress that those responsible for developing the package would do well to strive for a form that is compatible with a very wide range of possible long-run developments as well as with their own near-term recommendations.

MECHANISMS OF REPRESENTATION AND ACCOUNTABILITY

The demand for neighborhood government is part of a much broader program of democratic reform, one stressing the ideals of intimate scale, participation, and group representation as against those of areawide coordination, neutral competence, and "at-large" representation. As this program has emerged from a movement rather than an organization, it lacks a definitive statement. Actually, a good deal of poetic license is involved in speaking of one program rather than many. Each local incarnation is a variant; no one is authoritative. The basic aim is the same everywhere, and the core of recurring specifics is large. But on some points two or three options are more or less equally orthodox, and hosts of proposals that have not yet secured either widespread acceptance or rejection are in the air at any time. What I should like to do in this section is to review some of the ideas on representation that are most regularly put forward, and which seem to involve the most serious potential conflict with other widespread conceptions of "good" governmental procedures.

The most universal demand is for district representation, not only on the city council but on all other major policy committees—especially the school board and police commission —as well. District representation and neighborhood government should be tightly linked, so as to enhance the visibility of each and to reinforce popular awareness of the neighborhood as a political entity. It goes without saying, then, that part of the program is common district and neighborhood definition. Given the recent Supreme Court ruling that local government districts must be apportioned on a one man-one vote basis,[11] the satisfaction of this demand would go a long way toward resolving the issue of whether neighborhood boundaries should be conceived as permanent or as akin to legislative district definitions.

There is no standard position on whether citywide policy bodies should be composed *exclusively* of district representatives, or on how authority should be divided among the mayor, city council, and independent boards at the citywide level. In general, there is no hostility to strong mayoral authority within the scope of the city's jurisdiction, because chief executives are perceived as more friendly to Negro interests than most other policy-making units. (This may change if the trend that became discernible in 1969 toward election of "law and order" mayors continues.) What there is agreement on is that, insofar as cities make use of collegiate bodies, they should be constituted at least primarily on the basis of district representation. Where representation is at-large, the general preference is for selection by appointment rather than election, because at-large elections tend to shut minorities out entirely, whereas chief executives tend to balance their appointments among key interest groups.

Among those few I have encountered who have considered the issue, the common view is that power should *not* be fragmented at the neighborhood level by setting up numerous independent single purpose agencies. Design of the neighborhood system, they insist, should rather be aimed at providing a clear institutional focus for public attention. The expectation is that a concentration of neighborhood public authority in a single council and chief executive will enhance public interest, produce the largest possible voter turnouts, and thus maximize the neighborhood government's claim to speak and act for its constituency. The typical council, they add, will no doubt wish to divide into committees, to establish citizen advisory boards, and from time to time to appoint *ad hoc* task forces. These arrangements should rest upon, and be subject to alteration by, simple council decisions, however.

It is sometimes asserted that an important further step toward consolidation should be taken, that of having the same individual(s) lead the neighborhood government and represent the neighborhood on citywide policy bodies. There is a wide variety of ways in which such consolidation might be arranged. For example, the neighborhood's chief executive and its representative on the city council might be the same man; the chairman of its school board (or neighborhood council school committee) might represent it on the citywide school board; and so on. These combinations of authority would help rebut the criticism that community control equalled fragmentation of power; they would minimize the potential for city-neighborhood conflict; and they would provide the neighborhood with highly visible leaders.

Critics have argued that such reforms, while unifying the neighborhoods, would weaken the capacity of citywide bodies to act except by logrolling. The obvious reply is that any system of district representation would have this effect. The combination of city and neighborhood roles in the same men would be at least as likely to mitigate as to intensify it. If there were a great deal of concern about excessive fragmentation at the citywide level, the mayor's authority could be strengthened vis-à-vis that of the collegiate policy bodies.

Quite another line of criticism is that power should not be concentrated at the neighborhood level because the danger of majority tyranny is too great. Blacks respond that the alternatives are these: (1) fragmented power at both the city and neighborhood levels, or (2) concentrated power at the city but not the neighborhood level. If the former is contemplated, moves toward community control will be attacked as hopelessly fragmenting the governmental system. If the latter, city institutions will easily dominate those of the neighborhoods. The need, they argue, is for a combination of effective government with balance between city (or metropolitan) and neighborhood power. The latter is essential because the danger of majority tyranny has already been realized on the citywide level. Summing up, blacks consider this argument a simple ploy to render neighborhood government ineffective, thus keeping whites in control and discrediting the neighborhood concept. The critics who make it are particularly suspected of racism when they have records of urging improved coordination at the citywide and metropolitan levels.

Just as at-large representation is rejected for citywide policy bodies, so it is assumed that members of neighborhood councils should represent districts or "interests." There is substantial disagreement, however, about the precise manner in which they should be chosen. The main issues in controversy are: (1) Should representatives be elected or designated by organizations? (2) Should special provisions be made to ensure representation for key neighborhood minorities? (3) Should the neighborhood chief executive be a directly elected "mayor" or an ordinary councilman serving at the pleasure of his colleagues? (4) Should members of neighborhood councils and task forces receive compensation for attendance at meetings? and (5) To what extent, if any, should the principle of decentralization be applied to neighborhood government itself? Let us review these in turn.

Should representatives be elected or designated by organizations? The vast majority of sympathetic whites and a good many blacks feel that only elections will do. The predominant view among black activists, however, is that representatives should be designated by organizations. Among close observers of ghetto politics, some dismiss the activist position as self-serving. Others point out that the activists are a force to be reckoned with, and that the organizations are important mobilization mechanisms. This division has been reflected in the Community Action and Model Cities programs. Precise figures on the former are not available, but Arnstein and Fox report that two-thirds of the cities that had received Model Cities planning grants through July 1968 had opted for elections as the mechanism for choosing Model Neighborhood representatives.[12] Most of the others had solicited organizational nominations. A few had tried to get by with appointment by city officials.

Let us consider this debate in slightly greater detail. The supporters of organizational representation tend to argue (in the spirit of *realpolitik)* that the chief purposes of representation are (a) to satisfy specific articulate demands and (b) to co-opt the agitators who have rendered these demands important political issues. If the demand is for group representation, and it will take this to achieve the desired co-option, why fight it? What would be the benefit of insisting upon elections, only to have them effectively boycotted, or only to have them intensify the militants' sense of grievance? To answer the criticism that organizational representation was contrary to the majority will of the community, provision might be made for a referendum on the mode of representation whenever a specified proportion of the neighborhood's voters petitioned for one.

It may well be, they add, that the activists are the only residents of ghetto neighborhoods who really care what method of selection is used. Turnout in poverty elections tends to be quite low. In the first year of the Community Action Program, turnouts of 2 and 3 per cent were common.* Arnstein and Fox report that most Model Neighborhood elections through mid-1968 had turnouts in the 7 to 11 per cent

---

*Levitan writes: "During OEO's first year about a dozen cities held elections for membership on CAA boards, neighborhood planning councils, or both. The turnout for these elections was meager . . . Voter participation ranged from a low of 1 percent to a high of less than 5 percent of those eligible.

"A committee of the American Arbitration Association, which analyzed CAA elections during the first 18 months of OEO, concluded that the lack of participation stemmed from absence of issues or constituencies, from the fact that there were few contestants with charisma to inspire a large turnout, and from general skepticism of the poor that the new program would be more successful than previous efforts had been."[13]

In a detailed analysis of the CAP target area election held during this first year in Philadelphia, which elicited a turnout of 3 per cent, Paul Peterson emphasized the following factors: (a) the election method had been chosen over the objection of the area's organized groups; (b) the groups, consequently, did not take part in the election process; (c) this meant that all candidates ran as individuals rather than familiar symbols; and (d) it also produced a campaign without significant issues. The voters who turned out were those reached on a friends and neighbors basis by the individual candidates.[14]

range—though four ranged between 24 and 40 per cent.*[15] When very low turnouts occur, they leave the resultant councils highly vulnerable to the charge of being unrepresentative even though elected. If a system of organizational representation could render the charge harmless by its openness—that is, by its standing offer of a council seat to anyone who organized with moderate effectiveness in pursuit of one—it would merit very serious consideration, notwithstanding its unfamiliarity.

The proponents of election tend to counter these arguments as follows.

First, a system of representation through organizations would tend to rigidify and become less genuinely representative over time. At the beginning, every organization would be accorded a voice, with few questions asked; but in time the "charter members" would tend to arrange things so that their own seats were secure and newcomers had a hard time winning recognition.

Second, membership rolls would have to be open. Thus, a citizen would be much more susceptible to intimidation than in a secret ballot election. Intimidation is essentially a relationship rather than a neat category of acts that can be forbidden. Thus, even when the neighborhood governors gave no cause for intervention by higher authorities, many residents

---

*It is worth noting that comparable elections have low turnouts in the rest of America as well. Eugene C. Lee has reported on a survey of all local elections during 1961–1962 in cities larger than 25,000. Where city council elections were held independent of any other election, the median turnout was only 24 percent. Those cities in the lowest quartile averaged turnouts of 17 percent. Community size had no noticeable impact on voter turnout.[16]

It bears mention as well that in the neighborhood poverty elections held to date, less has been at stake than in city council elections. The responsibility of poverty boards has been confined to one program rather than many, and they have rarely had final authority to decide anything. The idea of electing a board to guide a single program is more unfamiliar and perhaps confusing to voters, moreover, than that of electing a city council.

would consider it imprudent to do anything that might displease them. And of course the governors *would* distribute the favors at their command with an eye to perpetuating themselves in office.

Third, even if organizational representation were the most effective method of forestalling charges of unrepresentativeness from within a particular neighborhood, it would tend to encourage them from without. Any group that wished to justify city or state intervention in neighborhood affairs would seize upon the fact that the neighborhood leadership had never been tested at the polls.

Fourth, just as a system of organizational representation would probably become less satisfactory over time, an electoral system would probably gather support. It is reasonable to expect that voting turnout would increase during the first few years as "the news" about neighborhood government spread—unless the news were that it had no significance. Election boycotts would rarely prove long-lived. Opposition to voting is hardly the sort of cause likely to command a mass following anywhere in America for long. Where militants did refuse to participate in a meaningful program of community control that called for elections, they would probably decline in significance as elected leaders began to act in areas of intense popular concern.

A final argument for elections (admittedly not to everyone's taste) is that they would tend to produce more moderate neighborhood spokesmen. At present, in this view, the decisive test of a "leader" is the space he commands in the mass media. For the media, the decisive test of newsworthiness is novelty. They have little knowledge of or curiosity about the real size of any leader's following. Thus, they focus at any time on whoever is most bizarre, and they tend to drive those who want coverage to think up ever more bizarre means of expression. Elections would show who did speak for the greater number of people. These would generally be moderates. (This thesis receives support, as noted above, both from the experience of ghetto elections to date and from numerous opinion surveys conducted among American Negroes.*) And those who did secure election, radical or not, would tend to be sobered by the experience and burden of responsibility.

For all the vigor of this debate, the pro- and anti-election positions may not be irreconcilable. One possible solution would be to permit organizational representation where the voters of a neighborhood opted for it in a referendum. The initial decision would not have to be final; provision could be made for subsequent referenda at stated intervals (say, not more frequently than once a decade) upon petition by a given percentage of registered voters in the neighborhood. Another possibility would be to have some representatives chosen by each method, with the elected representatives deciding after each election how many seats to allocate to each organization. Still a third possibility would be to arrange organizational representation in the manner of a multi-party, proportional representation election system. The weight of each organization's voice in a council so constituted would be fixed periodically on the basis of its membership. Each resident would be limited to a specified number of memberships, and membership would be ascertained by a system of voter registration—as political party membership now is—rather than by reliance upon organizational membership rolls. Such a system would presumably even meet the Supreme Court's apportionment standards.

Should special provisions be made to ensure representation for key neighborhood minorities? The specific minorities most frequently mentioned are those of race, ethnicity, extreme

---

*To illustrate: the Kerner Commission's 1968 poll, conducted before Martin Luther King's assassination, found King and Roy Wilkins approved by more than fourteen times as many Negroes as those who disapproved of them (72–5 and 50–3 per cent, respectively). By contrast, many more disapproved than approved the work of Stokely Carmichael and H. Rap Brown. Their approval-disapproval percentages were 14–35 and 14–45 respectively. This survey, it should be recalled, was conducted in fifteen large northern cities rather than nationwide—a circumstance which makes it particularly relevant to the present discussion.[17]

poverty, and youth. The arguments against explicit group representation on neighborhood councils are obvious and rather overwhelming. Such a reification of particular criteria for categorizing voters would eliminate from the system nearly all capacity to evolve; it would intensify and ensure the persistence of today's most salient group conflicts; and it would force many people into molds that they found Procrustean.

At the same time, a strong case can be made for neighborhood proportional representation systems, perhaps combined with reductions in the voting age, that might have similar effects in practice—depending on the importance that voters attached to these aspects of their identities. Given prevailing patterns of residential segregation, substantial racial and ethnic minorities would generally secure representation in the normal course of voting by district in any event.

The main argument against using a system of proportional representation is that it tends to promote disunity and indecisiveness. The organized factions or parties are encouraged by the system to cultivate narrow constituencies rather than to combine in search of majorities.[18] This suggests that although neighborhoods should be permitted, and in some cases even encouraged, to adopt proportional representation, they should no more be compelled to do so than cities themselves.*

---

*The New York City School Decentralization bill enacted by the New York State Legislature in 1969 does force proportional representation upon the "neighborhoods" (which will each have 250–300 thousand residents).

Elections to the citywide board, by contrast, are to be on a borough-wide basis. Not only is this procedure designed to minimize black representation. As it assigns each borough the same number of representatives (one), it also patently violates the Supreme Court's current apportionment standards. The largest borough (Brooklyn) had twelve times the population of the smallest (Staten Island) in 1960. The gap has doubtless narrowed since, but in 1967 Brooklyn still had more than nine times as many registered voters and public school students as Staten Island.

As the bill is also designed in numerous other ways to make "community control" a sham, the imposition of proportional representation on the neighborhoods in this case can with some confidence be labelled a hostile act—in the spirit of "Divide and rule."[19]

Should the neighborhood chief executive be a directly elected "mayor" or an ordinary councilman serving at the pleasure of his colleagues? The basic arguments for the former are: (1) that only direct election would normally provide the strength and continuity of leadership that a decentralized system will need to work effectively, and (2) that the addition of an at-large election for the top office in each neighborhood would elicit far greater public interest than councilman elections alone possibly could. The first of these arguments, of course, rests on the assumption that stable majorities will be rare on neighborhood councils; and that, consequently, pure parliamentary neighborhood governments might resemble nothing so much as miniature French Fourth Republics. Those who favor the parliamentary form, by contrast, stress that the movement for decentralization has received its impetus from a popular desire for greater responsiveness, not strong executive leadership.

This issue is intimately bound up with two others: whether the neighborhood's political chief executive (1) should serve also as its city councilman, and (2) should be supplemented with a professional "neighborhood manager."

(1) In a city where these two key political posts were combined, and the incumbents served at the pleasure of their neighborhood councils, the city council would be a mere conference of ambassadors. The city government would thus be sharply subordinated to those of the neighborhoods. Many supporters of community control believe that this would be a good thing, but it is clearly a vital factor to be considered.

(2) A professional neighborhood manager might provide adequate continuity at the summit of a neighborhood government system even if turnover in the political chief executive post were high. Some, therefore, envision such managers as permitting the objectives of high effectiveness and maximum responsiveness to be realized simultaneously. In response, it may be argued that these objectives are *inherently* antagonistic. If the manager ran the government while the politicians squabbled, the system would probably be less responsive, and it would certainly be less democratic, than if an elected chief

executive ran it while the neighborhood council squabbled. In such a system, moreover, elections might seem to have little influence on governmental content, thus compounding the tendency of the parliamentary form to reduce turnout. To oppose substantial reliance on professional managers to provide political leadership, of course, is not to oppose strong administrative support for the political chief executive. Many "strong mayor" cities in recent years have created the post of "city administrator" to provide such support, and this precedent would seem applicable to "strong mayor" neighborhoods.

Should members of neighborhood councils and task forces receive compensation for attendance at meetings?   Compensation has been rare in the Community Action and Model Cities programs. But the view is heard with increasing frequency that, in the absence of at least reimbursement for out-of-pocket expenses, the formal opportunity to participate has little meaning for the very poor. Some argue that stipends should be paid as well, to bolster the prestige and attractiveness of neighborhood office. It is pointed out that city officials are paid for their time, and that there is little tradition of sustained volunteer activity in most low income neighborhoods. In the absence of stipends, moreover, the regular participants, at least in black neighborhoods, are likely to be predominantly female. This is particularly unfortunate because it is the males who threaten the stability of the political order.* It is they whom community control must be perceived to pacify if it is to secure and retain widespread white support. Would stipends make a difference? Arnstein and Fox, who think so, report that in Denver, where stipends

---

*The Kerner Commission's fifteen-city survey found three times as many males as females reporting that they had ever participated in a riot.[20] Fogelson and Hill found that 89 percent of arrestees in the 27 disorders they studied were male. They contend that this figure overstates the extent to which the riots were male phenomena, however, because the police were apparently less inclined to arrest female offenders.[21]

of $15.00 a meeting are provided, 70 per cent of the Model Neighborhood representatives are male.[22] They neglect to provide any basis for estimating what the proportion would be in the absence of stipends, however.

To what extent, if any, should the principle of decentralization be applied to neighborhood government itself? The general view among proponents of community control is that people should have a chance to experience self-government in communities as small as several hundred or several thousand people wherever possible. Discussion of this issue has been casual and very general to date, however. If and when community control becomes reality, the potential for disagreement on the details of subdelegation will doubtless be realized. The key questions that will have to be addressed are the following: Should the formation and delegation of authority to subunits be purely at the discretion of each neighborhood government? If not, what should be the role of higher authorities? Should delegation be primarily to inclusive geographic units or to associations of program clients—for example, tenants' councils, school parents' councils, welfare mothers' councils? Should an effort be made to have subunit boundaries coincide with "cultural" boundaries—that is, with patterns of racial, ethnic, and class segregation—or should they be guided solely by such "culture-blind" criteria as equality of population, compactness, and physical barriers?

FINANCE

Speaking technically, there is no reason why neighborhoods of 50,000 or more people need have less fiscal independence than suburbs. There is a great deal to be said for an expansion of state and federal grants to offset inequalities of wealth among local jurisdictions, but this should be said regardless of whether community control is implemented. Federal and state aid formulas, incidentally, have long favored low income states and rural counties; and the recent trend (most explicit in the federal poverty and aid-to-education programs) has been to favor inner city slums as well.

Speaking politically, there are two major arguments against devolving responsibility for taxation upon the neighborhoods. The first, of interest primarily to those who are hostile to community control in any event, is that even partial devolution of the taxing function would be a long step in the direction of transforming the neighborhoods into full-fledged municipalities—and thus of rendering the larger city, unless it covered the whole metropolitan area, a rather anachronistic appendage. The second, of far greater interest to those who favor community control, is that fiscal disaggregation would render the cities far less able than they now are to redistribute resources from affluent to poor neighborhoods. Let us consider these arguments in turn.

The large cities are unlikely to fade away, if only because the organized groups with a stake in their survival are too powerful. The pressure for them to concentrate on a limited range of activities which require large scale, however, and perhaps to offer their services to all jurisdictions in the metropolitan area (either on a compulsory or a Lakewood Plan basis),* might well grow if neighborhood governments demonstrated a capacity for self-financing comparable to suburban jurisdictions. It is also true that neighborhoods which raised their own revenues would be sure to insist on spending them without city policy guidance or administrative supervision. (They would be susceptible, however, to influence via grant-in-aid matching requirements.) As they acquired confidence in their capacity for self-financing—if they did so—predominantly black neighborhoods in predominantly white cities might well demand full municipal status.

(In the future, it should be noted, demands for autonomy by white neighborhoods in black-dominated cities may become equally important. Their withdrawal would rarely constitute a net fiscal loss, so long as they left the main

---

*The Lakewood Plan is an arrangement whereby autonomous municipalities within Los Angeles County purchase services, in quantities of their own choosing, from the county.[23]

commercial and industrial districts behind. What it might do, however, would be to confine a growing black population in a fixed geographic area—unless the suburbs relaxed their hostility to black in-migration or the state intervened to make expansion space available. Insistence upon segregation by the society's dominant race is quite different in critical respects from the same insistence by a long-oppressed group trying to find its identity. Nonetheless, if white-dominated cities begin to concede to their predominantly black neighborhoods a high degree of autonomy, black mayors and city councils will have little choice but to follow suit.)

To hear them complain about the high cost of ghetto services compared to ghetto tax payments, one would expect most white residents of the big cities to be delighted at the prospect of fiscal disaggregation—whether as part of a general restructuring of local government or in the form of isolated ghetto secessions. It would be unwise to bet on this, however, in view of the recent record of resistance to far more modest demands for neighborhood authority. At the same time, it is not beyond imagining that in a few cities the demand for total autonomy might encounter less opposition than that for partial community control within the existing fiscal framework.

The redistribution argument is based on the premise that large sums flow from rich to poor today in the operation of city government, and that this redistribution is feasible only because it occurs by means that attract little notice. For example, the police department will normally concentrate its forces disproportionately in high crime areas without concern for who is paying the bill; the building inspection department is likely to devote most of its attention to the city's older structures; the board of education may invest heavily in compensatory programs for children from deprived backgrounds; and so on. Change this process into one in which the city council has to adopt explicit grant-in-aid formulas, the argument continues, and the poorer neighborhoods will come off far less well than they now do. Change it into one in which each neighborhood has to raise its own revenues from its own residents, and they will come off still worse.

The validity of this argument will vary from city to city, and from evaluator to evaluator. New York City's "special service" schools, for example, are frequently cited as models of compensatory spending. David Rogers concludes in a recent study, however, that these schools have been paid for mainly by neglecting other ghetto schools, and that overall the city continues to spend more per child in middle than lower class schools.*[24] In a city like Chicago, the case is simpler. The U. S. Commission on Civil Rights reported in 1962 that spending per child in predominantly white Chicago elementary schools was 27 per cent higher than in predominantly Negro schools ($342 vs $269). The number of children per classroom in the Negro schools was 52 per cent greater (47 vs. 31), and their percentage of uncertified teachers was more than twice as great (27 vs. 12).[26]

Moreover, the greatest inequalities are between cities and suburbs, not neighborhoods within cities. Thus, Alan Campbell reports that in a sample of 35 large metropolitan areas, suburban school expenditures per pupil averaged 35 per cent higher than those of the central cities in 1962. (The suburbs were averaging 32 per cent more in state aid as well.[27]) Christopher Jencks has estimated that the typical spread in spending per school child between the most affluent suburb and the inner city ghetto within each metropolitan area is

---

*More generally, Adam Walinsky has described the treatment of one black New York neighborhood as follows: In the Bedford-Stuyvesant ghetto of New York there are 450,000 people—as many as in the entire city of Cincinnati, more than in the entire state of Vermont. Yet the area has only one high school, and 80 percent of its teen-agers are dropouts; the infant mortality rate is twice the national average; there are over 800 buildings abandoned by everyone but the rats, yet the area received not one dollar of urban renewal funds during the entire first 15 years of that program's operation . . .

Clearly, Bedford-Stuyvesant has some special needs; yet it has always been lost in the midst of the city's eight million. In fact, it took a lawsuit to win for this vast area, in the year 1968, its first Congressman.[25]

of the order of 2 to 1.[28] And the U. S. Office of Education has published figures showing that in seventeen states, the highest spending school district spent more than four times as much per classroom unit in 1959 to 1960 as the lowest.*

Many black leaders argue as well that the apparent redistribution which now occurs within cities is of little value to the supposed beneficiaries. They contend, for example, that police who are both white and indifferent to community wishes constitute more of a provocation to disorder and violence than a preventative. They are inclined to add that, in light of the deference paid by public policy makers to police demands for job security and professional autonomy, the benefits of police salary payments should be viewed as accruing more to the individual payees than to the neighborhoods they patrol. More militant black spokesmen insist that the white police should be viewed as an army of occupation, concentrated in ghetto areas mainly to protect white-owned property, to impose white middle-class mores on the black community, and to let the blacks know clearly who is boss. These arguments are not accepted by all blacks, to be sure, but so long as they are asserted by many, and so long as the basic police decisions are made by white governors downtown, no "objective" assessment of financial costs and benefits is possible.** The same is true of all other services with respect to which community dissatisfaction is rife and the demand for community control strong.

For reasons such as these, some low income neighborhoods might quite coolly decide that autonomy was worth having,

---

*In 25 states, the ratio between the 98th percentile and the 2nd percentile exceeded 2–1. In 31 states, the ratio between the 90th percentile and the 10th percentile exceeded 1.5–1. These figures make no allowance for the number of children per classroom; nor do they distinguish between city, suburban, and rural school districts; nor do they reveal spending inequalities within school districts.[29]

**I am speaking of "objectivity," it should be clear, only in the very limited practical sense of being based on relatively noncontroversial premises.

even at substantial financial cost—or, more precisely, at substantial "benefit-in-kind" cost of disputed financial value. A neighborhood which made this choice, it need hardly be added, would normally seek to offset its loss with dollar grants-in-aid. It would very likely contend, for example, that tax revenues derived from the city's commercial and industrial (as opposed to residential) property should be thrown into a common pool and distributed among the successor governments, preferably according to a formula which favored the less affluent. It would also be zealous in its pursuit of state and federal grants.

Parenthetically, in the more limited situation where the city and the neighborhoods both exercised taxing power, it would also make sense to separate the residential from the commercial and industrial tax base. If the city government's primary base of support were the latter, a good deaī of heat might be drained from the redistribution issue.

Before leaving this subject, it should be noted that many ghetto residents suffer today from tax practices that are inequitable or that discourage slum replacement and maintenance. Some black neighborhoods, therefore, might be even more anxious to acquire control over the criteria of property taxation than the levels. For example, they would wish to ensure that ghetto tax assessment took account of declining property values. (A recent Boston study showed that ghetto property assessments averaged 75 per cent of market value, whereas assessments in two affluent neighborhoods averaged about 33 per cent.)*[30] More radically, they might wish to

---

*In a more complete and subtle analysis of assessment variations in Boston, David Black has found that assessments of ghetto residential property in 1960 averaged more than 70 percent higher than assessments elsewhere in the city. Using regression analysis, he found that the variations appeared mainly due to three factors: (1) systematically higher assessment of multi-family properties throughout the city, (2) failure to adjust for changes in value over time throughout the city, and (3) discrimination on the basis of race. The last seemed to account for about two-fifths of the total difference. Throughout the city, incidentally, new structures were assessed at a higher proportion of market value than old, the difference increasing their taxes by 10 to 20 percent. As the level of construction

concentrate taxation on land rather than on improvements, so as to encourage the latter. They might wish to offer special concessions to builders of new housing for low and middle income residents. And they might wish to do the same for investors who created jobs for their unemployed. Once having been alerted to the importance of tax criteria, they might also become vigorous lobbyists in the national arena, striving to have the federal tax benefits of real estate ownership confined (a) to one depreciation life per property, and (b) to properties not in violation of local codes.

Even if neighborhood governments were denied any power to tax, they might be accorded a substantial amount of budgetary autonomy. From the neighborhood standpoint, of course, the ideal mechanism of city support for neighborhood services would be the block grant. Between the total no-strings block grant and the minutely specified categorical grant, however, there is a very wide spectrum of possibilities. To illustrate: general grants might be made to each neighborhood for education; at the next greater level of precision, they might be divided into primary, intermediate, and secondary school categories; at the next, they might be divided by subjects; at the next, by types of items to be purchased (textbooks, maintenance services, etc.); at the next, by such specified items as textbooks listed by name; and so on. On another dimension, the grants might be allocated entirely by formula or varied to reward those neighborhoods which demonstrated unusual imagination and skill in dealing with high priority problems. It is vital (though perhaps tedious) to stress the great variety of options available, because some of the champions and nearly all the opponents of community control frequently speak as if the choice were all or nothing.

PERSONNEL

In this area the battle has already been joined. On the

---

activity was relatively low in the ghetto, this variation tended to offset the three previously mentioned.[31]

one hand, black communities are demanding: (1) the right to select and dismiss public employees assigned to their "turfs"; (2) representation at all levels of the public service more or less proportionate to their share of the population; and (3) a similar share of the profits and payrolls created by government contracts. On the other hand, associations of public employees are erecting barricades behind the principles of merit selection and promotion, job security, and citywide bargaining.

On both sides, the will to peace is in headlong decline, the determination to prevail is on the rise. Existing governmental institutions are perceived as instruments of selfish groups (sometimes majorities, to be sure), not of justice. Neither side is prepared to accept unfavorable decisions simply because they are the output of democratic processes. The only hope for peace is that both sides share some basic assumptions, and that both remain fearful of total war.

These minimal requisites of peace are by no means present everywhere. In most situations where they are, they will probably suffice only after both sides have faced each other at the brink for a terrifying moment. And the typical resolution will be a hasty patchwork, good for a truce but sure to be followed by new flareups in several days, months, or years.

All we can hope to do here is to review the key types of disputes that seem to be emerging, and to indicate a few of the approaches to reconciliation that seem most (if not always very) promising.

First, let us consider the tension between community control and public employee job security. Although it is frequently obscured by the heated rhetoric of the parties and the inattention to fundamentals of the mass media, blacks are not insisting on any general reduction in public employee job security. Most do believe, to be sure, that public service job security has been excessive, and that the granting of tenure has been virtually automatic (regardless of on-the-job performance) once the formal entrance examinations have been passed. They cite such examples as that during a recent five-year period in New York City, fewer than 1 in every 1,000 annual teacher ratings were "unsatisfactory," and that dismissals of tenured personnel ran about 1 in 10,000 each year.* But their strategy of change is focused on other objectives than getting currently tenured incompetents fired.

The two basic disputes in this area are about: (1) whether employees should be subject to involuntary transfer at the request of neighborhood boards, and (2) what form job security should take for those hired after the inauguration of community control.

The desire of white civil servants (and many blacks as well) to avoid ghetto assignments has long been notorious. Why, then, should the issue of involuntary transfers evoke such a hysterical response? The primary reason appears to be the traditional union fear—particularly intense among those who lived through the Great Depression—that there will not be enough jobs to go around. The concrete fear in this case is that employees driven out of one neighborhood would often prove unplaceable in any other—either because rosters were full or their incompetence was obvious. A secondary concern is doubtless that forced transfers would be painful to the egos of the employees affected.**

If forced transfers are permitted by community control schemes at all—given public employee militance, it seems unlikely that they will often be—not much can be done about the hurt egos. But it should be possible to give ironclad guarantees of placement. This would force neighborhoods to keep a few employees of whom they wished to be rid, but

---

*The first ratio was for tenured and nontenured personnel combined, the second for tenured personnel only. The average number of teachers in the system during this period was 54,235. Roughly 50 a year received "unsatisfactory" ratings, and 2 were fired.[32] Figures on the number denied tenure are not available.

**As opposed to these rank-and-file concerns, there are the lofty arguments about civil liberties and civil rights often deployed in public debate by union leaders. These arguments are indeed important—and they have

probably not many. Few large cities are due to have black majorities in the near future,* and predominantly Negro neighborhoods are unlikely to press for the transfer of all white employees. As noted previously, even the Ocean Hill-Brownsville district has been content with a teaching force 80 per cent white. The key issue was getting rid of specific individuals deemed hostile to Negro children or black community control.

In most local public services, moreover, turnover tends to be high. At one extreme, large city welfare departments frequently have turnover rates of 50 per cent a year and more.[34] Among the police, turnover rates of 20 per cent a year are common.[35] I have not seen any general figures on teacher turnover, but in New York City only about three-fifths of the teachers hold permanent licenses. Turnover in this group is about 5 per cent a year, but turnover among the remainder of the teaching force is much higher.

Needless to say, turnover rates are highest in the ghettos; new employees are typically assigned to them, and granted transfers as they acquire seniority. A 1963 study ranked Chicago's public high schools by the socioeconomic status of the neighborhoods they served. In the ten highest ranking schools (which averaged more than 90 per cent white), the median teacher had 12.3 years of experience. In the ten lowest ranking schools (which averaged about 90 per cent Negro), the median teacher had 3.9 years of experience.[36] Efforts in the past to compel or induce (with "combat" pay) more senior employees to accept ghetto assignments have been steadfastly, and successfully, resisted by the civil service unions.

---

been considered above, on pp. 34–37—but they hardly account for the membership passion. Nor have the union leaders themselves, for the most part, been particularly notable for their devotion to civil libertarian and civil rights causes in the past.

Congressional Quarterly has projected that only 1 of the nation's 50 largest cities will have a Negro majority in 1970, and that 6 more will have Negro proportions of 40 per cent or higher.[33]

As noted previously, moreover, the rates of turnover could be increased by measures that most public employees would consider beneficial (e.g., full vesting of pension benefits and the option of early retirement). Skolnick reports, for example, that most police officers retire as soon as they become eligible for a pension. When an early retirement provision came into effect in San Francisco, he adds, 11 per cent of the force (presumably almost every officer eligible) immediately applied to take advantage of it.[37]

Thus, the bases for compromise would seem to exist. To the extent that the predominance of white neighborhoods, the willingness of Negro neighborhoods to employ many whites, and high turnover rates failed to ensure places for all personnel who enjoyed tenure at the moment community control went into effect, the city could simply phase in community control gradually. That is, it could limit the proportion of employees in each occupational category who could be forced out of any neighborhood in a single year. It would be a rare city and category in which a rate of 10 per cent a year could not be handled comfortably. Given normal rates of voluntary departure, this would permit the typical ghetto neighborhood to phase out all its initial corps of tenured employees (if it wished) in three to five years.

How about employees hired after the inauguration of community control? Here the most plausible model would seem to be that such employees should have exactly the same guarantees of job security as suburban employees in the same metropolitan area. This would generally mean that state standards with regard to probationary periods and safeguards against arbitrary dismissal of tenured employees would apply. In other words, it would be harder for a neighborhood to get rid of an employee it had hired itself than of one who had previously been hired by the city. Provision might be made, parenthetically, for transfers from the latter category to the former, by mutual consent of individual employees and their respective neighborhood employers.

A second major area of dispute has to do with the relationship between community control and the merit principle. Here the contending positions are extremely far apart; and if means of reconciling them exist, they are far from obvious.

The problem is that the parties do not agree on the meaning of the central concept. The typical civil service union position is that "merit" should be defined in ways that exclude discretionary judgment (with its potential for favoritism). The basic approved indices are academic credentials, grades on written civil service examinations, and years of experience. Oral examinations and ratings by superiors are accepted as valid supplements, so long as they are used only to weed out obvious misfits and the judgements are made *solely by members of the career service involved.** In practice, the principle of civil service autonomy is taken much more seriously than that of objectivity. Even written examinations can be biased in the drafting, after all. The important thing is that they should be drafted by people committed to each service's concept of merit.

Advocates of community control, on the other hand, tend to argue as follows.[38] The "merit" criteria defended by public service unions bear little or no relation to the achievement of agency goals. They are typically products of ingrown tradition and status-striving rather than of research on the qualities associated with competent on-the-job performance.**

---

*Several "nonmerit" criteria, it should be added, are widely considered legitimate. In particular, disqualification of those with records of criminality, disloyalty, and/or sexual deviation is taken for granted. Veteran's preference is opposed where it is absent, but it is defended wherever a significant portion of a union's members are its beneficiaries (the usual case). Some Negroes argue that America owes no less a debt to them than to veterans, and that it should accord them similar preference in public service employment. Whatever the philosophic merit of this position, it has no visible support from civil service spokesmen.

**David Rogers writes of the New York City school system's Board of Examiners—which has recently been under severe attack from Negro groups, but which has been defended successfully by the teachers' union and supervisors' associations: "The Board of Examiners has developed

Thus, the written examinations typically require rote memorization of arcane texts and local codes. The formal academic requirements go up and up, creating shortages of personnel despite a total lack of evidence that years of education are useful predictors of job performance. The seniority criteria drive talented people away (because promotions are slow and real merit largely unrewarded). The oral examinations are frequently used to discriminate against members of ethnic groups not already well represented in the service.

The few criteria that *are* based on professional research are typically based on experience in white middle class neighborhoods. Not surprisingly, they normally show that the qualities of white middle class employees are the ones most closely associated with good job performance. Applied without adjustment, they are convenient mechanisms for excluding candidates who have something in common with ghetto clients. The same, incidentally, is true of techniques. For example, when teaching methods that have worked well with middle

---

the most standardized and elaborate measures imaginable, but the measures have little to do with identifying a competent supervisor. . . .

"Part of the problem lies in the nature of testing and personnel management as fields of scientific inquiry and application. Many psychologists themselves make the valid point that these disciplines are scientifically bankrupt. The main criticisms of selection techniques are that there is limited sensitivity about the work settings that people are being recruited for, and that there is a preoccupation with standardizing tests without thinking through what the tests are good for. . . .

"Actually, the Board of Examiners has never even tried to validate its tests and its personnel are not trained to do so. Thus, the tests can hardly be more than a ritualistic device to promote insiders. 'They have been urged repeatedly to validate,' an NYU researcher reported, 'from the Kandel Report in the late 1930's, to Strayer-Yavner in 1951, to Shinnerer in the late 1950's . . .'

"Few examinations are given outside the city. Neither the National Teachers Examination nor the New York State teaching certificate is allowed as a basis for eligibility. To become a regular teacher in New York City one must take a series of sequential exams that are given over two years, and there is no feedback until the entire sequence has been completed. Yet, if a candidate fails a single part, he is out completely. . . ."[39]

class white children fail to work in the ghettos, the blame is placed wholly (and, what is worse, fatalistically) upon the children and their socioeconomic backgrounds.

Nor do the advocates of community control take seriously the equation of civil service autonomy with political neutrality. The civil service unions, they believe, have largely replaced the old-style political machines.[40] Their members constitute the largest attentive publics of local government affairs. They are on the city payroll, they are assessed to support their organizations, they get out the votes of their friends and relatives when their group interests seem to be at stake. The last thing these unions are inclined to do is to stand by passively as politicians deliberate on policies of interest to them. They lobby vigorously; when lobbying fails, they demand referenda and mount passionate campaigns for voter support; at election time, they help their friends and seek to punish those who have defied them; increasingly, they demonstrate in the streets; and if sufficiently provoked, they strike. The activities of the police constitute a particularly interesting paradox. Their tendency is to attribute all unrest among other groups to "Reds" and "troublemakers." Yet they themselves are an extremely militant protest group. They commonly engage in all the activities listed above except striking. In place of the strike, however, they seem increasingly inclined to defy orders with which they disagree, to report sick in large numbers during contract disputes ("blue-flu" epidemics), and to take out their frustrations against black militant groups with acts of violence and vandalism.*[41]

To community control proponents, the objectives of public personnel policy should be civil service subservience, not autonomy. It is vital, they believe, to bring the public bureaucracies under democratic policy control. And nowhere

---

*This is not to say that police violence and vandalism in general are on the rise, only that their quasi-political uses in the northern civil rights struggle seem to be.

is this more necessary than in the area of appointment and promotional policy. Public service "merit," they insist, is at least as much a matter of rapport between citizens and their government as it is of technical skill. And it is unsafe even to leave the definition of technical skill entirely to ingrown bureaucracies. They are likely to be preoccupied with perpetuating their subculture and reserving all promotions for insiders rather than keeping up with the times.

In a society where race, ethnicity, and class are critical lines of political and social cleavage (the advocates of community control add), it is inevitable that these factors will affect public service personnel practice. When the politicians are passive, the bureaucrats simply discriminate. This could only be "nonpolitical" so long as the victimized groups themselves were passive.

To deny that personnel policy can be wholly nonpolitical is far from espousing a pure system of spoils. The "moderate" community control position is simply that neighborhood governments should have the sorts of discretion that suburban governments have now. That is, such appointments as the neighborhood police chief and school superintendent should be political (even if subject to statewide qualification standards). Key positions at the second and third echelon—down, say, to the level of school principal—should require political confirmation. And, in defining "merit," the neighborhoods should not be bound by the judgments of the particular professionals who happen to head the local career services.

The neighborhoods should be free, in this view, to propose "merit systems" that have been designed with the aid of experts whom they have selected themselves. Their proposals should be approved so long as a significant number of eminent professionals in the fields at issue would consider them reasonable. In particular, neighborhoods should have wide latitude to deemphasize formal academic qualifications, to make use of para-professionals, and to stress rapport with constituents as a test of competence. In each case, the decisive criterion of approval should not be consensus that the merit system proposed is the best possible, but only a finding that it is plausible and represents neighborhood democracy in action.

We have been concerned so far in this section with the establishment of neighborhood civil services. Let us turn now to the black demand for greater representation above the menial levels in citywide bureaucracies. The key question here is how the black demand for a greater share of middle and higher level civil service positions can be reconciled with the white demand (a significant retreat from the past, let it be noted) for equal treatment of individuals on the basis of merit. This dilemma may be susceptible to amelioration, but it is surely not likely to be resolved. Having said this, I would argue that the most promising paths to amelioration are the following.

(1) Recognize that representation in the public bureaucracy, at all levels where decisions are made that substantial numbers of people consider important, is a traditional and vital form of group participation in American government. Such decisions are regularly made by many officials whose hierarchical positions are below what is conventionally termed the "policy-making" level. The current furor over black representation is largely due to the widespread perception that journeyman teachers, police officers, social workers, building inspectors, and contracting officers make them.

At the same time, stress that bureaucratic representation must be pursued by limited means—which is to say, without abandonment of the merit principle, without formal quotas, and without programs that explicitly accord favors on the basis of race. Elaborate these principles as indicated below.

First, make special and vigorous efforts to recruit candidates from disadvantaged backgrounds for city positions. Provide them with special training for examinations, and whatever personal counseling they require to become effective employees. Wherever possible, waive formal requirements (e.g., of academic credentials and spotless police records) in favor of direct evaluation of a candidate's qualifications by personnel selection boards. Ensure that these boards have some black members, and that *all* their members are sympathetic to the program. Appoint citizens' task forces as well, with substantial black representation, to recommend specific means of enhancing access by the disadvantaged to responsible civil service positions without sacrificing competence.

The chances are that this sort of approach, implemented with zeal by a strong city administration, can have a major impact. To give one example: before the Detroit riot of 1967, that city's police force was little more than 3 per cent black.* Mayor Cavanaugh's administration had been concerned about this for some time, but had accepted police department assurances that qualified candidates to increase the proportion were unavailable. After the riot, a closer look was taken at the candidate selection process. It was discovered that the process included 32 screening stages, at each one of which discretion could play a role in disqualifying a candidate. After examining many individual cases, those around the mayor became persuaded that a systematic pattern of discrimination had long prevailed. At their prodding (with the mayor's vigorous support), the screening process was radically simplified, certain formal requirements were eliminated, and a major effort was begun to generate applications from the black community. By late 1968, the force was 7 per cent Negro. Officials close to the mayor who were interviewed reported that the police bureaucracy had hindered their efforts at every step of the way. It had even misled the mayor until he caught on, and began to check independently, about the actual racial breakdown of new recruit classes. He had kept the pressure on, however, and roughly two-thirds of the most recent classes had been black.

Had the merit principle been diluted? Perhaps, but this

---

*The city at that time was about 40 per cent black.

was unclear. There had been a critical shortage of capable recruits before, and an effort was being made to tap a new source of supply.* Resources were being spent on new recruitment and training programs, but this was quite another matter from abandoning the merit principle. In any event, a major threat to social peace was being dealt with effectively, and whatever dilution of the merit principle had occurred was obscure.** The principle was intact; if actual standards had been lowered, they could be raised again without fuss as conditions permitted.

(2) Turning from recruitment to promotion: make a very special, though informal, effort to achieve significant black representation in the highest echelons of the civil service—without waiting for today's junior recruits to rise to the top. Formal quotas should be avoided, but so long as Negro

---

*This is a national problem. Skolnick writes as follows: "One outstanding problem of the police is a decline in pay relative to comparable occupations. Correspondingly, the prestige of the occupation in the estimate of the general public has fallen sharply, and there has been a sharp decline in the quality and quantity of new recruits. Most departments have many vacancies . . .

". . . In many of our great cities the quality of recruits has actually been declining. In fact, matters are worse than they might appear, for while the average level of education among police recruits has been declining, the average level of educational achievement in the population has been increasing rapidly. Thus, new police recruits are being taken from an ever-shrinking pool of undereducated persons. . . .

"Even more bleak is the picture painted by Dr. Maurice Mensh, a physician who cares for the Washington, D.C., police: 'This is an uneducated group. You should read some of the essays they write. They can hardly write . . .' Moreover, such situations exist even in what are considered to be the most elite, competent, and educated police forces in the country. For example, in Berkeley, California, there has recently been a sharp decline in the educational level of recruits."[42]

Arthur Niederhoffer has noted that in 1940 more than half of New York City's police recruits had college degrees. In the early 1960's, by contrast, fewer than 5 per cent were college graduates.[43]

**The term "merit" is here used in its most narrow technical sense. The white police had proven incompetent to maintain order in the ghetto. Their rapport with the black citizenry was abominable. Thus, by any broader conception of merit, race itself was probably a relevant criterion.

representation is exceptionally low it may be useful to establish target rates of progress, deviations from which are to require special explanation from responsible officials. It must be recognized that negligible black representation at the top levels of a career service constitutes a severe threat to racial peace and evidence *per se* of past discrimination—if not by the bureaucracy specifically, then by American society generally. Either way, the same conclusion follows: it is equitable (as well as necessary) to waive regular procedures now for a time in order to demonstrate our present commitment to overcoming the legacy of past injustice.

The limit to this commitment should be a determination to maintain high standards of performance. The mechanisms of reconciliation between the objective and its qualifier should be: (a) to dispense with seniority and other requirements that have no demonstrable relation to job performance, (b) to look for qualified candidates outside as well as inside the local service, (c) to counsel potential black candidates for promotion, with the aim of encouraging them to strive for advancement,* and (d) to include, where appropriate, the ability to get along with specific racial and ethnic clientele groups in the definition of "good job performance."

Political parties apply the last mechanism when they send party workers to canvass neighborhoods which they match in race, ethnicity, and manner of speech. Survey research organizations today strive to do the same. They have not discarded the merit principle, but simply recognized that the components of merit vary from job to job, and include human relationships as well as technical skill variables. Police, edu-

---

*This would not constitute as much favoritism as it would seem at first glance. Numerous studies have found that black civil servants tend to avoid striving for promotion because they are so certain that discrimination will bar them. Supervisory officials often run informal coaching seminars for promotional candidates as well—which few Negroes in the past have been invited to join. All this is changing, but at radically different rates from one city and bureaucracy to another. The need for more precise knowledge in this area is great.

cational, and social work agencies, to name just three obvious local bureaucratic examples, would seem to have at least equal need for such flexibility.*

In a sense, of course, this does point toward a tempering of the strict merit principle with implicit, though imprecise, group quotas—in cases where the groups have become important political units and are insistent upon representation. Such tempering, one hastens to add, has been part of the American approach to public service merit from the start. State and national civil service agencies have always striven for rough proportionality in county and state representation respectively. So have state universities, the national military academies, and many private universities in their admissions policies.

Similarly, and perhaps more relevantly, public agencies have regularly consulted with their powerful interest group

---

*Pressed by its field personnel, Project Upward Bound, a component of the federal antipoverty program, adopted this principle in April 1968. In a memorandum to all key personnel, Thomas Billings, the national director of Project Upward Bound, ordered that henceforth, as a general rule, "Upward Bound programs with a plurality of any particular racial or ethnic group [are to] be directed by a person of that racial or ethnic group." Current directors were not to be fired, but as natural turnover occurred "every reasonable effort" was to be made to fulfill the objective.

In justification of the new policy, Billings argued, *inter alia:*

1. Upward Bound should be a model of integrated education, both in terms of students and staff.
2. Youngsters from racial/ethnic minorities, like other youngsters, need visible, successful 'role models' with whom they can identify quickly and confidently.
3. Teachers who have shared life experiences with youngsters are likely to be more sensitive to the social/educational needs of those youngsters. Racial and ethnic identity is an integral part of one's life experience in America . . .[44]

A personal observation: I would consider Billings' policy, focusing as it does directly on the race of directors rather than their capacity to relate to students, obnoxious except as an interim measure. Given the historic moment and the nature of his program, however, I would consider it infinitely preferable to a "merit" policy which ignored the racial variable entirely, and which (as most such do) ended up excluding blacks from positions of responsibility almost entirely.

clients before making top level civil service appointments. And many of the local career services which today most vigorously protest any tempering of the merit principle have long had a distinct ethnic flavor at the top levels. In New York City, for example, though other ethnic groups have long been well represented in the lower through upper middle ranks, the top police and educational positions remain firmly in Irish hands. This was the product of Irish political dominance originally, and it has been sustained by professional autonomy.

Wherever interviews and supervisor ratings are factors in the promotional process, human rapport—and hence such variables as race and ethnicity—will play an important role. Thus have Negroes, to a lesser extent Jews, and to a still lesser extent Catholics been kept from the top echelons of corporate power; thus did Ivy League WASP's long perpetuate their dominance of the foreign service; thus have non-Irishmen been excluded from the citadels of many big city bureaucracies in the Northeast;* and so on.

More generally, the ideal of totally dehumanizing personnel decisions has rarely been considered more than a weapon by its proponents—at least, those of its proponents with a managerial, as opposed to labor union, orientation—one useful to ward off intervention *by elected politicians* in personnel decision making. Although "good government" reformers have

---

*One illustration: Peter Schrag has recently noted of the Boston school system: "All but one member of the Board of Superintendents, the senior staff of the system, are graduates of Boston College, all have risen through the ranks and have been in the system for more than three decades, all are well over 50 years old, all are Catholics, and all, excepting only Superintendent William H. Ohrenberger with his German background, are Irishmen. . . . One leading critic, himself a Catholic, has privately . . . [noted that] to succeed in Boston 'you have to be a Catholic. It would be unthinkable to hire a non-Catholic as superintendent. This is a closed system. They never go outside and they never let outsiders in.' . . . Ohrenberger himself, it is sometimes said, is not fully accepted by some of his staff because he is not Irish, although, with his background as a Boston College football player and four decades in the system, he qualifies in every respect but name."[45]

championed it as an alternative to the spoils system, it has never occurred to them to rely mechanically on written tests in their own businesses. Similarly, top public bureaucrats have rarely believed that human judgment could safely be dispensed with in deciding whom to promote; but they have wanted the judgment exercised to be their own.* As a second best alternative, they have been willing to settle for reliance on test scores, so long as the tests emphasized what they considered important.

Tests, it should be noted, have also been a second best method from the standpoint of public employee associations. Their ideal has generally seemed to be a system in which, after initial selection, the only criterion for advancement is seniority. They have gradually striven, moreover, to reduce the importance of tests by confining eligibility for taking them to individuals with elaborately specified formal qualifications (academic degrees, specific courses, specific types and amounts of experience). It can be argued persuasively, in fact, that the aim of the typical public employee association is a system in which tests play a minor role and on-the-job merit, however defined, no role at all.

By comparison with the spoils system, bureaucratic autonomy has indeed meant a greater emphasis on merit. This has not been merit in any absolute or timeless sense, however,

---

*Again, let me quote Schrag on the Boston school system: "The rigid procedures are tempered with a personal style, with the private knowledge that an old self-perpetuating staff accumulates, and with the experience of people who know that the world cannot be organized solely according to points, forms, and procedures. As a consequence, the Boston School Department is really composed of two administrative networks, one formal, official, and apparently impersonal, the system that some civil service reformer dreamed about a half century ago; the other familiar, often friendly, and, in its own way, far more efficient . . .

"The machinery does not always work well, though it is probably as effective in abuse as in use. At any rate, it works better than the defensive administrators—often more Puritanically sanctimonious than the most severe Yankee—would like people to know. As they represent it—impersonal, mechanical, formal—it could hardly work at all."[46]

but rather merit as defined by each bureaucracy's subculture. The subcultures have generally been highly resistant to change by transient civilian commanders,* and the merit principle has operated within a range delimited by racial, ethnic, and religious prejudice. Such prejudice has generally been taken for granted within the organization, blithely denied to outsiders. When pinned to the wall, bureaucratic leaders have typically rationalized their behavior in terms of the attitudes of clients, fellow workers, and subordinates.

The walls of exclusion are gradually coming down, but this is primarily because Jewish and Negro groups, organized politically, have loudly and persistently called attention to discrimination and protested its injustice. The lesson is simply this. The ethic of universalism has never been more than one value among many in the American social system. At times, it has seemed to Jews, Negroes, career bureaucrats, "good government" reformers, and liberals generally an unmitigated good—given the enemies and possibilities of the moment. Time and experience have shown, however, that alternative definitions of "merit" can have a great impact

---

*James Q. Wilson has noted that certain bureaucratic systems give journeymen enormous discretion, very great job security, and limited opportunities for promotion. In such bureaucracies the subculture tends to be the dominant force shaping employee behavior, and to be unusually difficult for top officials to influence. Where the employees' work is dangerous and they are subject to a great deal of outside hostility, as in the case of the police, their drive to solidarity is intensified still further.[47]

In a related, more general, analysis, Michael Lipsky has characterized as "street level bureaucrats" those public employees: (1) who interact regularly with citizens, (2) who enjoy substantial on-the-job discretion, (3) whose decisions have a substantial impact on their clients, and (4) whose clients are non-voluntary. He notes that such bureaucrats are rarely dependent in the present governmental framework upon the approbation of their clients; that the clients do not constitute a primary reference group for them; and that, in consequence, they regularly misunderstand client motives and capabilities.[48] In part, of course, such estrangement is inevitable—most strikingly, in the case of crime control officials—but there is substantial reason to consider it excessive in the low income areas of American big cities today.

on the fortunes of groups, and that bureaucratic autonomy with respect to personnel tends to mean general insulation from political control. At the same time, Negro patience has worn thin, and attention has shifted from securing the outward forms of equal treatment to securing real progress toward equality.

In short, priorities have shifted, as they invariably do in politics. The paths of the "merit" issue and the race issue have crossed. Given their relative importance to Americans of all persuasions, it is hardly surprising that the cleavage lines of the latter should predominate. Many have altered their position recently on the merit issue, but only to bring it more closely into line with their positions on current racial disputes. I have in mind particularly, of course: (a) upper middle class liberals, who have backed off from their former devotion to bureaucratic insulation from the political process; (b) Negroes themselves, who formerly considered such insulation (when combined with strict adherence to merit system procedures) a bar against the grosser forms of discrimination; and (c) whites in the lower half of the socio-economic spectrum who have suddenly discovered the sanctity of the merit principle—just as, a couple of years ago, they elevated the neighborhood school concept to the highest level of American societal values.

The major exceptions to this proposition are some middle class civil service groups which were traditionally sympathetic to Negro aspirations, but which now see their own professional interests threatened. The New York City teachers are the most salient example. They have consistently sided with Negro groups when the latter have demanded pupil integration, smaller classes, and compensatory programs for the disadvantaged. Their past differences from Negro groups have centered on the handling of disruptive children (the teachers wanted authority to expel them) and the use of special procedures (mandatory assignments and/or "combat pay") to get experienced teachers into ghetto schools. Today, of course, the central issue is community control.[49]

Lower middle- and lower-class civil service groups have also intensified their pursuit of bureaucratic autonomy in the current crisis, of course, but few have memberships that were previously "liberal" on racial matters.

(3) Rapport between local governments and their black constituents must be sought by many other means as well as by increasing the number of black civil servants. Among the more interesting proposals for encouraging fair and sensitive behavior by bureaucrats in the ghettos that have come to my attention are the following:

(a) Representative black leaders might be appointed to citywide personnel boards, with the explicit function of monitoring civil service criteria and procedures to ensure that they do not conceal anti-Negro bias, and that success in client rapport is accorded great weight when promotional decisions are made. These appointments might be supplemented by the periodic appointment of special task forces, again with substantial black representation, to examine the relationship between democratically arrived at local objectives on the one hand and civil service practices and subcultures on the other. Obviously, this assignment would be far more difficult than the usual examination of formal procedures.

On the technical side, it would require painstaking social research and careful monitoring of the real impact that change efforts by local political leaders had over time. On the political side, it would require a task force which combined sophistication, authority, and representativeness of the main interests involved in near-optimal proportions, great leadership skill by its chairman, a profound commitment to change by the mayor, and at least some initial recognition that change was necessary by other key actors (ranging from leaders of the civil service unions to members of the relevant city and state legislative committees).

It follows that in many situations the best task force could not hope to have much impact. Where such is the case, blacks may have little choice but to engage in disruptive tactics, hoping thereby to force reconsideration of the costs of rigidity and to raise their demands to the top of the local political agenda. (The problem is that other groups, including the public service unions, have now learned this trick as well. Thus, the risk of chaotic stalemate on the political front, together with a worsening of actual civil service behavior, is high.)

(b) Representative neighborhood councils might be given a veto over top city appointments of field officers within the neighborhood. These might include such positions as the following: police precinct captain, district school superintendent, district health officer, district chief building inspector, district planning and urban renewal director, district public housing manager, and district fire chief. (Needless to say, some of these positions would have to be created and others would have to have their jurisdictions adjusted, in recognition of the new emphasis on neighborhood consultation.)

From the neighborhood point of view, this authority to veto would be second best to full community control. At the same time, it would represent a major concession to demands for neighborhood power. The actual range of alternatives about which city, organized labor, and neighborhood officials might negotiate is very wide. The right of the neighborhood might be to veto, to choose from a list of candidates submitted to it, or merely to advise. For some functions, neighborhood participation might be extended to the top several positions in each neighborhood rather than just one: all school principals, for example, rather than just the district superintendent. And there might be provision for third party arbitration wherever a stalemate developed.

(c) District offices of citywide agencies might be directed to keep neighborhood leaders fully informed of their activities, to consult with them on policy options left open by the central authorities, and to pay substantial deference to neighborhood desires wherever possible. The significance of such a directive would depend, of course, on the extent to which citywide authorities made clear that they took it seriously.

One method by which they might do so would be to pursue

a well-publicized policy of devolving responsibility upon district officials. Another would be to provide that neighborhood evaluations of a district chief's performance would be solicited periodically for his personnel file. A third would be to provide regular channels and mechanisms by which a neighborhood council might appeal a district chief's decisions or protest the inadequacy of his consultative arrangements.

(d) Agency quotas, combined with financial inducements, might be used to encourage civil servants assigned to districts with large low income and nonwhite populations to live within them.* Presumably, residence in a district would sensitize public servants to its cultural patterns and grievances. It might also increase their susceptibility to neighborhood social pressure, a healthy offset (it could very plausibly be argued) to the informal social pressures that operate within many of the bureaucracies today. Agency quotas, if they were set high enough, would also spur recruitment of individuals willing to live in such neighborhoods. In the normal course of events, most of those willing to live in black neighborhoods would themselves be black.**

In order to leave room for transfers within each citywide service, and perhaps also to make the system color-blind, it might work as follows. Special zones whose residents were underrepresented in a service (e.g., the police) would be designated as meeting the quota and bonus criteria. A mem-

---

*Lest this be too quickly dismissed, it bears mention that many cities currently require their employees to reside within them, and that many more did so when national unemployment rates were as high as those in the ghettos are today. Nor should the near-universal American practice be forgotten of requiring candidates for elective office to be residents of their districts.

**In their fifteen-city survey conducted for the Kerner Commission, Peter Rossi and four colleagues found (a) that Negro policemen assigned to predominantly Negro precincts were more than three times as likely to live in the neighborhood than white policemen (37–11 per cent), and (b) that Negro teachers in predominantly Negro schools were nearly seven times as likely to live in the neighborhood (27–4 per cent).

ber of the service who lived in such a zone when it was designated, or who moved into it thereafter while it remained designated, would be guaranteed bonus payments for a specified number of years. Renewal of an agreement at its expiration would depend on whether the house involved was still in a designated zone.

Citywide balance among the designated zones themselves might be pursued by having several bonus categories. In this case a zone's bonus rating might move up and down the scale automatically, in accord with its proportion of unfilled quota places and the recent strength of demand for them. Quite obviously, the range of possibilities (sizes of quotas and bonuses, length of bonus guarantee periods, zonal boundary definitions, etc.) is very great. Confidence in such a system would depend on widespread participation in the process of policy determination.

(e) More conventionally, financial and other incentives could be used to encourage civil servants to take courses in subjects thought likely to improve their capacity to deal sensitively with clients. These might range from the sociology of bureaucratic organizations to urban politics to the fictional treatment of race relations in American literature. Similarly, "confrontation seminars" between civil servants and client representatives might be sponsored by each agency. Un-

---

These findings should not be taken as more than suggestive. The total police sample size was only 437, and that of the teachers was only 273. Respondents were chosen in accord with quotas of race and position—one-quarter of the police sample and half the teacher sample were Negro —but it is doubtful that they were chosen randomly within these categories. The specific respondents were designated by the precinct commanding officers and school principals. Both were thought to have chosen fairly regularly with an eye toward projecting a favorable institutional image. The police sample covered only eleven cities, moreover, because of official noncooperation in the four others (Detroit, Boston, Chicago, and Milwaukee).[50]

fortunately, evidence is lacking that such courses and "confrontations" have much lasting effect.*

CONTRACTING

The black demand for participation in private sector profits and wages generated by government action is perhaps as vital an issue as that of black participation in government itself. It involves not just direct public purchases and contracts, but also private projects benefitting from such special public favors as tax incentives, mortgage guarantees, and the exercise of eminent domain.

Until the past several years, virtually all public authorities have winked at the private financial practices (e.g., refusal to bond or make loans) which made it virtually impossible for black firms to compete for government contracts,** and at the discriminatory labor practices (e.g., black exclusion from unions) which kept blacks from all but the poorest paying jobs on them.

Many public bodies have also cooperated positively in these practices. For example, it has been common for public

---

*Only a few have demonstrated even a short-term impact. One of the more notable of these was a Houston program in which 1,500 policemen were required to participate in "confrontation sessions" with ghetto residents. During the fifteen-month period during which the program was in progress, minority complaints against the police fell by 70 per cent. Upon its conclusion, however, they quickly began to rise again.[51]

**Dunbar McLaurin noted in 1968 that over 95 per cent of major construction in New York City's ghetto areas during the postwar period had been publicly funded or subsidized. Yet not a single prime contract had been let to a minority-owned construction firm. The city, probably the nation's most liberal on racial issues, had confined its efforts to securing jobs for individual skilled workers. It was true, of course, that no large minority-owned construction firms existed, but it was also true that the city had done nothing to facilitate their creation.[52]

vocational high schools to run apprenticeship programs in cooperation with labor unions, and to permit the unions to exclude black students from these programs. The limited evidence available suggests that most cities still manifest their indifference to (or support of) discrimination in these ways, despite federal pressure to change. To illustrate: according to a recent Office of Education study, the Chicago public school population is now about 54 per cent black; yet twenty times as many whites as blacks are enrolled in the school system's cooperative (with labor unions) apprenticeship programs.[53]

This is not to deny that there is some encouraging evidence of response to black demands. Some craft unions have initiated (or cooperated with) special programs to increase the number of black apprentices. Some school systems have ceased their participation in white-only apprenticeship programs. The federal government has led the way in terms of requiring "affirmative action programs" to bring the black proportion of the labor force on federally aided projects up to reasonable levels.

Neither space nor my knowledge permits here a comprehensive review of all the policies which might be undertaken to ensure blacks a more equitable share of the profits and wages generated by government action. Several of the more interesting ideas currently in the air, however, are described below.*

Eugene Foley (former Assistant Secretary of Commerce for Economic Development) and Dunbar McLaurin (an eco-

---

*Let it be noted that my concern in this section is with government contracting, not ghetto economic development strategies more generally. The latter is a critically important subject, but one outside the scope of this volume. Readers who wish to pursue it are referred to Theodore L. Cross's recent book, *Black Capitalism: Strategy for Business in the Ghetto.*[54] This study is rather weak in its treatment of the ghetto, but it is brilliant in its analysis of business motives and in its suggested program for encouraging black business development.

nomic consultant) have in separate analyses suggested that American governments institute "set-aside" programs for ghetto procurement.[55]

Foley notes that the Department of Defense and most other federal procurement agencies have long set aside certain contracts for exclusive bidding by small business, and have required prime contractors to demonstrate zealousness in striving to subcontract to small business. A 1960 order which is still in effect (though it has had little practical impact, due to lack of administrative follow-through) requires the Department of Defense to give preference, wherever prices are equal, to firms which will perform a substantial portion of their work in labor surplus areas. Unfortunately for urban blacks (especially as this is just one among many federal programs of aid to depressed areas), the federal government defines labor market areas in terms of one or more local political units. Subareas within cities are thus ineligible for designation as labor surplus areas, even though (as in the case of Harlem) they have many times the population of the typical area that is so designated.

McLaurin, writing about New York City, noted that it has a longstanding policy of purchasing from nonprofit companies which employ the blind—on a noncompetitive basis.

One might add, though these authors do not, that federal agencies today "buy American" even at very substantial cost in order to conserve dollars, and that most of the northern cities in which Negroes are concentrated require public contractors to use union labor, again frequently at substantial cost (not to mention Negro exclusion).

The explicit rationale of a set-aside program might be based on neighborhood poverty and unemployment alone, or on these in combination with race. The justifications for considering race a factor would be the same as those applicable to public hiring: severe current underrepresentation and a legacy of past injustice. The favoritism would be viewed as transitional. The targets would be designed to avoid charges that the door was being opened to demands that all government contracts be awarded on a group quota basis. This would be relatively simple, given the extremity of Negro underrepresentation today.*

McLaurin suggests that long-term government purchase agreements could be used to make a great deal of potential ghetto investment creditworthy. And he adds that the use of such agreements could be linked with other policies to ensure that the credit was in fact available. For instance, government bank deposits could be allocated to banks that agreed to make the necessary loans on favorable terms. And special subsidies could be offered to make sure that expert advice and services were available to the small businesses thus financed.**

Short of formal set-aside programs and long-term purchase agreements, public authorities in many cities might actively encourage minority-owned businesses to bid on government contracts, provide them with technical assistance, help them to secure loans and insurance bonds, and informally give them preference where it was possible to do so without violating the statutes requiring minimum price procurement. More explicitly and boldly, they might give preference within a specified price differential range to bidders (regardless of race) who pledged to hire and train substantial numbers of workers with long unemployment histories. Such programs of pref-

---

*The issue of quotas is dealt with in somewhat greater detail below, on pp. 181–82.

**Theodore Cross has proposed a similar plan for the private sector. The government's role would be to provide tax incentives. Hopefully, these incentives would encourage private corporations to sign long-term purchase agreements with minority-owned suppliers. These agreements would be similar to the long-term rental agreements that commercial real estate developers regularly use to secure favorable financing. Why, Cross asks, should not industrial developers get started in the same way? As supplements to this proposal, he suggests a number of other tax incentives designed to make bank operations in poverty areas profitable.[56]

erential purchasing might be linked with manpower training subsidies.*

Two recent contracting schemes which might serve as models (to be built upon, not merely imitated) are the Bradford Plan and the Newark Medical School agreement. The former has been reported by Foley and by Bradford himself, the latter by Leonard J. Duhl.[58]

In 1966, Foley, then Assistant Secretary of Commerce, employed Bradford, a former general manager of the *New York Times,* as a consultant to work out a method whereby the federal Economic Development Administration (EDA) might reduce unemployment in Oakland, California. The tools available were public works grants and low interest business loans. Within two years, EDA authorized more than $14 million in grants and $9 million in loans in accord with the scheme that Bradford drew up. It provided that each applicant (public and private alike) should file an employment plan stating the numbers and types of jobs for the long-term unemployed that the proposed investment would create, and describing the methods of recruitment and training that would be used to realize these targets.

To review these plans, an eight-man committee was established, consisting of five representatives of the poor (one from each of Oakland's Poverty Target Areas), one representative of business, one of labor, and one of EDA. After considering the advice of this committee, EDA decided whether or not to approve the application.** After approval,

---

*Appropriations for the multitude of federal manpower programs totalled about $2 billion in fiscal 1968.[57]

**Noting the fantastic delays that have invariably been involved in government loan and loan guarantee programs to date, Cross proposes a number of reforms. The most useful of these would be to permit reputable lending institutions to make the loans, subject to review for conformance with government specifications by a private accounting firm. The govern-

each employer was required to file a progress report each month. The contract with EDA provided that noncompliance with the employment plan would constitute a default, and that disputes were to be resolved by binding arbitration. Unfortunately, this plan was a one-shot effort, and as such amounted to little more than a flyspeck on Oakland's sea of troubles.* Its other critical flaw was that, in its single-minded focus on creating employment, it ignored the development of black-controlled business. Predictably, no such business secured a single loan or contract under the plan.

The agreement which resolved the Newark Medical School controversy was far more comprehensive. This controversy, it will be recalled, was cited by many as a significant cause of the 1967 Newark riot. The medical school concerned was a state institution. Its trustees had not desired an inner city location, but had agreed to one under "tremendous pressure" (in Duhl's words) from the city and from others concerned about Newark's employment, health, and "blight" problems. The project involved eminent domain, an urban renewal land cost writedown, and a large federal grant for construction, even aside from the state's basic support of the school. In its original form, the project destroyed a good many units of low-cost housing without creating any, provided no assurances of neighborhood employment or neighborhood health programs, and involved no consultation with neighborhood residents.

In a letter to Governor Hughes of New Jersey dated

---

ment's own audits would be conducted later, probably (like income tax auditing) on a sample basis. Where carelessness was uncovered, banks and accounting firms could be suspended from participation in the program. Where malfeasance was uncovered, the offending parties could be prosecuted.[59]

*Aaron Wildavsky, who is directing a major study of Oakland government, informs me that in recent years annual spending by all levels of government in Oakland has exceeded $500 million. The Bradford Plan expenditures were due to take place over several years.

January 10, 1968, the federal undersecretaries of HUD and HEW stated a number of conditions that would have to be met in order for the project to secure the approval of their respective departments. Summing up the impact of this letter, Duhl notes that "the school's very existence now hinged on that which before had been peripheral to the interests of medical education: housing, employment, and citizen participation."* Within the next two months, an agreement was worked out in consultation with community leaders. Among its many provisions were the following on employment and contracting:

(a) If at all possible, at least one-third of all journeymen and one-half of all apprentices employed in construction of the medical school were to be members of minority groups (i.e., Negroes and Puerto Ricans). To this end, a review council, composed of community representatives, union officials, contractors, and representatives of the interested public agencies, was to review contract bids and compliance with pre-contract promises.

All bidders on contracts and subcontracts were to submit employment projections with racial breakdowns and relevant union agreements. Any bidder whose projections fell short of the minority group employment targets was to file an "affirmative action" program. This would become part of the contract if his bid were successful. Affirmative action programs were to include intensive recruitment and pre-apprenticeship training programs, along with normal apprenticeship and on-the-job training programs. In the event of union resistance, the contractors were to hire the minority group workers directly, assign them to the job site, and pay them at prevailing union rates.

---

*Duhl, it should be noted, was at this time a special assistant to the Undersecretary of HUD, on loan from the U. S. Public Health Service, which is a component of HEW. He played an important liaison role between the two departments during the course of the medical school controversy.

(b) The review council was to develop an affirmative action program of its own to ensure that as many contracts as possible were placed with minority-owned businesses. This program was to include provisions for dividing contracts into small units, state action to ensure that minority group businessmen were able to secure adequate bonding, and state technical assistance to help such businesses prepare their bids.

(c) The review council was to hire a number of full-time compliance officers to police the construction integration program. These officers were to meet civil service standards and to serve officially as members of the state Treasury Department staff.

(d) Moving beyond the construction stage, the medical school agreed to pursue a long-range policy of filling as many positions as possible from the ranks of neighborhood residents. To this end, it pledged to develop new career ladders for nonprofessional employees, to develop training programs for the full range of hospital skills, and to establish a special recruitment and scholarship program to attract minority group students to the medical and dental professions. In carrying out these pledges, it agreed to work closely with the community health council. This council was to consist of nine community representatives and eight representatives of local medical institutions.

Both the Newark agreement and the Bradford Plan were rendered possible only by the intervention of federal bureaucrats with large sums of money to dispense. They were not, it should be noted, mere isolated incidents. They were, rather, advanced examples of a general trend in federal contract policy.

Under Executive Order 11246 of September 24, 1965, government contractors are required to practice nondiscrimination and to encourage minority group employment. Enforcement of this executive order has gradually gathered steam, most strikingly since the spring of 1968. On May 28, 1968, the Office of Federal Contract Compliance (which is located in the Department of Labor) issued an exhaustive and explicit set of regulations pursuant to the order, one which includes procedures for invoking the ultimate sanction—debarment from federal contract work—against companies which violate their affirmative action promises. Judging from outward appearances (speeches by officials of the major contracting agencies, official directives issued by these agencies, etc.), contracting officials throughout the federal government are taking this set of regulations very seriously indeed.

The most recent development, as this is written, is a federal plan to go beyond "affirmative action" to precise minority employment targets. It is being applied first (since September 1969) to seven skilled building trades in Philadelphia, but the expectation is that it will shortly be applied to other job categories, industries, and cities. The plan calls for the Office of Federal Contract Compliance to estimate the number of minority workers who are locally available in each job category, and then to establish specific hiring targets for each contract larger than one-half million dollars. Each contract bid is required to include a pledge that these targets will be met. If the successful bidder fails to meet these targets in practice, he will be subject to penalties unless he can demonstrate that he made a "good faith" effort to comply and that minority workers with the requisite skills were simply unavailable.*

It is indeed remarkable that a conservative federal administration should have come to the point of using quotas to combat racial discrimination. This is a measure both of the extent to which milder techniques have been evaded, and

---

*This plan was vociferously opposed by the Building and Construction Trades Department of the AFL-CIO. Justifying it, Assistant Secretary of Labor Arthur Fletcher, who signed the Philadelphia order, noted that the Philadelphia unions involved were more than 99.5 per cent white in 1967. Although their minority membership had since risen to 1.6 per cent, the Labor Department had found that "they continue to engage in practices, including the granting of referral priorities . . . which result in few Negroes being referred for employment."[60]

of the still growing national commitment to equal employment opportunity.* In fact, any program designed to increase the nonwhite proportion of a group (suburban residents, public employees, government contractors) involves at least an implicit conception of what share would remove the need for public concern. It is possible for many people to agree on the need for "more" now, however, without agreeing on the ultimate target. This is quite fortunate, because any program that depends upon proving discrimination in each case will, the record indicates, have negligible impact on the problem.**

We have concentrated in this section on federal and potential citywide contracting policies. There is no reason, however, why a good deal of purchasing authority might not be devolved upon neighborhood governments. The delays and red tape caused by excessive centralization of purchasing in large cities have frequently been criticized by students of urban government in any event. The citywide interest in economy could be reconciled with community control by such regulations and administrative mechanisms as the following:

(a) Forbidding the neighborhood purchasing department to pay more than 10 per cent above the price for any given item paid by central purchasing, except for reasons stated in

---

*In August 1969, the Nixon Administration submitted a proposal to Congress that would enable the Equal Employment Opportunity Commission to bring suit when it judged that conciliation had failed. The current law permits suit to be initiated only after the Department of Justice has independently found a pattern and history of job discrimination. The Senate Labor Committee seemed likely to report out an even stronger bill, giving the Commission authority (similar to that of most other federal regulatory agencies) to issue cease-and-desist orders.

This movement on the equal employment front was occurring at a time when the major news on the civil rights front was an easing of federal pressure for school desegregation.

**I would argue further that the liberal hostility to both minimum *and* *maximum* quotas will have to "give" if housing and school integration are ever to be achieved on a substantial scale. Without the former, evasion of integrationist policies is the norm; without the latter, racial "tipping" seems almost unavoidable.[61]

writing (as the size of the order rose, the allowable percentage might decline, and provision might be made for advance approval by central purchasing); (b) on contracts for non-standard items (such as buildings), requiring the neighborhood to follow the same competitive procedures as the city itself, and specifying the precise differential that it could pay in order to "buy neighborhood" (a differential might be permitted only in low income neighborhoods, and in these it might be supplemented by a wide variety of other business development aids); (c) providing an arbitration board to resolve disputes between the neighborhood and central purchasing officers with dispatch; and (d) subjecting the neighborhood's accounts to periodic city or state audit, with the usual provisions for punishment of officials responsible for any irregularities uncovered.[62]

THE FEDERAL ROLE

For some years now the federal government has been manipulating grant-in-aid incentives to encourage broadly oriented metropolitan decision making.* The proponents of

---

*I have reviewed this story through 1964 in an earlier book.[63] The most important recent developments are the following:

(i) The Housing and Urban Development Act of 1965 (Section 701g) authorized federal grants to support the activities of metropolitan councils of governments. In consequence, between mid-1965 and mid-1969 the number of such councils in the nation increased from 8 to 142.[64]

(ii) The Demonstration Cities and Metropolitan Development Act of 1966 (Section 204) included a requirement for areawide review—by a single general purpose planning agency—of nearly all applications for federal public works aid by jurisdictions lying within metropolitan areas. Each application must be accompanied (a) by the areawide planning agency's comments and recommendations, and (b) by a statement on the part of the applicant that such comments and recommendations have been considered prior to formal submission of the application. The legislation provides that the areawide planning agency should, wherever possible, be part of a general purpose metropolitan government or a regional council of governments.

community control would have it deploy at least equivalent incentives to encourage neighborhood participation in large city government.

Put forward as an objective for white and black neighborhoods alike, this idea might rather appeal to Congress. Organized labor would be hostile, and so would most big city politicians, but many of the latter might be mollified by careful drafting to preserve their "ultimate" authority and by the promise of large grants-in-aid. As noted previously, moreover, fewer than one-quarter of all Americans live in cities with populations over 250,000. The typical congressman is quite capable of waxing sentimental about the virtues of small-scale local government, and he has no other type within his constituency. The tradition of legislative courtesy, not to mention his interest in logrolling, will normally prevent him from overriding the wishes of his big city colleagues on matters of real interest only to them. Let them divide on the issue, however, at a time when the President, the relevant federal bureaucracies, and the communications media are pressing for passage of bills that include strong participation requirements (or inducements), and a good deal might become feasible that is not currently so.

Indeed, one can cite more than future possibilities. The whole current movement for neighborhood control was largely set in motion by the "maximum feasible participation" provision of the Economic Opportunity Act of 1964. It is true that the administration itself had no clear idea of what this phrase meant, that Congress endorsed it in a fit of over-

---

As of June 1968, 62 of the 209 designated review agencies were councils of governments. A high proportion of the others, however, were state governments or county governments in single-county SMSA's. (The reason why there were only 209 review agencies for the 233 SMSA's was that the state government agencies frequently handled more than one SMSA.)

(iii) The Intergovernmental Cooperation Act of 1968 (Section 402) provided that, wherever both special and general purpose units of local government are eligible to receive federal aid, federal agencies shall, in the absence of substantial reasons to the contrary, favor the general purpose units.

sight, and that both were rather horrified as it revealed its "revolutionary" potential.* But it has not been repealed. In fact, John Wofford has noted that in the year (1966) that Congress established a floor of one-third for representation of the poor on each CAA governing board, only 30 per cent of the current governing board members nationally were in fact such representatives.[66]

The Model Cities Program is perhaps a more relevant example. Congress authorized it after two years experience with

---

*Richard Blumenthal and Daniel Moynihan have identified four interpretations that had adherents within the administration in 1964:

One group, led by Paul Ylvisaker of the Ford Foundation and David Hackett, director of the President's Committee on Juvenile Delinquency, envisaged community action as a mechanism for enabling federal officials to exert leverage on city officials. They believed that institutional change at the local level would depend upon federal officials making such change a condition of grants-in-aid. They did not expect the poor to participate in policy making.

A second group, led by Richard Boone, formerly of the Ford Foundation and currently (1964) of the White House Special Projects Office, emphasized hiring the poor to help implement anti-poverty programs. Some of its members simply wanted to create employment, "new careers for the poor." Others emphasized that the subcultures of the public bureaucracies had to be transformed if an effective war on poverty was to be mounted. They judged that these subcultures were impervious to formal policy directives. But they hoped that the injection of large numbers of poor people into them would have a greater impact. Working alongside poor people, they theorized, the middle class bureaucrats might be infected with empathy for the poor.

A third group, centered in the Bureau of the Budget, emphasized the potential of community action as a mechanism of coordination. Coordination of federal activities from the "top down" had failed. The members of this group hoped that coordination from the "bottom up" might succeed. They envisaged each Community Action Agency as a council of the interested public agencies, intended to forge a consensus on local anti-poverty priorities and methods.

A fourth group, headed by Richard Cloward, a professor of social work at Columbia, believed that the need was to organize the poor, to help them become a potent pressure group in American society. Its model was the labor movement (though it perceived the current labor movement as a reactionary force). Its motto was "creative conflict." The administration's top decision makers were apparently unaware of this group's aims, and were certainly unaware of the extent to which the bill incorporated them, as the Economic Opportunity Act moved toward passage.[65]

"maximum feasible participation" in the poverty program, and has continued to treat it sympathetically (within the context of general budgetary stringency for domestic programs) through mid-1969. The legislation[67] provides for "comprehensive city demonstration programs . . . to rebuild or revitalize large slum or blighted areas." These areas are elsewhere defined as "entire sections or neighborhoods."* One of the listed criteria by which local applications for assistance are to be judged is "widespread citizen participation in the program."

In the legislative history, the phrase "widespread citizen participation" represented a retreat from "maximum feasible participation." In fact both phrases are equally vague and sweeping, however. And in practice the role of citizen participation has been comparable in the two programs. HUD's "Minimum Performance Standards for Citizen Participation in Model Cities," issued in 1967, provide that:

(i)   . . . there must be some form of organizational structure which embodies neighborhood residents in the process of policy and program planning . . .

(ii)   The leadership of that structure must consist of persons whom neighborhood residents accept as representing their interests.

(iii)   That structure must have sufficient information about any matter to be decided . . . so that it can initiate proposals and react knowledgeably to proposals from others.

(iv)   . . . the structure must have the technical capacity for making knowledgeable decisions. . . . Some form

---

*The original HUD guidelines confined the program to 10 per cent of any city. This was altered by the Nixon Administration in April 1969 to give city governments local option in determining what portion of their jurisdiction to include. The focus of the program is still to be on "poor and blighted neighborhoods," however. In cities where the Model Neighborhood is sufficiently comprehensive, HUD will favor the use of the Model Cities administrative system to administer all federal, state, and local programs for the poor.[68]

of professional technical assistance in a manner agreed to by neighborhood representatives shall be provided.

In 1968 the HUD Model Cities staff began to press hard for the use of elections to select the "representatives of the poor" on Model Neighborhood governing boards. Arnstein and Fox report that about two-thirds of the 75 localities which had received Model Cities planning grants through July 1968 either had held or were planning to hold neighborhood elections. Most of the others had sought to achieve representativeness by other means, such as inviting neighborhood organizations to designate governing board members. A few had gotten by so far with groups of neighborhood residents appointed as "representatives" by the mayor or City Demonstration Agency director.[69]

The Nixon Administration, like the Johnson Administration before it, has emphasized that ultimate local control of Model Neighborhood programs would rest with city governments. It has not let up the pressure for citizen participation, however. The most visible illustration of this has been the settlement of a long-standing dispute with the city government of Chicago. The city's plans submitted to Washington in 1968 called for the mayor to appoint all the members of Chicago's four Model Neighborhood governing boards. The Johnson and Nixon Administrations both balked at this proposal. In June 1969 the city agreed to election of half of the governing board members, and HUD announced a $38 million Model Cities grant to it.

There has also been a growing trend, in response to demands by governing board members, for local applications to provide for dollar grants to the boards for the hiring of staff and professional consultants. In at least several recent cases, moreover, OEO has made supplementary grants to Model Neighborhood governing boards for this purpose.

To recapitulate: the Model Cities Program does not give final authority to neighborhood bodies, nor does it require them to be elected. It is a competitive program, however; and the word has been communicated that programs which provide a large role for elected neighborhood representatives will be viewed most favorably. In elaborating and stressing this criterion, federal bureaucrats may well have gone beyond the congressional intent. But this is quite common. What is more important is that in doing so they have remained (it appears) within Congress's zone of indifference. And this in the midst of a rising conservative tide.

The next step would be for federal policy to encourage the establishment of representative, general purpose neighborhood authorities throughout large cities, rather than just in "poor and blighted neighborhoods." Congress would be most unlikely to make the existence of such authorities an absolute condition of federal aid. Quite conceivably, however, it might: (a) authorize grants-in-aid to help support neighborhood staff services (on the model of Section 701 grants to support local planning services);* (b) permit federal administrators to favor cities that have established such authorities in a wide variety of federal aid programs; and (c) require that, where neighborhood authorities exist, they should be given an opportunity to file advisory opinions (on the model of Section 204 area-wide review opinions) before policy departures and public works projects likely to have a significant effect on their constituents are approved. All of these elements, it should be noted, are already present to one degree or another in the Model Cities Program. And it has been officially billed a pilot program.

---

*This section (of the 1954 Housing Act, as amended), it should be noted, does not confine eligibility to state and municipal agencies. Also eligible, if approved by the governor, are (i) metropolitan and regional planning agencies, (ii) Indian tribal planning councils, and (iii) the Appalachian Regional Commission. Moreover, planning grants to state agencies can be channeled to "any group of adjacent communities, either incorporated or unincorporated, having a total population of less than 50,000" as well as to counties and municipalities.

More generally, of course, federal authorities have the primary roles to play in making resources available to low income communities, in establishing the tone of American responsiveness to black demands, in spurring program innovation, and in structuring incentives to encourage the flow of private resources (credit, investment, employment) to the nation's ghettos. These roles are critical to every aspect of the nation's poverty and racial crises, but they lie outside the concentrated scope of this book.

CHAPTER FIVE

A PERSONAL STATEMENT

SOCIAL science tends toward the static view. It is helpful in explaining how things got the way they are, but its understanding is too crude to support forecasts of where they will go from here. This is least so where trends are measurable and steady, but these qualifiers have little bearing on the present subject.

American social science, reflecting the stability of this country's social and political patterns, has tended to make of its limits an ideology. Its primary concern has been how to explain "fundamental" (i.e., stable) rather than transient phenomena or the process of change itself. Thus, it has been preoccupied (a) with the obstacles to change, (b) with the basic satisfaction of the American people, on which these obstacles have rested, (c) with the benefits of social peace and gradualism. It has tended till recently both to ignore the study of revolution and to deprecate the possibility of bringing about rapid change by illegal means.

I have been unable to surmount the basic limits of my calling, but, along with many of my colleagues, I have been alerted by recent events to the possibilities of rapid change and disorder, and to the acute dissatisfaction of at least some Americans. My concern has been with the options before us rather than with the obstacles to any change at all. I need hardly add, however, that the force of white resistance has been ever in my mind, shaping my view of which options were even worth discussing.

I have eschewed precise blueprints, judging that the needs at this point (and in a general volume of this nature) were rather for broad indications of direction, flexible approaches, and a great deal of experimentation. I would add the caveat, however, that designers of particular experiments will do well to specify rights and procedures with the most painstaking care. As S. M. Miller and Martin Rein have noted, ambiguity can be invaluable in getting a plan accepted initially. This benefit will normally be more than offset, however, by the battles born of misunderstanding which subsequently occur.[1] The tension between clarity and flexibility can hardly be exaggerated, but it is far from unique. It is rather similar, in fact, to that between liberty and law.

In the remainder of this chapter, I propose to set out the main judgments to which I have been led in preparing this volume. I trust that they do not strain the evidence presented in Chapters One through Four. Quite clearly, however, they draw upon it in highly selective fashion. The purpose of those chapters was to review a wide variety of relevant propositions, with supporting evidence for each, not to build a case. So I make no pretense that the judgments which follow are the only ones to which a careful reading might lead. They are simply my own, at the moment of completing this interim report.

*   *   *

The central issues, I would argue, are social peace and political legitimacy, not abstract justice or efficiency. No society adopts fundamental change because its dominant groups have suddenly acquired virtue or become horrified by waste. This is not to deny that some individuals act from idealistic motives, or that some societies are less rigid and brutal in their defense of established privilege than others. But it is to state predominant truths first.

White America has tolerated racial injustice on a grand scale for three centuries, and it has quite regularly placed other values before efficiency in its politics. Its resistance to housing and school integration, and to large-scale redistributive programs, remains overwhelming. The efficiency experts who call for metropolitan government continue to be ignored. For most Americans, ours is a society of abundance, not scarcity. We purchase things (such as small-scale suburban government) because they please us and their cost seems tolerable. We recognize that "efficiency" is a word with little meaning where values are problematic.*

Here is the crux of the problem. Whites (especially those who live in homogeneous jurisdictions) take the basic values of local government for granted. Blacks do not. Whites disagree on precise spending priorities, and they grouse about tax increases; but they do not question the system itself. Blacks do. Whites chuckle over bureaucratic inefficiency, but they assume that the objectives being sought are proper. Blacks do not. Whites are fundamentally satisfied because they sense that the institutions of American government have been shaped by men like them, for men like them. Blacks are not, because they do not. As Stokely Carmichael has observed, no one talks about white power because it goes without saying that power in America is white.

For Negroes, the issue is indeed justice—not abstract justice, justice for others, but justice for themselves. They are a small and isolated minority, however. Most whites are little moved by their moral claims. If they played entirely by the

---

*I confess that I do not believe any important political group cares much about efficiency. Many care about it a little, but almost no one cares about it a great deal. It has ever been so. The Progressive reform movement of the early twentieth century may seem an exception, but its primary value was democracy, and its appeal rested largely on its hostility to malefactors of great wealth and power. On the local scene, its main vote-getting theme was to "throw the rascals out."

rules of the democratic game, they would get little attention, let alone satisfaction. But ours is a highly interdependent society. Small, even tiny, minorities can disrupt a great deal. The riots have brought this lesson home, and raised black demands to the top of the national political agenda. At the same time, the riots have stirred white anger; they could lead the majority to seek peace by brutal repression.

Most whites, I believe, would prefer a peace of reconciliation to one of conquest. They—or rather, we—are a decent people; there are certain kinds of horrors we do not want in our midst; we have guilty consciences about the nation's racial record; we imagine that a peace based on compromise will be cheaper than one which permanently alienates one-ninth of the nation; and we fear that a sufficiently ruthless policy to bring peace would stamp out liberty for us all.

It makes quite good sense, of course, for a society to allocate its resources in accord with the "squeaky wheel" principle. Most people are instinctively opposed to social change; they dislike paying taxes; what privileges they have, they are loath to give up; they are full of self-serving rationales about the justice of their own claims and interests. In other words, resources are scarce, claims abundant; people are selfish, the consensus on priorities weak. This is not to say that the public lacks any sense of what is right and proper, or that this sense can be ignored. It is merely to say that this sense is extremely general, and is itself largely an indirect and lagged product of power relationships. It does not dictate an across-the-board attack on injustice. Its role is rather to help determine which of the passionate claimants deserve serious hearings, and to help define the range of plausible solutions. At every point, it interacts with power. The mix between morality and pragmatism in specific political settlements can never be fully sorted out.

The "squeaky wheel" principle works best when few people know about it, when general satisfaction is high, and when power relationships are stable. It is by no means cost-less to exploit. A group must expend enormous energy to attract notice, and its activity is likely to spur opposing groups to do likewise. The more extreme the means employed, the greater the risk of boomerang.

In urban America, however, the word seems now to have reached nearly everyone—a development for which the civil rights movement can probably take substantial credit. A great many people are angry. And power relationships (primarily because of the rapidity of technoeconomic change) are anything but stable. At times in the largest American cities it seems that we are on the verge of universal war: the war, that is, of all against all.

For this whites are inclined to blame blacks, calling on them to abide by the traditional rules of American political conflict. The trouble is that many young blacks are so angry that they are prepared to take enormous risks, and that they view the white demand for "law and order" as sheerest hypocrisy. The law itself, they argue, is an expression of power—the power of wealth and whiteness. The majority is content to see military force applied in support of American interests around the world, and it is indifferent to police brutality at home. Public employee strikes are increasingly common, despite laws forbidding them, and punishment is rare. Those who most loudly cry "law and order" are typically the most vociferous critics of the Supreme Court's efforts to protect the rights of accused criminals. Some of them have called for outright defiance of the Court's decisions on integration, reapportionment, and school prayers. But usually they are spared the embarrassment of having to challenge the law, because it is on their side.

It seems to most rebellious blacks that the majority demand is for black acquiescence in the status quo rather than rapid, orderly change. Looking around the world, they conclude that fundamental change rarely occurs except as the product of revolutionary pressure. Many cannot express this entire rationale, but they have absorbed key slogans which express its essence: that "power speaks through the mouth of a gun" and that "violence is as American as cherry pie."

They are aware, of course, of how little capacity to match white violence they have. This intensifies their frustration, but also keeps most of them searching for ways to make small gains. Just as the black mass desire for integration persists, so does the black activist recognition of the necessity for compromise. The public record often suggests otherwise, but it should not be overemphasized—any more than the rhetoric of white politicians. All over the country black activists are struggling patiently, against enormous odds, to develop ghetto wealth and political power by legal means.

I address myself to fellow whites who believe that this nation's highest priority must be to achieve a peace of reconciliation. The question for us is more than one of peace; it is one of legitimacy. It is first: how can we sustain the interest of blacks in peaceful compromise—in sharing laws, institutions, even a common nationality with the white majority? And it is second: how can we pursue this aim effectively within the American political system?

Blacks have a great many grievances, and they are making a great many demands. The need, I suggest, is for substantial positive responses to at least some of these. Permit me to draw an analogy. In a fascinating paper, based on a survey conducted in Watts following the 1965 riot, H. Edward Ransford has maintained that the willingness to use violence to correct racial injustice is a function of cumulative other factors. Highly educated* Negroes in his sample, whatever their other characteristics, were indisposed to use violence (though other studies have found them much *more* disposed toward participation in the organized civil rights movement). Among those with low degrees of education, however, three subjective conditions appeared to have a great impact: high dissatisfaction with their treatment as Negroes, a high sense

---

*The cutoff point was some college education. Respondents with a high school education or less were lumped together in the low education category.

of powerlessness, and a low degree of status-equal contact with whites. *The effect of combining these factors was much more than simply additive.* Isolation from status-equal contact with whites, for example, did not increase the propensity to use violence among those who were satisfied and had a high sense of efficacy. But it had a very substantial impact when combined with high dissatisfaction and powerlessness. More generally, among respondents with one or two of the subjective characteristics deemed conducive to violence, the actual willingness to use violence was only 24 per cent (vs. 12 per cent for those who had none of these characteristics). Among respondents with all three, however, 65 per cent expressed a willingness to use violence.*[2]

It is certainly true that concessions today will be followed by new demands tomorrow. But that is not the point. The aim must be to persuade Negroes that playing by the rules can produce some meaningful gains. If this involves revising the rules, so be it. The hope must be that we can domesticate American racial conflict as we have done with labor-management conflict. Labor makes new demands at every opportunity, but it is far from a revolutionary force.

How important is the participation issue in this context? How necessary is it to revise the political rules? I would judge that the answers depend more on white preferences than black. Blacks, to repeat, want many things. They want more and better jobs. They want massive redistributive public programs. They want integration. They want to own property. They want to be treated with respect by civil servants, employers, and merchants. They want to see their own kind in positions of power, prestige, and wealth. They want credit, insurance, and decent merchandise at prices com-

---

*Other studies have shown that those most likely to take part in riots are young unmarried males who have been raised in northern cities and who live in segregated neighborhoods. Income and employment status do not seem to have much independent effect. More conventional civil rights protestors tend to be middle class, among the better educated, northern and urban by upbringing, young, male, and socially mobile.[3]

parable to those paid by whites. And, of course, many of them want community control.

There is almost surely a good deal of substitutability among these wants. The tradeoffs cannot be specified with quantitative precision; but at some level, higher relative incomes would probably alleviate the intensity of black anger as effectively as integration. More responsive substantive policies could do as well as participatory reform. And even within the participatory realm, jobs, contracts, and elaborate consultation could doubtless reduce (even if not eliminate) the pressure for transfers of authority to the neighborhood level.

Why, then, give serious consideration to community control, in view of the powerful arguments that have been raised against it? The answer, I submit, is that for all the obstacles to it, it is probably the most feasible major demand that blacks are now making. White resistance to massive desegregation and redistribution is overwhelming, and it comes from all segments of white society. The resistance to community control, by contrast, is centered in the big city public bureaucracies. Many other whites are hostile—out of family, ethnic, or racial solidarity—but they really have no stake in who governs the ghettos.

A little progress can be made without massive redistribution and a willingness of whites to integrate, but only a very little. In the early sixties reducing unemployment was an alternative path to progress, but its potential has been exhausted now for several years. The current direction of policy, in response to inflation, is just the reverse. In any event, prosperity itself has little effect on relative incomes, and it is inequality (rather than absolute poverty) that is at the root of black unrest.*

The outlook for grand national reform, then, is bleak. What can be done at the local level? Certainly not much

---

*As is frequently pointed out, American Negroes are quite well off by world and historic standards. They think of themselves as Americans, however, and thus it is against contemporary American norms that they evaluate their lot.

about segregation and inequality. Central city whites are already in massive flight to the suburbs; vigorous efforts to promote integration simply hasten their exodus. The cities also lack resources to engage in much redistribution; and efforts to soak the affluent (again) just accelerate their pace of departure.

That leaves participatory reform. At the citywide level, a mayor can engage in elaborate consultation with black leaders, appoint some of them to citywide office, encourage black recruitment and rapid promotion by the career bureaucracies, seek to transform the bureaucratic subcultures, insist that Negroes secure employment on government contracts, and so on. Except where citywide Negro majorities exist, however, his efforts are likely to have a minor impact at best. He will find that he can consult, but he cannot pass ordinances, appropriate funds, make more than a few appointments, or dominate the civil service bureaucracies. In fact, he will normally find that the bureaucracies have far greater political strength in their respective spheres than he. They are much more likely to defeat him for reelection than he is to alter their subcultures. He may be a racial "statesman," but he will find that few members of the councils, boards, and commissions with which he must deal share his outlook. They will be more typical working through middle class whites. They will be determined not to give blacks any "special preference."

A single mayoral administration, of course, may surmount

It should be noted, parenthetically, that the relative incomes of the poor do improve during the upswing from a recession to high employment. Another way of putting this is to say that the poor bear a disproportionate share of the cost of recessions. In particular, they are the ones who get laid off as employment contracts.

After high employment is achieved, its maintenance (at any given level) has no further tendency to alleviate inequality. As incomes rise, the same degree of inequality (to repeat: a relative concept) involves larger and larger absolute differentials. In the most advanced modern economies, moreover, those at the bottom of the income pyramid have become liberated from peasant traditionalism and consumers of the mass media. Thus, they are intensely conscious of their poverty—and they question it.

these obstacles enough to achieve a fair rate of progress. In doing so, however (if the record to date is any indication), the mayor will stir widespread and bitter white antagonism. With his defeat or decision to retire, the pattern of city government will return to normal. Blacks may be left more bitter than ever, because they will have had their hopes raised and then dashed.

The hope of community control is that it might provide a base for long-term reform. It would provide an arena in which blacks might engage their energies and experience power. It would provide a mechanism for transforming the bureaucratic subcultures (by changing their basic lines of political dependence). It would provide a focus for black political organization. It might help to build black skills and self-respect. But most important, it would give blacks a tangible stake in the American political system. By giving them systems they considered their own, it would—hopefully—enhance the legitimacy of the whole system in their eyes.

What is to be said of the white liberal argument that community control would be a step toward increased separatism? Although I have made clear above (p. 131) that I do not think neighborhoods should be defined on racial lines, I accept the force of this argument. Small jurisdictions in large urban areas do have a tendency toward homogeneity, and the drive toward racial homogeneity within social units in our society is particularly strong. Were this not so, we could have small-scale local government and integration, too. As it is, we have extremely few integrated neighborhoods even within large jurisdictions. And the forced political mix in big city government appears on balance to be a force for increased friction rather than reconciliation.

The primary reason for this is white prejudice. The black desire for integration is well documented and overwhelming. Thus, liberals are faced with a bitter dilemma. They desire a peace of reconciliation and they also desire integration. They would like to pursue the former by implementing the latter. But they are a tiny minority within the white majority. (I am speaking now of the few who are truly prepared for massive desegregation—and in their own lives, not just those of the less affluent folk.) Thus, they cannot deliver integration. At least, they cannot deliver it at a rate that is nearly rapid enough.

Having long envisioned complementarity, they are unwilling to contemplate the possibility that their two primary values may have to be traded off. This is especially so because the facts are ambiguous. A plausible case can be made that community control will heighten, rather than alleviate, racial antagonism. And then there is the long history of liberal battle with the racist proponents of "states' rights." It is imperative, nonetheless, for white liberals to face the possibility that a tradeoff price exists. If it does, the reason is that most whites do not subscribe to liberal values, and thus would not consider the transaction in question a tradeoff at all. What liberals contemplate as a cost (setback for integration), they are more likely to contemplate as a benefit.

Let one point be absolutely clear. I have said that a tradeoff price in terms of liberal values *may* exist. not that it does. This is not to call for an immediate wholesale revamping of our local government structure to provide community control; but it *is* to call for a vigorous program of experimentation looking toward that possibility. Such a program might well include the use of federal incentives to bring about a total restructuring of local government in one or a few cities (and/or metropolitan areas).

On the very limited evidence to date, what might one expect the main products of community control to be? In particular: (1) Would it be conducive to racial peace? (2) Would it be conducive to the development of black skills and incomes, and to the improvement of other conditions (health, housing, security from crime, etc.) in the ghettos?

WOULD COMMUNITY CONTROL BE CONDUCIVE TO RACIAL PEACE?

My own view is that, where properly designed and after

an initial shakedown period, it would tend to be. This is not to say that it would be in every case, or to deny that great political battles will be necessary to achieve it (if it can be achieved at all). But it is to suggest a direction of probabilities, and to recall that every great transition involves a period of crisis and apparent chaos. The best such transitions, like the American Revolution and the acceptance of the labor movement into the American political mainstream, enhance tranquility within a few years even if not overnight.

The primary considerations on which I base this view are the following:

(a) The keys to legitimacy in the modern world are equality and self-determination.

There are many dimensions of equality, but of these the most important are equality of opportunity and equality before the law. With respect to the former, community control would open up a good many local, highly visible, opportunities to just those blacks who are the most articulate and skilled at organization.* The primary impact of community control, however, would be on the latter. On the day-to-day level, it would go far toward persuading blacks

---

*David Cohen has recently written of the special interest that black school professionals have in community control as follows: "Even in itself integration is a difficult path: it promises strain, tension, and unfamiliarity to black and white administrators and teachers equally, and hence it has never inspired real enthusiasm except among a few. Community control, on the other hand, avoids these pitfalls. It offers concrete gains long over-due—jobs and promotion to administrative and supervisory positions, without the accompanying discomfort of venturing into foreign schools and neighborhoods—under the ideological aegis of assisting in the development of one's own community. A more perfect coincidence of ideology and self-interest can hardly be imagined.

"The coming-of-age of the black professional class, a potent aspect of the struggle for community control, may turn out in the end to be the most important element in the battle over the schools, more significant than the substitution of parent for citywide boards, or community for bureaucratic control."[4] Community control would also, of course, extend numerous opportunities to black politicians, whether highly educated or not.

that governmental behavior toward them was not based on racial discrimination. More generally, blacks consider the existing situation a blatant denial of equality. The vast majority of whites enjoy small-scale, essentially neighborhood (by big city standards), local government. The black heritage is one of extreme oppression in the rural South, and more recently of exclusion from the northern suburbs. It seems to them that their permanent minority status is not simply a product of accident. Wherever it seems that equal application of the rules might permit them to enjoy local majority status, the rules are applied unequally. The last several years have witnessed a few exceptions—in long-established northern cities and southern towns where Negroes have won political control—but in general that's the way it is.

The current white policy is not in fact so consciously discriminatory. The problem is rather the incredible force of inertia. *It is possible neither to consolidate the suburbs nor to break up the central cities.* Add to this that blacks are confined to the central cities. Add also that the one central city in the nation with a Negro voting majority (Washington, D.C.) is also the one that lacks self-government. And it becomes readily comprehensible why many blacks view the present structure of American urban government as a barefaced gerrymander.*

---

*My stress here on the force of inertia is not meant to deny the critical role of prejudice in sustaining the status quo. It is undeniable, for example, that while Congressional rule of Washington, D.C. predates the Negro majority, the hostility of Southern Congressmen to that majority has been the decisive obstacle to home rule in recent years.

What I am denying is that the white determination to maintain racial superiority is today sufficient to revise the structure simply because it permits blacks to achieve some power. At certain extremes it may well be, but not in the ranges we can currently observe.

The problem, rather, is that our system is one of minority vetoes. It takes very large majorities to change the status quo in any fundamental way. Blacks, together with fair-minded whites (a category which includes many others in addition to hard-core liberals) seem to have reached the point where they can veto fundamental changes. But as a deprived group they want much more. And one heritage of the past is that the existing structure, on balance, is radically biased against them.

The primary need, then, is for parity between black and white "neighborhoods" in each urban area. My own preference would be for a two-tier pattern, on the model of metropolitan London.[5] The bottom tier authorities in such a system—today's suburbs and central city neighborhoods—would have less power than the suburbs now do. In particular, they would have less power to practice racial exclusion, to veto programs of great metropolitan interest, and to engage in tax competition for commercial and industrial investment. With respect to the last, taxation of commercial and industrial property would be a metropolitan function, so that tax rates might cease to be a factor in business location decisions (at least, within each urban region), and so that these decisions might become uncoupled from the distribution of public services.

But my preferences, quite clearly, are of little importance. The critical issue is what it will take to persuade blacks that the system is fair. To that end, some dramatic move toward parity would seem essential, whatever the precise nature of the design.*

If equality is one key to legitimacy in the modern world, the other is self-determination. Not every group, of course, desires or can have independent nationhood. We are fortunate that the vast majority of blacks are not yet making this demand. (But we had better keep an eye on its rate of growth.**) What they *are* demanding is that they sometimes, at the lowest tier of American government, be permitted the experience of majority status.

To endorse this demand is not to say that every group which comes forward with a similar demand in future should

---

*It is perhaps worth adding that one move toward parity (fortunately, the least likely) might actually exacerbate black anger. That would be to consolidate a city and its suburbs into a one-tier metropolitan gargantua. This would look like a transparent ploy to dilute black influence in the central city without offering anything in return.

**See above, p. 58.

be accorded the same privilege. The fact is that race is the most critical variable in American politics. To be a Negro is to have the fact of race pervade all of one's other roles. It is also to face constant exclusion and hostility. As the saying goes: we are faced with a condition, not a theory. The Constitution may be color-blind, but Americans are not. To be a Negro in white America is to be *always* in the minority. It is rather difficult to have much sense of self-determination in such a situation. This is especially so if one is poor, and cannot even exercise much choice in the marketplace. It is not significantly less so because the system is democratic. Where race is concerned, majority tyranny is much like any other.

To endorse this demand is also not to suggest that opportunities for integration should be curtailed, or that neighborhood boundaries should be drawn on racial lines. My own position is that the battle to extend integration opportunities for those who want them must be pressed more vigorously than ever, and that neighborhood boundaries should be drawn (and periodically reapportioned) like legislative districts. The aim must be not to promote separatism—though an incidental effect of community control may be to increase the present, almost total degree of segregation. It must rather be to provide blacks with the chance in some circumstances (and when they care enough) to experience majority status. Suburban-neighborhood parity would accomplish this aim. If the boundaries were drawn in color-blind fashion (e.g., for compactness and equal population), many members of each race would find themselves in neighborhood minorities. But there would be no racial bias to the system, and those who cared enough could move to neighborhoods that were predominantly of their own race.

(b) The bureaucratic subcultures, which produce behavior that so infuriates young blacks today, are unlikely to be transformed by any reform short of community control. At the citywide level in most cities (the exceptions are those few with Negro-white liberal voting majorities), the bureaucracies can count on majority support from the electorate and nearly all policy-making bodies. Even where they cannot, their power to veto and delay is generally sufficient to block fundamental change. Community control would not change them everywhere, but it would change them where it counted most—in the ghettos. Not only would it change them in fact, but it would change them very obviously. Blacks would be much less likely to see slurs where none were intended when dealing with employees of governments they considered their own.

(c) There is no reason to believe that neighborhood power would tend to increase black radicalism. Indeed, precisely the reverse hypothesis is more plausible.

The evidence suggests that elections would produce more moderate black leaders than the current process of screening for newsworthiness and support among the activists alone. Community control would give authority, resources, and newsworthiness to those who could win elections. It would also set them astride the channels of liaison with units of the larger society. They would be the logical and legitimate leaders for outsiders to deal with. This would both simplify matters for the outsiders and render the conclusion of bargains more feasible. (Consider the "exclusive bargaining agent" mechanism in labor-management relations.)

There is every reason to believe, moreover, that the possession of property and the exercise of responsibility are both "conservatizing" experiences. Power is a form of property; it gives its holders a great psychic stake in the system. Home and business ownership would probably be even more effective moderating influences on ghetto politics; it should be recalled that they are important parts of the full community control demand package. The exercise of responsibility would be a vital educational experience for black leaders. They would be forced to go beyond slogans, to grapple with ghetto problems in all their dull complexity. This would lead them to press higher levels of government for greater resources (as just about all city officials now do), but it would also decrease their confidence in simple, radical panaceas.

Community control might or might not facilitate ghetto

political organization. The reason it might not is that, in removing the "enemy" from immediate proximity, it would reduce the incentive to mobilize. On the other hand, it would provide a clear-cut set of rewards for successful mobilization. Let us assume for the moment, therefore, that the effect on balance would be to increase ghetto organization.

The critical point to keep in mind is that greater organization does not necessarily mean heightened black-white conflict. For one thing, a great deal of the increased black organization would be competitive. Alternative groups would be vying for power. For another, the most successful organizational leaders would probably be among the more moderate (for the reasons noted above). For a third, heightened organization in itself is generally a force for peace. The rioters, it will be recalled, have been drawn predominantly from the young, the unmarried, the politically inactive—i.e., those least integrated into stable social organizations. Those most involved in organized protest and political activity have been among the least likely to riot. Indeed, they have been the most likely to act as counterrioters when disorders have occurred. If one's aim is a peace without black political activism, then one's method must be ruthless repression. But if one's aim is a peace of reconciliation, the sensible thing is to concentrate on replacing violent disorder with nonviolent political and protest activity. That is the kind in which the labor movement engages. The best resolution of the current racial crisis for which we can hope is that the labor precedent will be emulated.

Finally, there is no reason to equate even separatism with heightened antagonism. Less contact has often in history meant less conflict. When the quality of contact is negative, the option of reducing its quantity is not to be sneezed at. Once again, this is not to oppose integration. It is just to deal with the facts as they are. When two parties both passionately insist on separation, who am I to refuse it? But of course the situation is really less extreme, so let me put it another way. Blacks have been an oppressed minority. I have championed their right to integration, and I still do. But

I can recognize why they might want something of their own while they wait; and I can see that having it might make the wait less infuriating.

WOULD COMMUNITY CONTROL BE CONDUCIVE TO THE DEVELOPMENT OF BLACK SKILLS AND INCOMES, AND TO THE IMPROVEMENT OF OTHER CONDITIONS IN THE GHETTOS?

This seems to me a more relevant way to put the question than to ask whether neighborhood governments would be as "efficient" as citywide governments?

There are tremendous disagreements over what the specific objectives of public policy in the ghettos should be. Thus, there is no basis for achieving consensus on what is efficient. But there is substantial agreement on what black aspirations are. So let us speak of outcomes, and arrangements that might be conducive to them, rather than of government efficiency.

Let us dwell on this point a moment longer. It is possible for a remarkably "efficient" government to produce disastrously negative results. Its objectives may be irrelevant, perverse, or self-defeating. Or it may simply be so overwhelming in its competence that it destroys the capacity of its clients to help themselves.

When spokesmen for the civil service bureaucracies speak of "efficiency," they typically refer to process rather than outcome variables—just as when they speak of "merit," they typically refer to degrees and test scores rather than on-the-job accomplishment. For example, they speak of police response times reduced, not crime rates. They speak of smaller classes and "better qualified" teachers, not student acquisition of skills and self-respect. They speak of ironclad guarantees against corruption, not the reduction of inequality, segregation, or racial bitterness.

It has long been a central tenet of the American tradition

that the best government is often no government, or at least government which confines itself to arranging environments rather than tending to every detail. Thus, we leave most economic decisions (other than the very largest) to the market-place. This leaves a great many decisions to be made by extremely unsophisticated actors; but most Americans be-lieve that it is highly conducive to "efficiency" on balance.

Similarly, Americans have always left the bulk of gov-ernmental decision making (national security affairs excluded) to state and local authorities. They have done so despite a widespread belief that state and local officials are less com-petent, less innovative, and more corrupt than those of the federal government. Why have they done so? They have judged that decentralization would produce a finer tuning of government to varied local tastes. By insisting on no more uniformity than was necessary, satisfaction with union would be maximized.* They have considered widespread participa-tion in government a value in itself, noting its utility as an instrument of democratic education and socialization. They have believed that distributing responsibility widely would spread competence throughout the society (even though the most competent might still gravitate toward the center). Those with a taste for the classics have frequently noted Tocque-ville's observation that the American system was very waste-ful but also incredibly vigorous, and that these were two sides of the same coin: decentralization.**

Finally, students of colonialism have frequently noted that people who do not have self-government somehow never seem ready for it. In part this is a prejudice of the colonial-

---

*They have also recalled the wisdom of the framers, who recognized that no union would be possible at all without numerous concessions to state separatist sentiment.

**The flavor of Tocqueville's moving defense of American localism may be gathered from the following key passages: ". . . Centralized administra-tion . . . may insure a victory in the hour of strife, but it gradually relaxes the sinews of strength. . . .

ists, but in part it is true. Countries new to self-government are rarely very good at it. Unfortunately, there does not seem to be any other way to learn than by practice. The colonialists

---

"Centralization imparts without difficulty an admirable regularity to the routine of business . . . maintains society in a status quo alike secure from improvement and decline; and perpetuates a drowsy regularity in the conduct of affairs, which the heads of the administration are wont to call good order and public tranquility. . . . Its force deserts it when society is to be profoundly moved or accelerated in its courses; and if once the cooperation of private citizens is necessary to the furtherance of its measures, the secret of its impotence is disclosed.

"Even whilst the centralized power, in its despair, invokes the assistance of the citizens, it says to them: 'You should act just as I please, and in the direction which I please. You are to take charge of the details, without aspiring to guide the system; you are to work in darkness; and afterwards you may judge my work by its results.' These are not the conditions on which the alliance of the human will is to be obtained . . .

"In America, the power which conducts the administration is far less regular, less enlightened, and less skillful, but a hundred-fold greater, than in Europe. In no country in the world do the citizens make such exertions for the common weal. I know of no people who have established schools so numerous and efficacious, places of public worship better suited to the wants of the inhabitants, or roads kept in better repair. Uniformity or permanence of design, the minute arrangement of details, and the perfection of administrative system, must not be sought for in the United States: what we find there is the presence of a power which, if it is somewhat wild, is at least robust; and an existence checkered with accidents, indeed, but full of animation and effort. . . .

"There are countries in Europe where the natives consider themselves as a kind of settlers, indifferent to the fate of the spot which they inhabit. The greatest changes are effected there without their concurrence, and (unless chance may have apprised them of the event) without their knowledge; nay, more, the condition of his village, the police of his street, the repairs of the church or the parsonage, do not concern him; for he looks upon all these things as unconnected with himself, and as the property of a powerful stranger whom he calls the government. . . .

"When a nation has arrived at this state, it must either change its customs and its laws, or perish; for the source of public virtues is dried up; and though it may contain subjects, it has no citizens. . . .

". . . A democracy without provincial institutions has no security against [disorder and despotism]. How can a populace, unaccustomed to freedom in small concerns, learn to use it temperately in great affairs? What resistance can be offered to tyranny in a country where each individual is weak, and where the citizens are not united by any common interest?

might have done well to transfer power gradually, but they rarely moved at all until confronted by revolution. Sound familiar?

What should we expect, then, of neighborhood government in the ghettos? Clearly, we should not expect high efficiency "in the small."[7] We should not expect the quality of political debate to be highly logical or the test scores of civil service candidates to improve. We should not expect more innovative programs or cleaner streets. We should probably not even expect lower crime rates or higher pupil reading scores.

We may hope, however, that community control will help cement the American union by providing an adequate outlet for racial pluralism. We may hope that it will help build black confidence in, and understanding of, our political institutions. We may hope that over time it will provide a mechanism for increasing competence throughout the black community.

There is substantial reason as well to hope for more specific benefits. A great many black problems are due to pathologies of the ghetto spirit—or rather, more accurately, to behavior patterns that are adaptive to the ghetto as it is, but which constitute severe obstacles to improving it.[8] These problems are the products of black self-hatred, despair, fatalism, and alienation from authority much more than of poverty itself. (Many other groups have been poor, and still are around the world, without experiencing the social disorganization of the American ghetto.) These characteristics have been fostered primarily by oppression, but also by paternalism. The active oppression is decreasing rapidly, but the legacy of the past will be spinning out its consequences for a long while to come.

Those who dread the license of the mob, and those who fear absolute power, ought alike to desire the gradual development of provincial liberties."[6]

There is almost surely a greater potential for improving the ghettos by transforming their spirit than by inundating them with paternalistic programs. This is not to deny that resources are essential. Quite obviously, rapid change will be impossible without massive infusions of outside aid. But it is to maintain that resources are not enough. It seems quite obvious that the existing system is not getting any mileage at all (except perhaps in reverse) from its expenditures of resources in terms of transforming the ghetto spirit. Self-determination might not produce any better results. But a great many people, including just about all the nation's black leaders, believe that it would. It would certainly seem to merit serious trial.

Let us be more specific. How might self-determination lead to improved outcomes in specific policy arenas, even if it operated with less qualified personnel by existing civil service standards?

George Sternlieb has shown that by far the most impressive way to improve ghetto housing is to replace absentee ownership with resident ownership. He has based his argument not on conjecture, but on painstaking analysis of the histories of large numbers of specific properties.[9] Home and tenement ownership also builds management skills, and it provides a powerful incentive to become active in neighborhood improvement efforts. Thus, it is likely to produce leadership as well as more narrow business skills, and to channel energies into sober, constructive political efforts. Sternlieb notes that a public policy which encouraged resident ownership would have precedents dating to the Homestead Act and beyond.* Note that such a policy would not require a

---

*The owners studied by Sternlieb, of course, were far from typical ghetto residents. Without unusual drive and skill, most of them would never have become owners. But their number has been growing, and Sternlieb argues convincingly that the process could be accelerated to a very marked degree without a serious dilution of benefits.

large bureaucracy, nor would it give the recipients of aid any sense of being on the dole. The beneficial outcomes which ensued would be viewed as more the products of free enterprise in action than "efficient" government.

Theodore Cross has recently noted that black lending institutions can operate much more effectively in the ghettos than white. The reason is simple. To break even in the ghettos, let alone make a profit, it is necessary to charge higher interest rates than elsewhere. The reasons: high bad debt rates, very small average loans, the need for intensive counseling of customers, a resource base of very small and highly active accounts, the need to devote a great deal of effort to community improvement activities. White banks are afraid to charge higher interest rates in the ghettos, recognizing their vulnerability to charges of racial discrimination. Thus, they have tended to stay out of the ghettos entirely, except for token money-losing operations undertaken for public relations purposes.

The result has been to make credit virtually unavailable in the ghettos, except from loan sharks, small loan companies, and individual merchants. In part, the answer to this problem should be subsidies to enable private banks to make profits lending in the ghettos on the same terms as elsewhere. Realistically, however, the subsidies will not be sufficient to meet the demand for a long time to come (if ever). Thus, a very sensible alternative, to which some large white financial institutions have already turned, is to channel resources for ghetto lending through black banks. This at least can make bank-style credit available, and at rates only 1.5 or 2 percentage points higher than elsewhere, instead of 30, 50, or 1,000.*[10] Cross notes, incidentally, that the same phenomenon operates in retailing. The large white-owned

---

*Credit from loan sharks typically comes at prices ranging from 5 per cent a week to $1.00 a week for each $5.00 borrowed. The former works out at 260 per cent a year, the latter at 1,000 per cent a year.

chains avoid the ghettos, and brand names tend to be unavailable because their manufacturers refuse to permit them
to be sold at higher than list prices. The primary results:
ghetto residents buy shoddy, nonname brand merchandise
from small and frequently shady merchants.[11] Community-
owned black retailing operations would have a much better
chance to secure permission from the brand-name manufacturers to charge what they had to; they would also have
a better chance to secure subsidies (perhaps from government,
perhaps from the manufacturers themselves) to enable them
to break even while charging list prices.

Christopher Jencks has recently noted that, although most
of the debate on ghetto education focuses on specific skills,
there is little evidence that these skills have much bearing
on earning capacity:

> If you ask employers why they won't hire dropouts . . .
> they seldom complain that dropouts can't read. Instead,
> they complain that dropouts don't get to work on time,
> can't be counted on to do a careful job, don't get along
> with others in the plant or office, can't be trusted to keep
> their hands out of the till, and so on. Nor do the avail-
> able survey data suggest that the adult success of people
> from disadvantaged backgrounds depends primarily on
> their intellectual skills. If you compare black men who
> do well on the Armed Forces Qualifications Test to those
> who do badly, for example, you find that a black man
> who scores as high as the average white still earns only
> about two-thirds as much as the average white earns.
> Not only that, he hardly earns more than the average
> black. *Even for whites, the mental abilities measured by
> the AFQ account for less than a tenth of the variation in
> earnings.*[12]

If Jencks's reading of the evidence is correct—and I believe it is—black poverty and unemployment are much more products of poor socialization (by the standards of the job market) than of poor reading and arithmetic skills.* The likelihood that the current citywide educational bureaucracies will be able to alter the socialization patterns of ghetto youth is nil. The problem is not one of qualifications. It is one of trust and rapport. It is essentially political, not technical. Black-controlled educational systems might fail to do any better, but they could hardly do worse. In all honesty, it is hard to believe that they would not do better.

If unemployment is a product of socialization, how much more obviously so are crime and disorder.** So long as it is *de rigeur* for all black leaders to view the police as armies of occupation, no one is likely to have much success in altering the socialization patterns involved. Nearly all students of police work agree, moreover, that the most important variable determining effectiveness is community cooperation.*** Existing citywide police forces are the least likely agencies to secure such cooperation. They even have great difficulty using their black personnel effectively, because black police are widely perceived by ghetto residents as having "sold out." Critics of the black participation movement frequently speak as if this showed the unimportance of black police recruitment. Actually, what it suggests is the need to

---

*They are also, doubtless in very large part, products of discrimination, but that is outside the scope of the present discussion.

**This is not to judge the ultimate responsibility of institutions vs. individuals, but simply to point out that the institutions have failed to inculcate behavior patterns conducive to their peaceful survival, and to persuade the individuals of their legitimacy.

***For example, James Q. Wilson—an opponent of community control on other grounds (see above, pp. 29-38)—writes as follows: "The police can do relatively little about preventing most crimes, and those they can help prevent—street crimes—are precisely the ones that require the greatest knowledge of local conditions and the greatest support, in terms of a willingness to report offenses and give information, from the populace." [13]

link black recruitment with political reform to enhance the legitimacy of the whole police system.

So far as civil disorder is concerned, the police have often been less than ineffective. They have themselves been a major source of disturbance.

As Burton Levy notes, nearly every recent disorder has begun with a police incident. The police have often not been particularly blameworthy in these incidents (and, in any event, every organization contains some rotten apples). But that is not the point. What matters is that such particular events have been able, because of the context of hostility within which they occurred, to trigger such general disorder. To quote Levy: "Whatever the factual reality is—as contrasted to the belief systems—clearly the cops serve as the 'flash point' for black anger, mob formation, and civil disorder."[14]

Once again, then, the problem appears to be primarily political (though it could doubtless be stamped out with sufficient force). For those of us bent on a peace of reconciliation, the overwhelming need is not for better equipment but for rapprochement. With respect to personnel policy, it suggests less emphasis on academic degrees, test scores, and seniority, and much more on relationships of trust with the community.

Would community control increase efficiency? The issue, it seems, is less clear-cut than it sounds. The answer will largely turn on whose conceptions of problem and purpose one adopts. From a somewhat different perspective, it is likely to depend on whether one interprets the question to be about efficiency "in the small" or "in the large."

It goes without saying that we can foresee very little. One of the more useful research efforts that might be undertaken in the next few years would be a series of case studies examining the record of Community Action, Model Neighborhood, and community control designers in forecasting even the very short-run consequences of their actions. One need have little doubt that these will be, from the standpoint of would-be social planners, quite discouraging tales.

But like sailors in a hurricane, we can ill afford to drift. We must estimate our bearings, on the meager information we have, and act. We may have a little time for experimentation. If so, we would do well to exploit it vigorously. But we probably will not. Societies are transformed by revolution and inadvertence, but they rarely conduct experiments to improve political forecasting. In the end, if community control becomes reality, it will probably do so little more because of experimental findings than white altruism. It will be a product of protest and pragmatic compromise.

NOTES

ONE: THE ISSUES

[1] *New York Times,* September 3, 1968, p. 1.

[2] For a less sympathetic view, see Nathan Glazer, "The Negro's Stake in America's Future," *New York Times Magazine,* September 22, 1968, pp. 1, 30.

[3] Angus Campbell and Howard Schuman, "Racial Attitudes in Fifteen American Cities," in *Supplemental Studies for The National Advisory Commission on Civil Disorders* (USGPO, 1968), pp. 1–67. The tables cited appear on pp. 29–30.

[4] *Boston Globe,* September 1, 1969, p. 19. Material reprinted by permission of the Chicago Tribune-New York News Syndicate, Inc.

[5] *Newsweek,* October 6, 1969, p. 45.

[6] Cf. Irving Kristol, "Decentralization for What?" *The Public Interest,* Spring 1968, pp. 17–25. The reference is to p. 25.

[7] Robert L. Crain, *The Politics of School Desegregation* (Aldine, 1968), chs. 10–13; and Robert L. Crain and James J. Venecko, "Elite Influence in School Desegregation," in James Q. Wilson, ed., *City Politics and Public Policy* (Wiley, 1968), pp. 127–148.

[8] Cf. Donald B. Rosenthal and Robert L. Crain, "Structure and Values in Local Political Systems: The Case of Fluoridation Decisions," in Wilson, *op. cit.,* pp. 217–242; and Harvey M. Sapolsky, "Science, Voters, and the Fluoridation Controversy," *Science,* October 25, 1968, pp. 427–433.

[9] Cf. Raymond E. Wolfinger and Fred I. Greenstein, "The Repeal of Fair Housing in California: An Analysis of Referendum Voting," *American Political Science Review,* September 1968, pp. 753–769.

[10] Harry Scoble, "Effects of Riots on Negro Leadership," in Louis H. Masotti and Don R. Bowen, eds., *Riots and Rebellion: Civil Violence in the Urban Community* (Sage, 1968), pp. 329–346. The point cited appears on p. 331.

[11] Campbell and Schuman, *op. cit.,* p. 33.

[12] Everett F. Cataldo, Richard M. Johnson, and Lyman A. Kellstadt, "Social Strain and Urban Violence," in Masotti and Bowen, *op. cit.,* pp. 285–298. The point cited appears on p. 293.

[13] Joel D. Aberbach and Jack L. Walker, "The Meanings of Black Power: A Comparison of White and Black Interpretations of a Political Slogan," paper delivered at the annual meeting of the American Political Science Association, September 1968, mimeo. The point cited appears at p. 12.

[14] Cataldo, *et al.,* in Masotti and Bowen, *op. cit.,* p. 293.

[15] *Newsweek,* June 30, 1969, p. 20. It should be emphasized that these findings are not strictly comparable to those of the 1968 SRC survey, so no trends can be inferred.

[16] Reynolds Farley and Karl E. Taeuber, "Population Trends and Residential Segregation Since 1960," *Science,* March 1, 1968, pp. 953–956.

[17] Karl E. Taeuber, "Residential Segregation," *Scientific American,* August 1965, pp. 12–19.

[18] U. S. Bureau of the Census, *Current Population Reports,* Series P-23, No. 24 (USGPO, October 1967), p. 8; and No. 27 (USGPO, February 1969), p. 3.

[19] *Ibid.* The Bureau's surveys are designed to provide reliable information on national population trends. The smaller any population group within the nation is, the less reliable are the data bearing on it. Thus, far more confidence can be placed in the data showing an acceleration of the white exodus from the central cities than in that showing a Negro breakthrough in securing access to suburban housing.

[20] Cf. Seymour Martin Lipset, *Political Man* (Anchor, 1963), pp. 200–202; Lester Milbraith, *Political Participation* (Rand McNally, 1965), p. 119; and Jay Schulman, "Ghetto-Area Residence, Political Alienation, and Riot Orientation," in Masotti and Bowen, *op. cit.,* pp. 262–284, esp. p. 281.

[21] Campbell and Schuman, *op. cit.,* p. 20.

[22] *Ibid.,* p. 19.

[23] Aberbach and Walker, *op. cit.,* pp. 3–9.

[24] *Newsweek,* June 30, 1969, pp. 9, 20, 22.

[25] *New York Times,* July 4, 1969, p. 35.

[26] U. S. Bureau of the Census, *Current Population Reports,* Series P-23, No. 27, pp. 2, 7.

[27] Campbell and Schuman, *op. cit.,* p. 26.

[28] *Newsweek,* June 30, 1969, p. 21.

[29] *Report of the National Advisory Commission on Civil Disorders* (Bantam, 1968), pp. 315–316.

[30] *New York Times,* June 25, 1969, p. 39.

[31] Campbell and Schuman, *op. cit.,* p. 19.

[32] Cf. Kristol, *op. cit.,* p. 21.

[33] *Varieties of Police Behavior* (Harvard, 1968), pp. 288–290.

[34] Daniel P. Moynihan, *Maximum Feasible Misunderstanding* (Free Press, 1969), esp. pp. 132–139.

[35] Cf. *The Federalist* No. 10 for the classic statement of Madison's view; Alexis de Tocqueville, *Democracy in America,* Vol. I, ch. 15; Richard Hofstadter, *The Age of Reform* (Knopf, 1955); and, among others, Daniel Bell, ed., *The Radical Right* (2nd ed., Doubleday, 1963), chapters by David Riesman, Peter Viereck, Herbert Hyman, and Seymour Martin Lipset.

[36] Judith May, "Citizen Involvement in Urban Affairs," Department of Political Science, University of California at Berkeley, August 1968, dittoed, p. 15. She supports the passage cited with an analysis (pp. 15-24) of Lipset's books from *Agrarian Socialism* (1949) through *Union Democracy* (1956) and *Political Man* (1963); and of Dahl's from *Congress and Foreign Policy* (1950) through *Preface to Democratic Theory* (1956) and *Who Governs?* (1961).

[37] Leonard Fein, "Community Schools and Social Theory: The Limits of Universalism," paper prepared for the Brookings Institution Conference on Community Schools, Washington, D.C., December 1968, p. 1. Fein is here making his point by quoting the words of Myron Lieberman, as expressed in *The Future of Public Education* (University of Chicago Press, 1960), p. 60.

[38] *Ibid.,* p. 1.

[39] Wilson, *op. cit.,* pp. 286-293.

[40] Personal communication from Patrick Murphy to the author. Murphy has been Chief of Police in Syracuse, Deputy Chief Inspector in New York City, Assistant Director of the U. S. Law Enforcement Assistance Administration, and Director of Public Safety in Washington, D.C. He is currently director of research on law and public order at The Urban Institute.

[41] It should be noted that only the last two sentences of this paragraph are based on Wilson.

[42] *Op. cit.,* pp. 19-21.

[43] Burton Levy, "Cops in the Ghetto: A Problem of the Police System," in Masotti and Bowen, *op. cit.,* pp. 347-358. The quotation is from p. 349.

[44] Joseph Lohman, "Law Enforcement and the Police," in Masotti and Bowen, *op. cit.,* pp. 359-372. Lohman, a former sheriff of Cook County (Chicago), at the time of his death in 1968 was dean of the University of California (Berkeley) School of Criminology.

[45] Levy, in Masotti and Bowen, *op. cit.,* p. 348.

[46] Arthur Niederhoffer, *Behind the Shield: The Police in Urban Society* (Doubleday, 1967), chs. 2, 3.

[47] *New York Times,* September 11, 1968, p. 37. They were aggrieved because Huey Newton, a Panther leader accused of killing a policeman, had just been convicted of manslaughter rather than first-degree murder, and thus could not receive the death penalty.

[48] Jerome Skolnick, *Justice Without Trial* (Wiley, 1966), pp. 80,

81. Skolnick noted, parenthetically, that even on this force the ordinary patrolman's job was mainly keeping the peace rather than enforcing the law.

[49] Gary T. Marx, "Civil Disorder and the Agents of Social Control," paper prepared for the annual meeting of the American Sociological Association, August 1968, mimeo, p. 42 (forthcoming in the *Journal of the Social Issues).* See also Paul Jacobs, *Prelude to Riot* (Random House, 1966), pp. 13–60.

[50] *Op. cit.,* p. 20.

[51] Sidney Verba, "Democratic Participation," *The Annals,* September 1963, pp. 53–78. The quotation is from p. 75.

[52] I have considered the logic, within the present framework, of so responding in my book, *The City Planning Process: A Political Analysis* (Cornell, 1965), pp. 409–411.

[53] On the balance between the strengthening of chief executives and the weakening of parties within cities, cf. Edward C. Banfield and James Q. Wilson, *City Politics* (Harvard, 1963), pp. 78–81, 335–336.

[54] Robert C. Wood, *1400 Governments* (Harvard, 1961), pp. 112–113.

[55] For suggestive evidence tending to support the latter point, cf. J. David Greenstone and Paul E. Peterson, "Reformers, Machines, and the War on Poverty," in Wilson, *City Politics and Public Policy,* pp. 267–292.

[56] Verba, *op. cit.,* p. 75

[57] Cf. Altshuler, *op. cit.,* chs. 6–8.

[58] James Q. Wilson, *Negro Politics* (Free Press, 1960), pp. 63–4.

[59] *New York Times,* July 10, 1969, p. 1. Leading scholarly analyses of the Chicago machine and its products are the following: Edward C. Banfield, *Political Influence* (Free Press, 1961); Harold F. Gosnell, *Machine Politics: Chicago Model* (2nd ed., with a Foreword by Theodore J. Lowi and a Postscript by Gosnell, University of Chicago Press, 1968); James Q. Wilson, *Negro Politics op. cit.;* Harold M. Baron, "Black Powerlessness in Chicago," *Trans-Action,* November 1968, pp. 27–33; Charles and Bonnie Remsberg, "Chicago Voices: Tales Told Out of School," in Raymond W. Mack, ed., *Our Children's Burden: Studies of Desegregation in Nine American Communities* (Vintage, 1968); and Greenstone and Peterson, in Wilson, *City Politics and Public Policy.*

[60] Cf. Scott Greer, *Metropolitics* (Wiley, 1963), pp. 30, 52, 80, 94–95; and Edward Sofen, *The Miami Metropolitan Experiment* (2nd ed., Anchor, 1966), pp. 77–78.

[61] Martin Rein, "Community Action Programs: A Critical Reassessment," *Poverty and Human Resources Abstracts,* May–June

1968, pp. 2–8. The quotation is from pp. 6, 7 (italics in the original). The last sentence is separated by several paragraphs from the remainder of the quotation, but is intended to conclude and summarize the entire section of which it is a part.

[62] Moynihan, *op. cit.,* pp. 136–137.

[63] S. M. Miller, Martin Rein, and Mary Morgan, "The Future of Community Participation," mimeo, May 1969, p. 22. Miller goes on to note that given current levels of ghetto hostility, however, numerous services may be unable to deliver at all if they fail to accommodate black demands for participation. Thus, in succeeding (by threatening paralysis), the demand for participation may produce less efficient service delivery than would have existed had it never been made.

[64] Cf. David Cohen, "The Price of Community Control," *Commentary,* July 1969, pp. 23–30, esp. p. 26; and Christopher Jencks, "Private Schools for Black Children," *New York Times Magazine,* November 3, 1968, pp. 29 ff. Cohen and Jencks are both at the Harvard School of Education. The former is senior author of a forthcoming volume in the present series.

[65] Betsy Levin, Communication to the Editor, *Commentary,* September 1969, p. 6.

[66] Moynihan, *op. cit.,* pp. 156–157.

[67] Cf. Andrew H. Greeley and Peter H. Rossi, *The Education of Catholic Americans* (Aldine, 1966).

[68] *Newsweek,* June 30, 1969, p. 20.

[69] Center for Urban Education, *Community Attitudes in Bedford-Stuyvesant: An Area Study* (Center for Urban Education, 1967), p. 75.

[70] Campbell and Schuman, *op. cit.,* p. 16.

[71] Cohen, *op. cit.,* p. 29.

[72] Louis Harris and Associates, Inc., News Release, January 30, 1969, p. 3. This poll was financed by the Center for Urban Education. By and large, the press seems to have ignored it. I am grateful to Norman Fainstein for bringing the news release to my attention.

[73] *Ibid.,* p. 7.

[74] *Newsweek,* June 30, 1969, p. 25 (italics added).

[75] *New York Times,* July 6, 1969, Section I, p. 32 (italics added).

[76] Campbell and Schuman, *op. cit.,* p. 55.

[77] Robert M. Fogelson and Robert B. Hill, "Who Riots? A Study of Participation in the 1967 Riots," in National Advisory Commission on Civil Disorders, *Supplemental Studies,* pp. 217–248. The reference here is to pp. 230–231 and some calculations of my own based on data presented there.

[78] In defining power, authority, and influence, I have myself

been influenced by the usage of Banfield and Wilson in *City Politics (op. cit.;* see esp. p. 101). However, I define power as they define influence, and vice versa. I do so not to be different, but because I believe that my usage better corresponds to everyday usage.

[79] Cf. Verba, *op. cit.,* p. 54.

TWO: THE FRAMEWORK

[1] Cf. Peter F. Drucker, *The Age of Discontinuity* (Harper & Row, 1968), chs. 10, 11; James Q. Wilson, "The Bureaucracy Problem," *The Public Interest,* Winter 1967, pp. 3-9; and Charles E. Lindblom, "The Rediscovery of the Market," *The Public Interest,* Summer 1966, pp. 89-101.

[2] Nathan Glazer, "For White and Black, Community Control is the Issue," *New York Times Magazine,* April 27, 1969, pp. 36-54. The comparative discussion is centered on pp. 42-44.

[3] Cf. Charles Tilly, "Collective Violence in European Perspective," in Hugh Davis Graham and Ted Robert Gurr, eds., *Violence in America: Historical and Comparative Perspectives* (Bantam, 1969), pp. 4-45. See esp. p. 10.

[4] *Ibid.,* p. 41.

[5] *Ibid.,* p. 42.

[6] Cf. Robert E. Brown, *Middle-Class Democracy and the Revolution in Massachusetts, 1691-1780* (Cornell, 1955), pp. 21-99, 401-408.

[7] William Riker, *Democracy in the United States* (2nd ed., Macmillan, 1965), pp. 3, 35-36.

[8] Elie Halevy, *England in 1815* (Barnes & Noble, 1961), p. 148. Cited by Tilly, *op. cit.,* p. 6.

[9] Benjamin Disraeli, preface to *Alton Locke,* as cited by Tilly, in Graham and Gurr, *op. cit.,* p. 22.

[10] Cf. Robert L. Lineberry and Edmund P. Fowler, "Reformism and Public Policies in American Cities," in Wilson, *City Politics and Public Policy,* pp. 97-123.

[11] Robert Salisbury, "Schools and Politics in the Big City," *Harvard Education Review,* Summer 1967, pp. 408-424. The quotation is from p. 413.

[12] *Ibid.*

[13] *Municipal Yearbook,* 1968, p. 59.

[14] Grant McConnell, *Private Power and American Democracy* (Knopf, 1966), p. 68.

[15] Theodore J. Lowi, *The End of Liberalism* (Norton, 1969), p. 95. Lowi, too, it should be noted, is hostile to this doctrine.

[16] Lewis Lorwin, *The American Federation of Labor* (Brookings, 1933), p. 355. Cited by J. David Greenstone, *Labor in American Politics* (Knopf, 1969), p. 19.

[17] Philip Taft and Philip Ross, "American Labor Violence: Its Causes, Character, and Outcome," in Graham and Gurr, *op. cit.,* pp. 281–395.

[18] *Ibid.,* p. 381.

[18a] *Cf.* Scoble, *op. cit.,* pp. 331–333.

[19] Greenstone, *op. cit.,* pp. 19–20. On the harshness of American slavery by comparison with that of other lands and historic periods, and the source of that harshness in Protestant individualism, see Stanley Elkins, *Slavery* (University of Chicago Press, 1959).

[20] *Op. cit.,* p. 43. See also Taft and Ross, in Graham and Gurr, *op. cit.,* pp. 348–361.

[21] *Report of the National Advisory Commission on Civil Disorders,* p. 116.

[22] Gary T. Marx, "Civil Disorder and the Agents of Social Control," p. 61.

[23] U. S. Bureau of the Census, *Historical Statistics of the United States: Colonial Times to 1957* (USGPO, 1960), p. 683.

[24] Walter Dean Burnham, "The Changing Shape of the American Political Universe," *American Political Science Review,* March 1965, pp. 7–28. The data cited appear on p. 10.

[25] Thomas F. Pettigrew and Kurt W. Back, "Sociology in the Desegregation Process: Its Use and Disuse," in Paul F. Lazarsfeld, *et al., The Uses of Sociology* (Basic Books, 1967), pp. 692–722. The analysis cited appears on pp. 703–704.

[26] Cf. Moynihan, *op. cit.,* pp. 96, 144; and Richard Blumenthal, "Antipoverty and the Community Action Program," in Allan P. Sindler, ed., *American Political Institutions and Public Policy* (Little, Brown, 1969), pp. 128–179. The reference here is to pp. 173–174.

[27] The key cases are: *Baker* v. *Carr,* 369 U. S. 186 (1962); *Wesberry* v. *Sanders,* 376 U. S. 1 (1964); *Reynolds* v. *Simms,* 377 U. S. 533 (1964); and *Avery* v. *Midland County,* 338 U. S. 905 (1968).

[28] *Newsweek,* June 30, 1969, p. 20.

[29] Quoted in W. E. B. DuBois, *Black Reconstruction* (Harcourt, Brace, 1935), pp. 14–15.

[30] Cf. U. S. Commission on Civil Rights, *Housing* (USGPO, 1963), pp. 95–103; and Charles Abrams, *Forbidden Neighbors* (Harper, 1955), ch. 17.

[31] Cf. Irving Kristol, "The Negro Today is Like the Immigrant Yesterday," *New York Times Magazine,* September 11, 1966, pp. 50 ff.

[32] The following discussion is based on Lerone Bennett, Jr., *Confrontation: Black and White* (Penguin, 1965), chs. 1, 2; Harold Isaacs, untitled memorandum submitted to the National Advisory Commission on Civil Disorders, October 22, 1967, dittoed, section entitled "The Options of Despair;" and Theodore Draper, "The Fantasy of Black Nationalism," *Commentary,* September 1969, pp. 27–54.

[33] *Op. cit.,* p. 29.

[34] Bennett, *op. cit.,* p. 60.

[35] From a letter to William Lloyd Garrison, cited by Isaacs, *op. cit.,* pp. 6, 7.

[36] Cited by Bennett, *op. cit.,* p. 89.

[37] Cf. Arthur Waskow, *From Race Riot to Sit-In* (Doubleday, 1966), esp. chs. 8–10; and Marx, *op. cit.,* pp. 13–26.

[38] Cited by Bennett, *op. cit.,* p. 125.

[39] Cited *ibid.,* p. 126.

[40] Cf. Congressional Quarterly, *Revolution in Civil Rights* (Congressional Quarterly Service, 4th ed., 1968), p. 14; and Thomas Wagstaff, Preface to his edited volume, *Black Power: The Radical Response to White America* (Glencoe Press, 1969).

[41] John C. Donovan, *The Politics of Poverty* (Pegasus, 1967), p. 64.

[42] Cf. Nathan Glazer and Daniel P. Moynihan, *Beyond the Melting Pot* (M.I.T. Press, 1963), esp. pp. 12–20, 288–290.

[43] Cf. Edward O. Laumann, "The Social Structure of Religious and Ethnoreligious Groups in a Metropolitan Community," *American Sociological Review,* April 1969, pp. 182–197.

[44] Cf. Raymond Wolfinger, "The Development and Persistence of Ethnic Voting," *American Political Science Review,* December 1965, pp. 896–908, esp. pp. 897–898.

[45] Michael Parenti, "Ethnic Politics and the Persistence of Ethnic Identification," *American Political Science Review,* September 1967, pp. 717–726.

[46] *Ibid.,* p. 720, drawing primarily upon C. B. Nam, "Nationality Groups and Social Stratification in America," *Social Forces,* May 1959, pp. 328–333; and Dale Hiestand, *Economic Growth and Employment Opportunities for Minorities* (Columbia, 1964).

[47] *Op. cit.,* pp. 37, 43–44, 155–166.

[48] Wolfinger, *op. cit.,* pp. 904–906.

[49] *Ibid.,* p. 906.

[50] Parenti, *op. cit.,* pp. 721–722.

[51] Martin Diamond, "On the Relationship of Federalism and Decentralization," in Daniel J. Elazar, *et al.,* eds., *Cooperation and Conflict: Readings in American Federalism* (Peacock, 1969), pp. 72–81. See esp. pp. 75–77.

[52] *Ibid.*, pp. 77, 78.

[53] Morton Grodzins, *The American Federal System* (ed. Daniel J. Elazar) (Rand McNally, 1966), pp. 258–260.

[54] The large city population estimates are taken from Congressional Quarterly, *Revolution in Civil Rights*, p. 117. In line with numerous studies, I have assigned a 1970 national population of 205–210 million, with Negroes accounting for 11 per cent.

[55] U. S. Bureau of the Census, *Current Population Reports,* Series P-23, No. 27 (USGPO, February 1969), p. 4.

[56] *Gallup Political Index,* March 1966, p. 23.

[57] *City Politics,* p. 123.

[58] Gabriel A. Almond and Sidney Verba, *The Civic Culture* (Princeton, 1963), p. 185.

[59] *Ibid.*, p. 191. I have consolidated cells, reducing the number in each column (excluding totals) from ten to five. The numbers in each column's individual cells add up to more than the "total percentage" which appears at the foot because some individuals gave more than one answer.

[60] *Ibid.,* p. 203. The same explanatory notes apply.

[61] *Ibid.,* p. 109.

[62] *Ibid.,* p. 219.

THREE: THE INTERESTS

[1] Cf. Joseph Featherstone, "Choking Off Community Schools," *New Republic,* July 19, 1969, pp. 16–18; and Marilyn Gittell, "New York City School Decentralization," *Community* (published by the Institute of Community Studies, Queens College), May 1969, pp. 1–2.

[2] Herbert Kaufman, "Administrative Decentralization and Political Power," paper delivered at the annual meeting of the American Political Science Association, September 1968, mimeo, pp. 12–13.

[3] The legislative history and general political background of the Green Amendment are reviewed in the *Congressional Quarterly Almanac,* 1967, pp. 1058–1081.

[4] On the original legislative history of "maximum feasible participation," see Blumenthal, "Antipoverty and the Community Action Program," in Sindler, *op. cit.,* pp. 129–179, esp. pp. 169–172; and Donovan, *The Politics of Poverty,* pp. 33–51. On the subsequent attacks, see Donovan, pp. 54–61, 65–68, 78, 83–88, 137.

[5] *New York Times,* September 24, 1968, p. 42.

[6] *Ibid.,* September 1, 1968, pp. 1, 28.

[7] *Ibid.,* July 30, 1969, p. 23.

[8] *Ibid.,* October 13, 1968, pp. 1, 80.

⁹ Cf. Paul Peterson, "Forms of Representation: Participation of the Poor in the Community Action Program," Department of Political Science, University of Chicago, ditto, n.d., pp. 42–44.

¹⁰ Banfield and Wilson, *op. cit.,* pp. 303–307.

¹¹ Almond and Verba, *op. cit.,* pp. 230–257.

¹² Michael Parenti, "The Black Muslims: From Revolution to Institution," *Social Research,* Summer 1964, pp. 175–194.

¹³ Almond and Verba, *op. cit.,* pp. 230–257.

¹⁴ Cf. F. J. Roethlisberger and William J. Dickson, *Management and the Worker* (Harvard, 1939).

FOUR: PLAUSIBLE OPTIONS

¹ Cf. Suzanne Keller, *The Urban Neighborhood* (Random House, 1968), pp. 99–102; and Herbert Gans, *The Levittowners* (Pantheon, 1967), pp. 154–165.

² *Ibid.,* p. 87.

³ Robert A. Nisbet, *The Sociological Tradition* (Basic Books, 1966), pp. 47–48.

⁴ H. L. Ross, "The Local Community: A Survey Approach," *American Sociological Review,* February 1962, pp. 75–84. Cited by Keller, *op. cit.,* p. 99.

⁵ See, for example, Gans, *op. cit.,* pp. 45–48, 154–181; and William Dobriner, *Class in Suburbia* (Prentice-Hall, 1963), pp. 11–16.

⁶ Cf. Scott Greer, "Individual Participation in Mass Society," in Roland Young, ed., *Approaches to the Study of Politics* (Northwestern University Press, 1957), pp. 329–342; and Melvin Webber and Carolyn C. Webber, "Culture, Territoriality, and the Elastic Mile," in H. Wentworth Elredge, ed., *Taming Megalopolis* (Doubleday, 1967), Vol. I, pp. 35–54.

⁷ *Ibid.,* p. 37.

⁸ *Ibid.,* pp. 40–44.

⁹ John B. Lansing and Eva Mueller, *The Geographic Mobility of Labor* (Survey Research Center, University of Michigan), ch. 10. See esp. pp. 270–271.

¹⁰ Cf. Wilbur R. Thompson, *A Preface to Urban Economics* (Johns Hopkins, 1965), ch. 7; and Robert A. Dahl, "The City in the Future of Democracy," *American Political Science Review,* December 1967, pp. 953–970.

¹¹ *Avery* v. *Midland County, Texas,* 390 U. S. 474 (1968).

¹² S. Arnstein and D. Fox, "Developments, Dynamics, and Dilemmas," internal staff memorandum on citizen participation in the Model Cities Program, Department of Housing and Urban Development, August 1968, mimeo, p. 9.

¹³ Sar Levitan, *The Great Society's Poor Law* (Johns Hopkins, 1969), p. 114.

[14] Paul Peterson, "Forms of Representation: Participation of the Poor in the Community Action Program," pp. 23–26, 45.

[15] *Op. cit.,* p. 11.

[16] Eugene C. Lee, "City Elections: A Statistical Profile," in Duane Lockard, ed., *Governing the States and Localities* (Macmillan, 1969), pp. 62–76. The turnout figures cited appear on p. 72.

[17] Campbell and Schuman, *op. cit.,* pp. 1–67. The data cited appear on p. 21.

[18] Maurice Duverger, *Political Parties* (2nd ed., Wiley, 1959), pp. 245–255, 301–304, 325–330.

[19] The best analysis of the bill's provisions that I have seen was prepared by the United Bronx Parents (791 Prospect Avenue, Bronx, New York). It is mimeographed, undated, and simply entitled "Summary and Analysis of School Decentralization Bill." I am indebted to Norman Fainstein for bringing it to my attention.

[20] Campbell and Schuman, *op. cit.,* p. 54.

[21] Fogelson and Hill, *op. cit.,* pp. 234, 245. Cf. also p. 240.

[22] *Op. cit.,* p. 21.

[23] Cf. Samuel K. Gove, *The Lakewood Plan* (University of Illinois Institute of Government and Public Affairs, 1961); and Robert O. Warren, "The Lakewood Plan," in Joseph F. Zimmerman, ed., *Government of the Metropolis* (Holt, 1968), pp. 316–324.

[24] David Rogers, *110 Livingston Street* (Random House, 1968), p. 214.

[25] Adam Walinsky, review of Moynihan, *op. cit., New York Times Book Review,* February 2, 1969, p. 2.

[26] U. S. Commission on Civil Rights, *Public Schools: Negro and White* (USGPO, 1962), pp. 217, 221–222, 241, 247.

[27] Alan K. Campbell, "The Socio-Economic, Political and Fiscal Environment of Educational Policy-Making in Large Cities," paper delivered at the annual meeting of the American Political Science Association, September 1966, pp. 4, 8.

[28] Christopher Jencks, "Is the Public School Obsolete?" *The Public Interest,* Winter 1967, pp. 18–27.

[29] Forrest W. Harrison and Eugene P. McLoone, *Profiles in School Support: A Decennial Overview* (USGPO, 1965), pp. 14–65, as cited by Arthur E. Wise, "The Constitution and Equal Educational Opportunity," in Charles U. Daly, ed., *The Quality of Inequality: Urban and Suburban Public Schools* (University of Chicago Center for Policy Study, 1968), pp. 27–46. The data cited appear at pp. 28–30.

[30] Oliver Oldman and Henry Aaron, "Assessment-Sales Ratios Under the Boston Property Tax," *National Tax Journal,* March 1965, pp. 36–48.

[31] David E. Black, "Inequalities in Effective Property Tax Rates: A Statistical Study of the City of Boston," doctoral dissertation,

Department of Economics, M.I.T., September 1969. See esp. pp. 90, 147–149, 152–157.

[32] Rogers, op. cit., pp. 336–337.

[33] Congressional Quarterly, Revolution in Civil Rights, p. 117.

[34] Edgar May, The Wasted Americans: Cost of Our Welfare Dilemma (Harper & Row, 1964), pp. 109–110.

[35] Jerome Skolnick, The Politics of Protest (Ballantine, 1969), p. 255. This study was a task force report submitted to the National Commission on the Causes and Prevention of Violence.

[36] Report of the National Advisory Commission on Civil Disorders, p. 428.

[37] Skolnick, The Politics of Protest, pp. 254–255.

[38] Some key sources which tend to support the assertions listed in this paragraph and the next are: Norman I. and Susan S. Fainstein, "The Promise of Community Control," Queens College Institute for Community Studies, mimeo, 1969, pp. 11–16; Rogers, op. cit., pp. 285–297; Drucker, The Age of Discontinuity, pp. 278–285, 329–333; Ivar Berg, "Rich Man's Qualifications for Poor Man's Jobs," Trans-Action, March 1969, pp. 45–50; and Wilson, Varieties of Police Behavior, pp. 281, 291.

[39] Rogers, op. cit., pp. 291–292 (italics added).

[40] For a scholarly argument to this effect, see Theodore J. Lowi, "Gosnell's Chicago Revisited Via Lindsay's New York," Foreword to Gosnell, Machine Politics: Chicago Model.

[41] Cf. Skolnick, The Politics of Protest, pp. 258–288.

[42] Ibid., pp. 253–254.

[43] Niederhoffer, op. cit., p. 16.

[44] Office of Economic Opportunity, Memorandum from Thomas A. Billings, Director, Project Upward Bound, mimeo, April 29, 1968.

[45] Peter Schrag, Village School Downtown (Beacon, 1967), pp. 55–56. Cf. also Rogers, op. cit., pp. 287–289, 295–296.

[46] Ibid., pp. 58–60.

[47] Wilson, Varieties of Police Behavior, adapted from pp. 7–9, 29–30, 73–75.

[48] Michael Lipsky, "Toward a Theory of Street-Level Bureaucracy," paper delivered at the 1969 Annual Meeting of the American Political Science Association, mimeo, September 1969.

[49] Cf. Rogers, op. cit., pp. 192–201.

[50] Peter H. Rossi, Richard A. Berk, David P. Boesel, Bettye K. Eidson, and W. Eugene Groves, "Between White and Black: The Faces of American Institutions in the Ghetto," in Supplemental Studies for the National Advisory Commission on Civil Disorders, pp. 69–215. The points cited appear at pp. 113, 138, 151–153.

[51] New York Times, June 9 1969, pp. 1 ff.

[52] Dunbar S. McLaurin, *Ghetto Economic Development and Industrialization Plan* (City of New York, Human Resources Administration, April 1968), p. 44. I am indebted to Margaret Power for bringing this document to my attention.

[53] Remsberg, "Chicago Voices: Tales Told Out of School," in Mack, *op. cit.,* pp. 275–386. The point cited appears at p. 291.

[54] (Atheneum, 1969). A recent paper of great interest is Robert Crandall and Duncan MacRae, "Urban Development Banks and Corporations," Laboratory for Environmental Studies, Massachusetts Institute of Technology, ditto, 1968.

[55] Eugene Foley, *The Achieving Ghetto* (National Press, 1968), pp. 126–130; and McLaurin, *op. cit.,* pp. 41–46.

[56] Cross, *op. cit.,* pp. 159–170, 190–192.

[57] *Congressional Quarterly Weekly Report,* May 10, 1968, p. 1067.

[58] Foley, *op. cit.,* pp. 63–69; Amory Bradford, *Oakland's Not for Burning* (McKay, 1968); and Leonard J. Duhl, with the assistance of Nancy Jo Steetle, "Newark: Community or Chaos: A Case Study of the Medical School Controversy," School of Public Health, University of California at Berkeley, mimeo, 1968.

[59] Cross, *op. cit.,* pp. 142–147.

[60] U. S. Department of Labor, Office of the Assistant Secretary for Wage and Labor Standards, memorandum to the heads of all federal agencies on the subject, "Revised Philadelphia Plan for Compliance with Equal Employment Opportunity Requirements of Executive Order 11246 for Federally-Involved Construction," June 27, 1969. This document was elaborated and ordered into effect in a subsequent Memorandum dated September 23, 1969. For a review of the political background, see the *New York Times,* September 24, 1969, p. 1.

[61] For a similar argument, see Anthony Downs, "Alternative Futures for the American Ghetto," *Daedalus,* Fall 1968, pp. 1331–1378, esp. pp. 1338–1341.

[62] This paragraph is based partially upon an analysis prepared by Anthony Kettaneh during the summer and early fall of 1968 for an advisory committee on decentralization (of which I was chairman) to the Boston Model Cities Administration.

[63] Altshuler, *The City Planning Process: A Political Analysis,* pp. 419–429.

[64] Cf. Royce Hanson, *Metropolitan Councils of Governments,* an Information Report of the Advisory Commission on Intergovernmental Relations (USGPO, August 1966); and B. Douglas Harman, *Councils of Governments: Trends and Issues* (International City Management Association, Urban Data Service, August 1969).

[65] Cf. Blumenthal, "Antipoverty and the Community Action Program," in Sindler, *op. cit.,* pp. 129–179, esp. pp. 137–140; and

Moynihan, "What is Community Action?", pp. 3-8. Moynihan deals with only two of these conceptions (the third and fourth), and he identifies one that I have not included: the "peace corps" approach, which emphasized sending idealistic young people into America's "underdeveloped" areas. Though significant, particularly in view of Sargent Shriver's background, this concept seems more relevant to other aspects of the "war" on poverty than the Community Action Program.

For other treatments of the Community Action Program's political history, see Donovan, *The Politics of Poverty*, pp. 33-41, 59-80, 136-138; and James L. Sundquist, ed., *On Fighting Poverty: Perspectives from Experience* (Basic Books, 1969), articles by Sundquist, Adam Yarmolinsky, and William C. Selover.

[66] John G. Wofford, "The Politics of Local Responsibility: Administration of the Community Action Program—1964–1966," in Sundquist, *op. cit.,* pp. 70-102. The point cited appears at p. 82.

[67] Title I of the Demonstration Cities and Metropolitan Development Act of 1966. The quotations are from Sections 101 and 103.

[68] The quotation is that of HUD Secretary George Romney, at a news conference called to explain the revised Model Cities guidelines. Cf. *New York Times,* April 29, 1969, pp. 1, 20.

[69] Arnstein and Fox, "Developments, Dynamics, and Dilemmas," p. 9.

FIVE: A PERSONAL STATEMENT

[1] S. M. Miller and Martin Rein, "Participation, Poverty, and Administration," *Public Administration Review,* January-February 1969, pp. 15-25. The point cited appears at p. 23.

[2] H. Edward Ransford, "Isolation, Powerlessness, and Violence: A Study of Attitudes and Participation in the Watts Riot," *American Journal of Sociology,* January 1968, pp. 581-591. Unfortunately, Ransford did not adjust for education in his analysis of the cumulative effect of the three factors. Presumably, however, doing so would not have altered the finding of a combination effect. All it might have done was to show that low education plus two of the other three variables sufficed to bring it into operation.

[3] Cf. Bowen and Masotti, eds., *Riots and Rebellion,* articles by Jay Schulman, E. S. Evans, and T. M. Tomlinson; Robert M. Fogelson and Robert B. Hill, "Who Riots? A Study of Participation in the 1967 Riots," in *Supplemental Studies for the National Advisory Commission on Civil Disorders,* pp. 221-248; Gary T. Marx, *Protest and Prejudice* (Harper & Row, 1967), ch. 2; and John M. Orbell, "Protest Among Southern Negro College Students," *American Political Science Review,* June 1967, pp. 446-456.

[4] Cohen, "The Price of Community Control," pp. 23–32. The quotation is from p. 30.

[5] Cf. Frank Smallwood, *Greater London: The Politics of Metropolitan Reform* (Bobbs-Merrill, 1965).

[6] Alexis de Tocqueville, *Democracy in America* (Mentor Edition, 1956; first published in 1835), pp. 64–71.

[7] My usage of this phrase follows that of Banfield and Wilson in their book, *City Politics.* See esp. pp. 18–22.

[8] For an elaboration of this theme, see Lee Rainwater, "Crucible of Identity: The Negro Lower-Class Family," in Talcott Parsons, ed., *The Negro American* (Beacon, 1966), pp. 160–204.

[9] Cf. George Sternlieb, *The Tenement Landlord* (Rutgers, 1966), and George Sternlieb, "Slum Housing: A Functional Analysis," *Law and Contemporary Problems,* Spring 1967, pp. 349–356.

[10] Cross, *op. cit.,* pp. 45–55, 168, 214–219.

[11] *Ibid.,* pp. 33–34.

[12] Christopher Jencks, "A Reappraisal of the Most Controversial Educational Document of Our Time [the Coleman Report]," *New York Times Magazine,* August 10, 1969, pp. 12 ff. The quotation is from p. 44. Cf. also Peter Blau and Otis Dudley Duncan, *The American Occupational Structure* (Wiley, 1967), ch. 6; and Michael J. Piore, "Public and Private Responsibilities in On-the-Job Training of Disadvantaged Workers," Department of Economics, Massachusetts Institute of Technology, Working Paper No. 23, June 1968.

[13] Wilson, *Varieties of Police Behavior,* p. 295. Cf. also The President's Commission on Law Enforcement and Administration of Justice, *The Challenge of Crime in a Free Society* (USGPO, 1967), pp. 99–103.

[14] Levy, in Masotti and Bowen, *op. cit.,* p. 349.